Culture and Customs of Laos

Laos. Courtesy of Bookcomp, Inc.

Culture and Customs of Laos

ARNE KISLENKO

Culture and Customs of Asia
Hanchao Lu, Series Editor

GREENWOOD PRESS
Westport, Connecticut • London

Library of Congress Cataloging-in-Publication Data

Kislenko, Arne.
   Culture and customs of Laos / Arne Kislenko.
      p.   cm.—(Culture and customs of Asia, ISSN 1097–0738)
   Includes bibliographical references and index.
   ISBN 978–0–313–33977–6 (alk. paper)
   1. Ethnology—Laos.   2. Laos—Social life and customs.   I. Title.
   GN635.L28K57   2009
   306.09594—dc22   2008040735

British Library Cataloguing in Publication Data is available.

Library of Congress Catalog Card Number: 2008040735
ISBN: 978–0–313–33977–6
ISSN: 1097–0738

First published in 2009

Greenwood Press, 88 Post Road West, Westport, CT 06881
An imprint of Greenwood Publishing Group, Inc.
www.greenwood.com

Printed in the United States of America

The paper used in this book complies with the
Permanent Paper Standard issued by the National
Information Standards Organization (Z39.48–1984).

10 9 8 7 6 5 4 3 2 1

The author and the publisher gratefully acknowledge permission for use of the following material:

Thao Worra, Bryan. *Touching Detonations: An E-Chapbook*. Published On-line by Sphinx House Press,
2004, at http://members.aol.com/thaoworra/poetry.htm.

For McB—*still* the Queen of *tom yam kung*—and that guy with the milkshakes in L.P.

Contents

Series Foreword

GEOGRAPHICALLY, ASIA ENCOMPASSES the vast area from Suez, the Bosporus, and the Ural Mountains eastward to the Bering Sea and from this line southward to the Indonesian archipelago, an expanse that covers about 30 percent of our earth. Conventionally, and especially insofar as culture and customs are concerned, Asia refers primarily to the region east of Iran and south of Russia. This area can be divided in turn into subregions, commonly known as South, Southeast, and East Asia, which are the main focus of this series.

The United States has vast interests in this region. In the twentieth century, the United States fought three major wars in Asia (namely the Pacific War of 1941–1945, the Korean War of 1950–1953, and the Vietnam War of 1965–1975), and each had a profound impact on life and politics in America. Today, America's major trading partners are in Asia, and in the foreseeable future the weight of Asia in American life will inevitably increase, for in Asia lie our great allies as well as our toughest competitors in virtually all arenas of global interest. Domestically, the role of Asian immigrants is more visible than at any other time in our history. In spite of these connections with Asia, however, our knowledge about this crucial region is far from adequate. For various reasons, Asia remains for most of us a relatively unfamiliar, if not stereotypical or even mysterious, "Oriental" land.

There are compelling reasons for Americans to obtain some level of concrete knowledge about Asia. It is one of the world's richest reservoirs of culture and an ever-evolving museum of human heritage. Rhoads Murphy, a prominent Asianist, once pointed out that in the part of Asia east of Afghanistan and south of Russia alone lies half the world, "half of its people and far more that half of its historical experience, for these are the oldest living civilized traditions." Prior to the modern era, with limited interaction and mutual influence between the East and the West, Asian civilizations developed largely independent from the West. In modern times, however, Asia and the West have come not only into close contact but also into frequent conflict: The result has been one of the most solemn and stirring dramas in world history. Today, integration and compromise are the trend in coping with cultural differences. The West—with some notable exceptions—has started to see Asian traditions not as something to fear but as something to be understood, appreciated, and even cherished. After all, Asian traditions are an indispensable part of the human legacy, a matter of global "common wealth" that few of us can afford to ignore.

As a result of Asia's enormous economic development since World War II, we can no longer neglect the study of this vibrant region. Japan's "economic miracle" of postwar development is no longer unique, but in various degrees has been matched by the booming economy of many other Asian countries and regions. The rise of the four "mini dragons" (South Korea, Taiwan, Hong Kong, and Singapore) suggests that there may be a common Asian pattern of development. At the same time, each economy in Asia has followed its own particular trajectory. Clearly, China is the next giant on the scene. Sweeping changes in China in the last two decades have already dramatically altered the world's economic map. Furthermore, growth has also been dramatic in much of Southeast Asia. Today, war-devastated Vietnam shows great enthusiasm for joining the "club" of nations engaged in the world economy. And in South Asia, India, the world's largest democracy, is rediscovering its role as a champion of market capitalism. The economic development of Asia presents a challenge to Americans but also provides them with unprecedented opportunities. It is largely against this background that more and more people in the United States, in particular among the younger generation, have started to pursue careers dealing with Asia.

This series is designed to meet the need for knowledge of Asia among students and the general public. Each book is written in an accessible and lively style by an expert (or experts) in the field of Asian studies. Each book focuses on the culture and customs of a country or region. However, readers should be aware that culture is fluid, not always respecting national boundaries. While every nation seeks its own path to success and struggles to maintain its own identity, in the cultural domain mutual influence and integration among Asian nations are ubiquitous.

Each volume starts with an introduction to the land and the people of a nation or region and includes a brief history and an overview of the economy. This is followed by chapters dealing with a variety of topics that piece together a cultural panorama, such as thought, religion, ethics, literature and art, architecture and housing, cuisine, traditional dress, gender, courtship and marriage, festivals and leisure activities, music and dance, and social customs and lifestyle. In this series, we have chosen not to elaborate on elite life, ideology, or detailed questions of political structure and struggle, but instead to explore the world of common people, their sorrow and joy, their pattern of thinking, and their way of life. It is the culture and the customs of the majority of the people (rather than just the rich and powerful elite) that we seek to understand. Without such understanding, it will be difficult for all of us to live peacefully and fruitfully with each other in this increasingly interdependent world.

As the world shrinks, modern technologies have made all nations on earth "virtual" neighbors. The expression "global village" not only reveals the nature and the scope of the world in which we live but also, more importantly, highlights the serious need for mutual understanding of all peoples on our planet. If this series serves to help the reader obtain a better understanding of the "half of the world" that is Asia, the authors and I will be well rewarded.

Hanchao Lu
Georgia Institute of Technology

Preface

DURING THE VIETNAM War an American diplomat working in Laos once referred to the country as "the end of nowhere." Foreshadowing what became the sad reality for Laos during nearly twenty years of war and revolution, he added, "We can do anything we want here because Washington doesn't seem to know it exists."[1] In some respects he was right. Over much of its history Laos has been caught in a vortex of internal divisions, imperial rivalries, and ideological struggles. Given its small size, population, and relatively isolated location, many people outside the region know almost nothing about the country. They are surprised to discover its rich heritage, a remarkable ethnic and cultural diversity, and the brutal fact that it was the scene of a long "secret" war that saw it become the most bombed country in history.

Some are also surprised to learn that Laos is one of the few remaining communist states in the world. Indeed, given the trappings of an ever-growing tourist trade, many travelers to Laos probably do not realize that an authoritarian government is in power. Nor would they understand that in some parts of the country an armed insurgency, more than thirty years old, against that government continues today. The pace of development and the exposure to foreign influences is such that few visitors can tell that the country opened up to tourists only slowly over the past twenty years. Nor would many guess that Laos today faces very difficult choices for the future. As one of the world's poorest nations its need for economic growth is obvious and immense. However, that necessitates outside involvement, which the current government views with suspicion, especially when it comes to managing its economic resources or introducing new political ideas.

Yet despite all these enormously complicated issues, Laos is also a very simple and traditional place. It is a remarkably relaxed country to travel, with places so beautiful, pristine, and remote that one really does feel that he or she is in the middle of nowhere. Some people say that being there is like going back in time. The pace of things is noticeably slower than almost anywhere else, even in relation to its Southeast Asian neighbors. The Buddhist faith has, for many Lao, been the one constant over decades of turmoil, and it remains a major influence for most people in everyday life. Various cultural traditions and the central role of the family also remain strong, particularly in the face of tremendous change.

This book is designed to introduce Laos and to present the traditional culture and customs of its peoples in the context of the twenty-first century world. As it quickly should be apparent, defining the country and its culture is a problematic exercise. With a population that represents multiple ethnic and linguistic groups, establishing a national identity for Laos is no simple task. Moreover, surrounded by much larger and more developed neighbors, Laos has for centuries existed in the cultural, economic, and political orbit of others. Devoid of the beaches, big cities, and high-profile tourist industries that draw millions to places like Thailand every year, Laos also has remained off the beaten path for most Westerners, even in an age of increasingly easy travel. Although there is a sizable expatriate Lao community, particularly in the United States, it is dwarfed by other Asian populations like the Chinese and Japanese. Even communities from other Southeast Asian countries, like Vietnam and Cambodia, have a more established and recognizable presence abroad. Aside from the occasional news report or documentary on the Vietnam War era, Laos rarely captures much international attention.

However, this by no means suggests that the country is unimportant. Both historically and in the contemporary sense Laos is worth careful study. In many respects it is a crossroads of cultures in Southeast Asia. Its ancient history reveals an impressive kingdom that safeguarded some of the most important Buddhist sites, relics, and traditions. In modern times the revolution and war that ravaged its neighbors consumed the country, and thus Laos offers much to those studying colonialism, decolonization, and cold war conflict. The diversity of its people is quite remarkable and presents a host of issues about identity and the state. Although it will never be a major economic or political power, Laos has always been key in the complex relationships of those on its borders, particularly Thailand and Vietnam, and therefore it has considerable regional significance. With some of the last untouched wildernesses in Southeast Asia, Laos also will be an important case for environmental protection in the midst of pressing economic development.

In fact, on many fronts Laos is a microcosm of globalization. The spread of outside influences, although not all negative, threaten traditional ways of life in the country. Democratic freedoms as they are known in the West do not exist, and many both in Laos and abroad are anxious for fundamental political change. Despite the ravages of war and a period of severe repression under communist rule, Laos never witnessed the extremism of Cambodia or Vietnam. In some respects it was the first Asian communist nation to experiment with economic and political reforms, ahead of both China and Vietnam. Today many problems remain, most centered on the fact that for nearly two hundred years Laos lagged far behind other states in the region in terms of development. Its commercial infrastructure is small, and it lacks major industries and exports. Corruption is a serious problem, as are prostitution and the drug trade, albeit mostly for export. Human rights abuses are all too familiar. Perhaps most difficult are questions about identity and a well-defined, independent Lao culture after centuries of foreign domination. These matters are all integral to the nature and existence of the state, particularly as it continues to open up the country after decades of isolation.

Of course, the best way to understand Laos, its cultures, and the issues it confronts is to go there. Even for the seasoned traveler Laos will impress and amaze. In fact, many say that Laos is one of the last relatively untouristy places left on earth, especially outside its few major cities and towns. Standing almost anywhere in the country, one is struck not only by the physical beauty and magnificent temples but also by the genuine friendliness and relaxed nature of its people. To be sure, Laos today faces incredible changes that will continue to challenge, if not undermine, its cultures and traditions. However, there is still a certain mystery to the country that makes it one of the most interesting places on earth—and far from nowhere.

NOTE

1. Charles A. Stevenson, *The End of Nowhere: American Policy towards Laos since 1954* (Boston: Beacon Press, 1972), 240.

Acknowledgments

MANY PEOPLE HAVE helped me in researching, writing, and editing this book. I am grateful to two excellent research assistants at Ryerson University in Toronto: Angela Wallace and Samantha Goodspeed. Angela got things off to a great start, while Sam's enthusiasm and dedication were indispensable to see this project through. Another Ryerson student, Jeffrey Phisanoukanh, showed me what learning is really about by attending my class all term, without enrolling, just because he was interested. He and his family then gave me valuable insight into Laos and its communities. Jeff and his family members— Nene Phisanoukanh, Kham Wong, and Simon Wong—also contributed some of the photographs for this book. Other photographs have been drawn from gifted artists who deserve special thanks: Christina Smit, Martine Duprey, Alfred Molon, Rick Madonik, Danny Callcut (Sticky Rice Travel Photography), and several professionals coordinated by Bob Turner, of Art Directors and Travel UK. I would also like to thank Jason Sahlani, Tony and Kerry Barlow, and David Begg for contributing photos to the selection process as well. I am grateful to Bookcomp Inc., which provided the map illustration, and I would like to extend sincere thanks to librarians at the University of Toronto, the Royal Ontario Museum, and the Freie Universität Berlin. Very special thanks are owed to Bryan Thao Worra, who gave permission to include some of his remarkable poetry in this volume.

Financial support for this project came from the Faculty of Arts and the Department of History at Ryerson University, and I am grateful to both. For her endless patience, kindness, and tremendous help in seeing this book through, I would like to warmly thank Kaitlin Ciarmiello, acquisitions editor at Greenwood Press. I am also grateful for the assistance of my copy editor, Katherine Faydash, at Aptara Corporation. Last but not least, I want to say thanks to my family and friends for just about everything in life, and to no one more than my wife, friend, travel partner, adviser, editor, and much more: Christine McCullough.

Note on Transliteration, Names, and Dates

THERE IS NO official method or single convention for transliterating the Lao language, which makes research on the country problematic. Many Lao sounds do not have an equivalent in English. Some Lao vowels do not exist in Western languages. Moreover, the first transliteration was based on the French colonial system, which bears little semblance to how an English speaker would phonetically sound out words. For example, the capital of Laos, Vientiane, would be pronounced in English as Wieng Chan or Wieng Jan, given that the *v* sound in Lao is closer to that of the English *w*. French does not have a written consonant that corresponds to the *w* sound, so the *v* was employed instead. Similarly, the *ch* or *j* sound in French is represented by *ti*. Confusion continues with the vowel *ou* in French, which sometimes translates into English as *u* and other times as a *w* sound. Luang Prabang can appear as Louang Prabang. An *o* is often used for a short *aw* sound in Lao, so *Bo* would be pronounced *baw*.

Some scholars follow *System for the Romanization of Lao, Khmer, and Pali*, published by the American National Standards Institute in 1979, and others use a hybrid of this and the French systems. In the former, *s* is used instead of the French *x*. Thus, Lan Sang can be Lan Xang, with identical pronunciations. Both the public and the private sectors in Laos are adopting a more universal system based on the Royal Thai General Transcription, given similarities between the two languages. However, problems still occur. Where an *l* or *h* sound in Lao is appropriate, an *r* sound in Thai is often employed because

Lao symbols closely resemble it, and an equivalent *r* in Lao does not exist.[1] Accordingly, Luang Prabang can also appear as Luang (or Louang) Phabang.

This book tries to follow the sound-based system commonly used in English-language works based on the Royal Thai General Transcription, although occasionally other styles may be used. Alternate phonetic spellings are given in brackets. The conventional contemporary spellings of Vientiane and Luang Prabang are used in this book, while the more Lao spelling *Phabang* is used in reference to the sacred image. Given their complexity to those unfamiliar with tonal languages, accents on Lao words have not been placed. Lao refer to themselves by their first names, and that is reflected in this book. Surnames and honorary titles are given when applicable. Proper names and most place-names have not been translated, but alternative names and rough English language meanings have been given when appropriate.

It is also important to note the usage of *Laos*, *Lao*, and *Laotian*. Given that the Lao language has no *s*, some foreigners refer to the country as Lao. The term *Laos* first appeared in the texts of Portuguese missionaries, and it is probable that French and English explorers followed this source. Also, in European languages the addition of the *s* is useful in transforming the adjective *Lao* into the country *Laos*. Some also use the term *Laotian* as an adjective. Literal translations of the Lao terms for their country are Muang Lao or Pathet Lao, which mean simply "Lao land." However, for reasons that remain unclear, this reference never took root. The *s* in the word *Laos* for the Lao is unnecessary because the word *Lao* is almost always joined with another word that it describes. Thus, *khon Lao* refers to a Lao person. There is no official Lao government position on the matter, although most publications, businesses, and media sources in the country refer to the country as Laos.[2] Historians and anthropologists use the word *Tai* in referring to the people inhabiting Laos and Thailand in the period before the creation of unified political entities. This also signifies a common linguistic and cultural identity between peoples in the region. In this book I refer to the Tai people prior to the establishment of modern kingdoms and states such as Laos.

Dates in this book follow the Gregorian calendar, the (unofficial) global standard. It uses the notations B.C.E. (before common era) and C.E. (common era) in reference to year 1 of the calendar where the context requires specification. Dates given without designation are otherwise all in the common era. Where exact dates are unknown or a matter of dispute, the abbreviation *ca.* (the Latin *circa*), indicating "approximate," is used. Dates of rule are given for most kings, while life spans are indicated for the most prominent political figures in modern Lao history.

NOTES

1. Joe Cummings, *Lao Phrasebook* (Footscray, Australia: Lonely Planet Publications, 2002), 11–16.

2. Grant Evans, *A Short History of Laos: The Land in Between* (Crows Nest, Australia: Allen and Unwin, 2002), xiii–xiv.

Chronology of the History of Laos

ca. 40,000 B.C.E.	Permanent hunter-gatherer sites established in Southeast Asia.
ca. 20,000–10,000 B.C.E.	Agricultural settlements emerge in Southeast Asia.
ca. 10,000 B.C.E.	Language and culture differentiate in Southeast Asia.
ca. 3,000 B.C.E.	Iron working and pottery emerge in northeastern Thailand, and wet-rice paddy growing in Southeast Asia.
sixth century C.E.	Chinese sources refer to Tai people living in southern China and Southeast Asia.
ca. sixth to ninth centuries	The rise of the Dvaravati civilization.
ca. eighth to ninth centuries	The rise of the Nan-Chao kingdom in southern China and northern Southeast Asia.
ca. ninth to thirteenth centuries	The rise of the Khmer civilization.
ca. eleventh to thirteenth centuries	The rise of the Pagan empire in Burma.
ca. eighth to thirteenth centuries	Southern Tai peoples expand through Thailand, Laos, Burma, and northeastern India, supplanting the Mon and Khmer.

ca. eleventh to thirteenth centuries	The rise of small Tai-speaking states on the frontiers of pagan and Khmer empires.
1253–1300	Mongol armies invade Southeast Asia, undermining Pagans and Khmer.
1279–1298	Sukhothai Tai kingdom established.
1281–1292	Lan Na Tai kingdom established.
1353	Kingdom of Lan Xang is founded.
Fourteenth to sixteenth centuries	Ayutthaya Tai kingdom enters expansion phase.
1421–1520	A succession of weak rulers, internal divisions, and wars occurs in Lan Xang.
1479	The Vietnamese invade Lan Xang.
1520	King Phothisarat reunifies the kingdom.
1545–1546	Lan Xang and Lan Na are unified briefly.
1558–1569	Burmese armies sack Tai kingdoms.
1560	Capital of Lan Xang moves to Vientiane.
1563–1575	Burmese armies sack Luang Prabang (1563), Vientiane (1565), and Ayutthaya (1568–1569).
1610–1688	The height of Ayutthaya's expansion.
1638–1695	The golden age of Lan Xang during the reign of Surinyavongsa.
1641–1642	The first Europeans to leave records appear in Vientiane.
1688–1733	Ayutthaya further expands in Cambodia and Laos.
1707–1713	Lan Xang separates into three kingdoms: Luang Prabang, Vientiane, and Champasak.
1760–1767	Burmese armies invade Tai kingdoms; Ayutthaya is destroyed (1767).
1763–1769	The Siamese control northern Laos, including Luang Prabang, while the Vietnamese Nguyen dynasty controls central Mekong, including Vientiane.
1767–1768	Thonburi Tai kingdom founded.

1768–1782	Thonburi campaigns against the Burmese; Chiang Mai captured (1776); Tai influence expands in Cambodia and Laos (1778).
1785–1793	Wars continue with the Burmese; Tai kingdoms consolidated under Siam.
1800–1822	Siam controls most of Laos; Chao Anuvong attempts to establish independent Lao kingdom.
1820–1840	Earliest Hmong migrations into Laos occur.
1826–1828	Chao Anuvong's war fails and he is executed; Siamese armies ravage central Laos.
1860–1885	Haw Wars in Laos; Vientiane sacked (1885).
1861	French explorer Henri Mouhot arrives in Luang Prabang.
1867	French expeditions take place to map the Mekong River.
1875–1887	Three Siamese campaigns are carried out to crush the Haw in Laos; the Haw sack Luang Prabang (1887); the Lao King Unkham appeals to the French for aid.
1893–1907	The Franco-Siamese conflict (1893); treaties give France all Lao territories east of the Mekong River.
1900–1939	The French encourage Vietnamese migration to Laos; the territory becomes a colonial backwater.
1908–1922	Ethnic minorities in Laos revolt periodically.
1933–1936	Kommadam rebellion occurs in the Bolaven region.
1939–1945	World War II occurs, and Japanese gain control of Southeast Asia.
1941	The nationalist government in Thailand (renamed from Siam in 1939) launches attacks on French Laos; Japan mediates treaty that gives Thailand parts of Laos.
1945	Japanese overthrow the French government in Laos and push for Lao declaration of independence (September); Lao Issara provincial government formed (October).

1946	French troops retake Laos (March–April) and occupy west bank of Mekong following Thai withdraw (November).
1947	Laos becomes a constitutional monarchy with a national assembly under French rule (August).
1949	Laos declared independent within the French Union (July).
1950	Laos receives international recognition; the communist Pathet Lao reject the government and ally with Vietnamese communists.
1952–1953	The Pathet Lao insurgency against the French occurs in the Northeast; Vietminh communists invade Laos (1953).
1954	French forces withdraw following the Geneva agreements (July), leaving Laos divided between the Pathet Lao and royalists.
1955	Laos is admitted to the United Nations; the Lao People's Party is formed.
1956	The Lao Patriotic Front is founded.
1957–1960	Souvanna Phouma leads three coalition governments; the United States periodically suspends aid to Lao government and provides covert assistance to right-wing militarists who take power (1958–1960).
1960	A series of coups overthrow the right wing and destabilize Laos; the Pathet Lao insurgency intensifies.
1961	Neutral and Pathet Lao forces seize the Plain of Jars region (January); the John F. Kennedy administration backs neutralization of Laos (March); the Geneva Conference on Laos begins (May).
1962	Right-wing forces are defeated at Nam Tha (May); coalition government returns (June); Geneva Conference ends (July).
1963	Communist forces in North Vietnam use the Ho Chi Minh trail through eastern Laos to fight in South Vietnam; U.S. forces respond with covert military operations in Laos.

1964	A failed right-wing coup occurs (April); Pathet Lao forces neutralists from Plain of Jars and U.S. strategic bombing of Laos begins (May).
1965	First overtly deployed U.S. combat troops in Vietnam (March).
1966	Political turmoil and new election in Laos continue (September); Pathet Lao gains more control.
1969	Hmong forces with American direction take the Plain of Jars (September).
1970	Pathet Lao and North Vietnamese forces take the Plain of Jars (February).
1971	South Vietnamese forces invade Laos to interdict the Ho Chi Minh trail (February).
1972–1973	Multiparty negotiations on coalition government lead to cease-fire (February 1973).
1973	U.S. forces begin withdrawal from Vietnam and the secret war in Laos stops.
1975	Communists gain control of government; King Savangvatthana abdicates (December); Lao People's Democratic Republic proclaimed (December).
1975–1989	Hard-line communist policies are implemented, and many flee the country.
1977	Hmong uprising occurs (February); the king is imprisoned (March); Laos and Vietnam sign the Treaty of Friendship and Cooperation (July).
1978	Forced collectivization program begins (May); Laos supports Vietnam in conflict with Cambodia and its supporter, China.
1984	Border conflict with Thailand breaks out (June).
1986	Economic reforms and market liberalization introduced.
1989–1990	The collapse of the Soviet Union leads to economic and political reform in Laos.
1992	President Kaysone Phomvihane dies, which leads to further liberalization in Laos; émigrés

	are encouraged to return, and tourism and foreign investment begins.
1994	The Friendship Bridge linking Laos and Thailand across the Mekong opens.
1997	Laos is admitted to the Association of Southeast Asian Nations (ASEAN).
1999	Vietnamese influence in Laos wanes as Thai investment and cultural links grow.
2001–present	Reforms continue, as does the opening up of the country; small-scale insurgencies and attacks by rebel groups occur.

SOURCES

Griffiths, Clare, ed., *Insight Guides: Laos and Cambodia* (London: Apa Publications, 2005), 18–19.

Northern Illinois University Center for Southeast Asian Studies, "Resources for Lao Studies," http://www.seasite.niu.edu.

Stuart-Fox, Martin, *A History of Laos* (Cambridge: Cambridge University Press, 1997), x–xiii.

1

Introduction: Geography and People

GEOGRAPHY

SLIGHTLY LARGER THAN Great Britain or the state of Utah, Laos is in the heart of mainland Southeast Asia, covering an area of just more than 235,000 square kilometers (90,700 square miles). Laos borders the People's Republic of China (PRC), Myanmar (Burma), Thailand, Cambodia, and Vietnam. The country comprises sixteen provinces (Phongsali, Luang Nam Tha, Luang Prabang, Udomxai, Hua Phan, Sainyabuli, Xiang Khuang, Vientiane, Saisombun, Bolikhamsai, Khammuan, Savannakhet, Salavan, Sekong, Champasak, and Attapeu) and the national capital, Vientiane. Officially known as the Lao People's Democratic Republic (Lao PDR), Laos is the only landlocked country in the region and thus has always been more insulated and remote than its neighbors have been. The predominantly mountainous and forested terrain adds to that isolation: More than 90 percent of the country is 180 meters (585 feet) or more above sea level, and high plateaus dominate 70 percent of that area.[1] Rugged mountain ranges slice Laos into narrow river valleys, particularly in the north, giving way to lowland floodplains in the south.

Most of the many rivers in Laos eventually flow into the Mekong River (Mae Nam Khong, in Lao), the world's twelfth-longest river, which forms the borders with Burma and Thailand. The Mekong stretches 4,350 kilometers (2,720 miles) from the Tibetan Plateau through China into Laos. It then passes into Cambodia and Vietnam before emptying into the South China Sea. The Mekong has the tenth-largest volume of water among rivers in the world, but that volume fluctuates considerably depending on the season. At its widest in Laos, near Si Phan Don in the south, the river reaches 15 kilometers (9 miles) across during monsoons, but it can be shallow and difficult to traverse in its upper reaches in drier months.[2] The Mekong has always been the economic and cultural lifeline of the country. The word itself reflects that: *Me* is an old Lao word meaning interchangeably "giver of life," "chief," "the biggest of all," and "female" (as in one who bears life). *Kong* is a Khmer word meaning "river," derived from the holiest river in India, the Ganges (Kong-ka, in Khmer).[3] Laos's major cities and towns, including Vientiane, Luang Prabang, Thakhek, Savannakhet, and Pakse, lie on the banks of the Mekong. The river provides the lowland floodplains with fertile silts that enrich the soil, essential for a predominantly agricultural country. As it has been for centuries, the Mekong remains the major conduit for trade, transportation, fishing, irrigation, and, increasingly, tourism.

Geographically, Laos is also defined by the jagged limestone peaks of the Annamite Cordillera that runs through the country from northwest to southeast and has historically provided a buffer from neighboring Vietnam. These mountains extend nearly 1,100 kilometers (688 miles) and, in effect, divide the Mekong from the South China Sea. Many peaks exceed 2,000 meters (6,500 feet) in height, the highest of which is Phu Bia at 2,820 meters (9,165 feet). At the foot of the mountains is the Xiang Khuang Plateau, the single largest geographical feature in the country. This series of rolling grassland hills is best known for the mysterious stone "jars" that dot the landscape, which has earned it the nickname the "Plain of Jars" (see Chapter 2).[4] There are also important plateaus in central and southern Laos, such as the Khammuan and the Bolaven, the latter extending 10,000 square kilometers (3,860 square miles) at an elevation of about 1,000 meters (3,250 feet). Much of the country's mountain rice, coffee, and tea cultivations are based here. Almost all other rice and many other agricultural products are grown in the floodplain between Sainyabuli and Champasak: the flattest and most tropical part of the country.

ENVIRONMENT

Laos has a tropical climate with three distinct seasons based on the annual monsoons. The wet season begins between May and July and runs through November. Rainfall, particularly in the southern lowlands, can be heavy and result in severe flooding, but without this period of intense precipitation, rice cultivation—the staple of Lao agriculture—would be impossible. From November to March is the dry season, during which most places are relatively cool and precipitation is low. From March to May the hot season brings substantially increased temperatures with little rain. It often reaches 40 degrees Celsius (104 degrees Fahrenheit) throughout the country. Mountainous areas are almost always cooler and drier than the low-lying plains. During the dry season the temperature can dip down to single-digit Celsius temperatures.

Among the most important environmental features of the country are its forests. Laos still has extensive tracts of virgin forest, despite illegal logging over the past few decades. According to the International Union for Conservation of Nature and Natural Resources (IUCN), unmanaged vegetation covers as much as 85 percent of the country, with 50 percent of that being native forest. In terms of the percentage of natural forest cover, Laos ranks eleventh highest in the world. Only Cambodia has a higher proportion of natural forest cover in Southeast Asia.[5] It is not surprising that forestry is one of the most important sources of revenue in the country, and the vast majority of timber is destined for foreign markets like Thailand and Japan. Hardwoods like teak and rosewood are particularly prized. About 50 percent of the gross domestic product (GDP) of Laos comes from natural resource products, much of it forestry, and agricultural production accounts for almost 40 percent. Nearly 80 percent of the labor force in Laos works in these two sectors, and the vast majority in farming.[6]

The forests of Laos are also important for biodiversity and tourism, as they are home to one of the most diverse collections of animals left in Asia. There are an estimated five hundred wild Asian elephants in the country, probably the biggest number left in the world. Laos is also home to a number of endangered or threatened species, including macaques, monkeys, flying squirrels, wildcat, deer, martens, tigers, gibbons, langurs, lesser pandas, pygmy lorises, and raccoon dogs. There are 69 verified species of bats, 437 types of birds, and numerous varieties of snake and lizards. To illustrate how remote some of the forests in Laos are, as recently as 1994 new and rare animal species were being discovered, such as the spindlehorn (*nyang* in Lao: a horned, deerlike mammal thought to be extinct for centuries). A few Javan and/or Sumatran rhinoceroses are thought to live in the Bolaven Plateau, while koupreys—wild oxen extinct elsewhere in Asia—have been reported in areas around Attapeu and Champasak.[7]

Laos does have a surprisingly extensive environmental protection program. Since 1993 it has established twenty official National Biodiversity Conservation Areas, covering nearly twenty-six thousand square kilometers (sixteen thousand square miles), or 14 percent of the nation's territory, much higher than in most Western countries. The conservation areas are not technically preserves but rather are managed environmental zones. Some are reserved for forestry and others for conservation; the latter are particularly important to the burgeoning tourism trade. Unfortunately, despite fairly substantial laws protecting the areas, illegal logging within their boundaries is increasing. Further development of the Mekong River for hydroelectric power exacerbates the problem, as large swaths of forest are cut down to make way for facilities and roads connecting towns on the power grid. Slash-and-burn agriculture on forest peripheries also threatens environmental balance.

Still, the majority of people in Laos today get their food from the forest and not farms. Many environmental experts fear that this dependency will eventually destroy ecological systems. Overfishing of lakes and rivers and illicit international trade in wildlife adds significantly to the problem, as does rampant government corruption, a weak judicial system, and a lack of environmental awareness throughout the country.[8] For example, Laos has still not ratified the United Nations Convention on International Trade in Endangered Species of Wild Flora and Fauna (CITES) and does very little to educate the public about environmental issues. Moreover, even today the environmental effects of the Vietnam War era are unclear. Large tracts of northern and eastern Laos were damaged from herbicides and chemical defoliants that American forces used extensively for nearly twenty years. Tourism may in fact be the best tool with which to protect the flora and fauna of Laos, but to date its effects seem negligible. In fact, over the past few years the Lao government has yielded to developers and allowed large-scale resorts, hotels, and even casinos aimed at prospective tourists.

ECONOMY

Beyond forestry and hydroelectricity, the Lao economy's main exports are coffee, spices, tin, gypsum, garments, and handicrafts such as silver jewelry, pottery, silks, carvings, and wicker. Agricultural production, for both domestic consumption and export, includes rice, corn, tobacco, cotton, beans, and fruits. Mining (tin and gypsum) along with cement manufacturing are the primary industrial activities, although the production of cigarettes, bricks, tiles, and beverages has increased over the past few years. The chief export markets are Thailand, Vietnam, China, Japan, and Europe. Laos imports almost all other goods, including foodstuffs, fuel, manufactured goods, and machinery.[9]

After two decades of isolation under communism, Laos began opening up to foreign investment in the mid-1990s. Since then Thais, who control much of the current economic stimulus, have displaced Vietnamese interests. Japanese and, more recently, Chinese investment, particularly in natural resource development, have also increased. In fact, external trade is growing at an annual rate of 10 percent. Economic growth, driven largely by foreign investment, has averaged 6.3 percent annually since 2002. Real growth in the GDP is projected to be about 7 percent between 2006 and 2010.[10]

However, Laos still ranks very low on the U.N. index for human development; as of 2003, it placed at No. 135 of 175 countries. It ranks No. 23 on the U.N. Least Developed Countries Index. Between 1966 and 2001, Laos absorbed US$950 million in loans from just the Asian Development Bank (ADB), and today it takes in more than $250 million annually in combined aid, which is why some experts refer to it as a "sponge."[11] It also has a thriving black market, estimated to control nearly 20 percent of all wealth in the country. Through a host of economic initiatives launched with the assistance of the United Nations, the International Monetary Fund, the ADB, and the Association of Southeast Asian Nations (ASEAN), the Lao government rather ambitiously hopes to end its status as a developing country by 2020. Planners are hoping that Laos will emerge as the pivot point in expanding overland transportation between China, Vietnam, and the rest of mainland Southeast Asia. They are also hopeful that tourism, which paradoxically revolves around the country's isolation and untouched wilderness, will also provide for economic development in the coming decade.

THE PEOPLES OF LAOS

As of 2007, the population of Laos had reached an estimated 6 million people. One-third of the population lives in the Mekong River Valley, mostly in four cities: Vientiane, Luang Prabang, Savannakhet, and Pakse. Another one-third lives along rivers like the Nam Ou, Set Don, and Nam Seuang.[12] With slightly more than twenty people per square kilometer (nine per square mile), Laos has one of the lowest population densities in Asia. Its annual growth rate since 2000 has averaged 2.3 percent, but numerous problems, most stemming from widespread poverty, continue to affect its population. Gross national income per capita is only about US$400. More than 20 percent of the population suffers from malnutrition. Life expectancy is just fifty-eight years for men and sixty for women. Only a very small percentage of the population is over the age of sixty, and slightly more than 45 percent of the population is under the age of fifteen, which makes Laos's population among the youngest in the world. The mortality rate for children under five years of age is ninety-one per thousand births, one of the highest in Asia. The literacy rate for men is 76 percent, but it is just 53 percent for women. Only 20 percent of the population has access to electricity, and health care in the country is rudimentary at best, even in the bigger towns and cities.[13]

The ethnic diversity of Laos is staggering. In fact, the exact number of groups is a matter of considerable debate. In 1995 the government of Laos recognized forty-seven separate ethnicities with 149 groups within them. The opposition group Lao Front for National Construction (LFNC), which operates in exile, recognizes forty-nine ethnicities and 160 groups. Most independent research suggests that there are anywhere between 40 and 170 separate ethnicities in Laos. The range in estimates stems from a lack of in-depth research on many groups given their physical isolation and the fact that revolution and war have made Laos a difficult place to conduct studies for the past sixty years. Indeed, a definitive study of all the country's ethnic groups and their numerous branches has yet to be completed.[14] Estimates are also wide ranging because in some circumstances there exist only slight linguistic and cultural differences between groups. Some observers merge groups together, whereas others identify the groups as separate. However, it is clear that even with the most conservative assessment, Laos has tremendous ethnic diversity, which has given rise to the contention that the country is more of a collection of tribes than it is a nation.

About 50 percent of the population is ethnic Lao, known locally as Lao Lum (or Lao Loum), who are closely related to Lao speakers in northeast Thailand and, more remotely, to the Thais. In fact, distinctions between the Lao and Thai are historically blurry and relatively recent creations designed for political purposes. There is no question among ethnologists that the two groups are from the same family, but many Lao resent Thai suggestions that they are their "little brothers." The traditional defining lines between the Lao Lum and other groups in the country have been location, agricultural practice, and religion. The Lao Lum dominate the lowland river valleys and grow wet rice, whereas most other ethnic groups live in the highlands and are sustained by dry-rice farming, hunting, gathering, and slash-and-burn agriculture.[15] The Lao Lum are also Buddhists, and most follow the Theravada practice (see Chapter 3), but many other groups practice other religions. About 20 percent of the population belongs to closely related ethnic subgroups of the Lao Tai, who live at slightly higher elevations and farm dry rice. These include the Tai Dam (Black Tai), Tai Daeng (Red Tai), and Tai Khao (White Tai). It is important to note, however, that the Lao government considers the Lao Lum and Lao Tai inseparable.

The Lao Theung (Lao Thoeng), literally "those Lao approaching the top of the mountain" but more often called "upland Lao," comprise another 15 to 20 percent of the population. They are also sometimes referred to derisively as *kha*, or "slave," by the Lao Lum. The Lao Theung are predominantly people of Mon and Khmer lineage that live at still-higher elevations and practice animism rather than Buddhism. About 9 percent of the country's population is Lao Sung (Lao Soung), or "high Lao." The Lao Sung live in communities more than 1,000 meters (3,200 feet) above sea level. Often referred to collectively as "hill tribes" in Laos, Thailand, and Vietnam, this group includes quite distinct ethnicities like the Hmong, Yao (Mien), Akha, and Lahu. Laos is also home to sizable communities of ethnic Vietnamese (Viet Kieu) and Chinese (Hua Chiao), both of which are concentrated in urban centers and are most closely identified with commercial interests. There are small communities of Chinese Muslims (Chin Haw), mainly traders living in low mountain areas, and South Asian Muslims, who are primarily businesspeople in Vientiane.

ETHNICITY AND IDENTITY

The diversity of populations is an extremely important factor shaping Laos. It has produced at times a violent history and remains a complicating factor in the national identity of the country. Indeed, one of the foremost experts on Laos, the anthropology professor and historian Grant Evans, points out that the paradox about studying the country is whether a common identity even exists. The historian Arthur Dommen once described Laos as a collection of tribes. The respected journalist Bernard Fall characterized it in the 1950s as "neither a geographical nor an ethnic or social entity, but merely a political convenience." A former official in the administration of the American President John F. Kennedy, Arthur Schlesinger Jr., said that the Lao state in the 1960s was simply a "diplomatic courtesy."[16] Not surprisingly, some nationalist historians in Laos have claimed the opposite. Writing in 1995, the director of the Institute of Culture in Laos, Houmphanh Rattanavong, argued that Chinese texts confirmed the existence of Ailao, a clearly Lao kingdom dating from the second and third centuries B.C.E. However, most experts believe that the Lao are Tai people—historically, ethnically, and culturally extremely close if not indistinguishable from their neighbors in Thailand. In this light, the definition of Laos and the Lao people is a creation of more modern times. Still, scholars like the historian Martin Stuart-Fox have tried to establish a truly Lao identity through its diversities, arguing, in effect, that the country's ethnic and cultural mix has produced a unique "Lao-ness."[17] It is also important to note that the question of identity is by no means only for Laos. Many countries and people around the world confront similar dilemmas, often with even more difficulty.

Complicating matters further, the geographic borders of Laos today are creations of more than a century of French colonialism, regional wars, revolution, and foreign interventions. The boundaries of old kingdoms throughout Southeast Asia have, for the most part, long disappeared, and they do not reflect the ethnic dispersion of people in the region. The best illustration of this is the fact that more Lao speakers live in northeastern Thailand (19 million) than in Laos itself (3 million). Often referring to themselves as *khon Isan* (people of the Isan region in northeastern Thailand) to be distinguished from Thais, Lao speakers demonstrate the historical dislocation of Lao peoples.

The current Lao government has done little to clarify questions of history and identity. Officially, authorities in Vientiane consider the Lao Lum and Lao Tai one large group, which thus constitutes a clear majority of the population (60 percent). The Lao Theung and Lao Sung are considered separate groups, making up about 34 percent of the population, whereas the Vietnamese and Chinese make up the remaining 6 percent. The government has further distinguished populations by linguistic categorization. All ethnolinguistic Tai groups are considered Lao Lum. Thus, there is no official recognition of the Lao Tai at all. Those from the Mon-Khmer ethnolinguistic group are deemed Lao Theung, whereas people from the Sino-Tibetan (Tibeto-Burman) or Hmong-Yao (Mien) language families are considered Lao Sung.[18] In doing so, it is apparent that government authorities have consciously tried to create a Lao identity by downplaying divisions, and, in the process, they have entrenched a dominant political, social, and cultural narrative in the country. Vatthana Pholsena, a leading scholar of modern Laos, points out that there are important cultural and political implications in definitions of ethnic groups, nationality, and nation, particularly when used by the government. She also notes the role that language has in determining such concepts. The term *Lao* is often used to describe both ethnicity and nationality, and thus applies to the whole population, despite the fact that in many respects it refers to one specific ethnic group. Officially, however, the diversity of peoples in Laos is recognized. The government still quotes its first communist leader: "each ethnic group has a nice and beautiful culture and belongs to the Lao national community, just as all kinds of flowers grown in a garden of various colors and scents."[19] Recently, the government has begun to promote ethnic diversity, primarily to attract tourism and improve its international image with respect to human rights.

For many who study Laos, the problem of whether *Lao* is even a legitimate ethnolinguistic term remains. Countries like Vietnam and China define dominant groups (Kinh and Han, respectively), but in both instances there are well-documented historical references to support them. The absence of a definitive separation from the broader Tai ethnolinguistic grouping makes this much more problematic in the case of the Lao. These distinctions are not simply academic. They speak to the very concept of national identity. For example, although Laos and Vietnam have been extremely close politically since communist takeovers in 1975, traditional cultural and historical animosities persist. Some experts see the Annamite Cordillera not just as a mountain range or the boundary between the two countries but as a kind of cultural fault line that divides Southeast Asia between its two greatest influences: India and China. Whereas the Lao (along with the Thai, Burmese, and Khmer) have absorbed more Indic traditions, the Vietnamese are more

Sinitic, or closer to the Chinese. A number of proverbs reflect this division, such as the old Lao saying "Lao and Vietnamese: Cat and Dog," or the adage "the Vietnamese plants the rice, the Khmers watch them planting, but the Lao listen to the rice grow."[20]

More pragmatic considerations have also played a part in shaping the relationship between Laos and Vietnam. The Vietnamese have always been more numerous and expansionist, something the Lao and especially the Khmer view with great suspicion. The period of French rule did little to change this, given the primacy of Vietnam in all matters and the fact that Laos (like Cambodia) was considered an appendage of its much larger neighbor. Moreover, French administrators encouraged, and indeed forced, the migration of Vietnamese into the rest of Indochina. Many came to dominate the commercial and bureaucratic elites in Laos, with rather predictable resentment from the Lao. This also dramatically changed the shape of Lao society as a whole. By the time of independence from France in 1953, more than half of the population of Vientiane was Vietnamese or Chinese. Thakhek and Pakse had even higher proportions: 89 percent and 85 percent, respectively.[21] Although many of those immigrants have returned home over the past fifty years, there remains a strong ethnically Vietnamese presence in places like Vientiane, and their profile in the economy continues to draw Lao resentment. In contrast, most ethnic Chinese in Laos have blended in over time and do not provoke the same reaction.

Lowland Lao relations with Lao Theung peoples undermine the government's insistence that they are part of the same family. Although some have been integrated into a more mainstream existence, most Lao Theung remain culturally distinct with different languages, religions, and practices. The largest of these groups is the Khmou (also spelled *Khmu*, *Kmhmu*, *Khammu*, *Khamu*, and *Kammu*), who, according to a 1995 government census, number slightly more than five hundred thousand, or 11 percent of the national populace. *Khmou* means "person," so many subgroups distinguish themselves by additional names, such as Khmou Rock, Khmou U, Khmou Khrong, or Khmou Mae. The Khmou are among the oldest inhabitants of northern and central Laos, having migrated during the first millennium c.e. from either Burma or southern China. The Khmou claim to be the founders of the ancient Lao capital at Luang Prabang. They speak a Mon-Khmer language and follow animist religious beliefs. Other larger Lao Theung populations include the Katang (roughly 110,000), Bru (70,000), Kui (52,000), Laven (40,000), Mal (24,000), Phai (15,000), Katu (15,000), Lave (13,000), Ngae (12,000), Jeh (8,000), Khuen (8,000), and Jeng (7,000). The Alak, Ir, Kasseng, and Khlor all number between four thousand and six thousand people, whereas the Aheu, Bo, Halang Doan, Hung, Xinh Mul, and Khua number between two thousand and four thousand people each. Smaller groups include the Arem, Bit, Chut, Maleng, and a host of other tribes.[22] Today, some of these tribes live in very remote locations and have a traditional hunter-gatherer existence. Many Lao Lum consider such remote groups to be strange peoples who engage in black magic, bizarre rituals, and even human sacrifices. For example, as traditional, nomadic hunters, the Mlabri are derisively referred to *khon pa* ("jungle people") by Lao who still view them as "savages."[23]

Relations between the Lao Lum and Lao Sung, or hill tribes, have also been problematic. The ethnic groups that make up the Lao Sung have consistently been the poorest and most marginalized in the country. Some have also forcibly resisted attempts to be integrated into the mainstream Lao Lum majority. In fact, as discussed in Chapter 2, the Hmong were important combatants throughout French rule and the Vietnam War era, when many worked with American forces against the communists. Not surprisingly, following the communist takeover in 1975 the Hmong were persecuted.

The Lao Sung are relative newcomers to Laos, most having migrated there in the early nineteenth century from southern China. As discussed in the section on languages, the Lao Sung stem from two distinct linguistic families: Tai and Sino-Tibetan. The Hmong make up the largest group, numbering about 320,000. They are best known to travelers by their array of colorful costumes and unique handicrafts. There are actually four subdivisions of Hmong: the White, Red, Black, and Striped Hmong. They live primarily in nine northern provinces and are most concentrated in Hua Phan, Xiang Khuang, and Luang Prabang. Most Hmong practice slash-and-burn agriculture to grow dry rice and corn, as well as to raise livestock.[24] However, many also cultivate opium poppies, which are integral to the international narcotics trade of which the Golden Triangle of Laos, Burma, and Thailand is a major producer. Despite recent attempts by the Lao government to showcase the Hmong as part of the country's ethnic diversity, the reality is that they and other Lao Sung remain problematic for authorities in Vientiane. They are notoriously independent and suspicious of the Lao majority. Their history in Laos is a painful one, full of betrayed promises and almost continuous war. Tens of thousands of Hmong fled the country after 1975 and many still reside in camps in Thailand, which muddies relations between Vientiane and Bangkok and, from the Lao point of view, constitutes a potential threat to national security. This is particularly true in light of the intermittent insurgency led by Hmong who reject accommodations with the Lao Lum and aspire to varying degrees of autonomy within Laos.

The Yao (also known as the Mien, Lu Mien, and Man) come from the same linguistic family as the Hmong but are generally more Sinitic, as they use Chinese script for writing and incorporate Taoist deities into their faith. The

Yao number approximately fifty thousand, mostly in the north. They engage in the same farming practices as the Hmong, including opium production. There is also a population of about five thousand Kim Mun people, closely related to but distinct from the Yao, in Laos. Within the Sino-Tibetan family the Lao Sung are primarily represented by the Kaw (60,000), Lahu (10,000), Kaduo (5,000), and Lisu (4,000). There are also smaller populations of Hani, Phana, Si La, and Kado.[25]

No discussion on the peoples of Laos would be complete without mentioning sizable émigré communities outside the country. More than 10 percent of the entire population, or some four hundred thousand people, fled the communist takeover in 1975.[26] Perhaps even more taxing was that this exodus included nearly 90 percent of those with formal education.[27] Some estimate that as many as 50 percent of various Lao Sung groups left to seek save haven elsewhere. The large ethnically Lao populace of northeastern Thailand and the large Hmong communities scattered along the Laos–Thailand border are of concern to authorities in Vientiane. So, too, are the considerable numbers of Lao and Hmong who eventually resettled abroad, primarily in the United States and France. By some accounts there are almost the same number of Lao speakers in the United States as there are in Laos itself. One the one hand, the Lao government has viewed these communities as potential threats. More recently, however, it has come to view them as possible assets for the economic development of the country, even encouraging successful Lao émigrés to return and open businesses. Moreover, as discussed in Chapters 4 and 5, overseas communities, especially in the United States, are extremely important to the literature and art of Laos.

LANGUAGES

Given such ethnic diversity it is not surprising that there are at least eighty distinct languages spoken by the different ethnic populations of Laos. Experts differ on the precise classification of all languages, especially considering the numerous groups, subgroups, and dialects found in the country. However, most sources identify three major language families in Laos: the Tai-Kadai, Austroasiatic, and Sino-Tibetan. Within the Tai-Kadai family there are two groups: the Tai and the Hmong-Yao (Mien). Each is in turn divided into branches and numerous sub-branches, making any discussion on language in Laos rather complicated. For example, the Tai-Kadai has three principal branches based on geographic region: the northern, southwestern, and "unclassified" Tay-Tai. Within the northern branch are at least twenty-three sub-branches, while the southwestern branch numbers approximately fifteen sub-branches. The Austroasiatic family of languages is represented in Laos by only one group: the Mon-Khmer, which has six major branches and at least forty sub-branches. Sino-Tibetan languages include two major branches, the Han (Sinitic) and Lolo-Burmese, both of which have several sub-branches.[28]

The official language of Laos is Lao, part of the Tai-Kadai group, as spoken and written in Vientiane. There are also a multitude of "tribal" languages spoken among the many ethnic minorities in the country, representing the other linguistic families and groups. Lao serves as the lingua franca between these groups. Linguists identify five major dialects of Lao according to regions: Vientiane, northern, northeastern, central, and southern. Northern Lao dominates the provinces of Sainyabuli, Bokeo, Phongsali, Luang Nam Tha, Udomxai, and Luang Prabang. Northeastern Lao is spoken primarily in Xiang Khuang and Hua Phan, whereas central Lao is heard in Khammuan and Bolikhamsai. The regions of Champasak, Salavan, Savannakhet, Attapeu, and Sekong are home to the southern Lao dialect.[29] There are many subdialects and different vocabularies as well. As part of the Tai-Kadai family of languages, Lao is similar to Thai. Spoken Thai is easily understood in Laos, especially in the Mekong River Valley, given the influence of Thai culture. Many of the words in both languages are the same, although the two are not mutually intelligible given differences in grammar, usage, and pronunciation. The Lao used in the Isan region in northeastern Thailand is exactly the same as the standard or Vientiane form. However, the written languages diverge slightly. Most educated Lao also understand written Thai given that the majority of texts used in Lao colleges and universities are from Thailand.

Lao is a monosyllabic, tonal language. Tones differentiate the meaning of words. For example, the word *sao* means "girl," "morning," "pillar," or "twenty," depending on the tone used.[30] There are six tones in Lao: three level tones (low, mid, and high) and three inclined tones (rising, high falling, low falling). Languages like Thai, Mandarin, and Cantonese are similar in this respect, although standard Thai has five tones, while Mandarin has four and Cantonese has nine. The tones are relative to the speaker, in that each speaker can give different pitches to each tone.

The Lao script is fairly new, first developed during the Lan Xang period. It was devised from Tai script, which was itself based on Khmer and earlier Indian scripts. Prior to the communist takeover in 1975 there were multiple writing systems in Laos. As most published material was in French, Thai, or Vietnamese, no standardized Lao script existed. Since 1975 government authorities have established a common system, but variations based on region continue. Although there is some debate, many scholars agree that the written form today has thirty-three consonants based on twenty-one sounds and twenty-eight vowels and diphthongs (various combinations of vowels used to form special sounds) based on twenty-seven sounds. It has also four diacritic marks used with other symbols to indicate the six spoken tones.[31] As indicated in the note on transliteration at the beginning of this book, translating Lao words into a romanized alphabet can be extremely difficult because of unique vowel sounds. It is important to note that other scripts are still in use today in Laos, including *lao tham* (*dhamma lao*), for writing ancient religious scripture in the Pali language of Theravada Buddhism, and assorted Thai tribal systems, such as Thai Neua, the standardized language form of the Thai language in southern China.

Languages of the Lao Theung all come from the Austroasiatic family and are of Mon-Khmer origin, which many scholars consider indigenous to large parts of Southeast Asia. Linguists count 147 separate Mon-Khmer languages among the 168 in the Austroasiatic family, the most widely spoken of which are Vietnamese and Khmer. Six major branches are found in Laos, including the Bahnaric, Katuic, Khmuic, Palaungic, Viet-Muong, and Lavy. There are at least thirty groups within these branches. For example, the Htin, Khmou, and Mlabri are part of the Khmuic branch, whereas the Brau, Chieng, Sedang, and Sou are Bahnaric.

Lao Sung languages stem from both the Tai-Kadai and Sino-Tibetan family. The former is represented by the Hmong-Yao (Mien) group, which, as the name suggest, has two principal branches. Hmong speakers are further grouped into three categories—the Chuanqiandian, the Qiandong, and the Xiangxi—upon which Hmong tribal divisions are based. The Hmong Do (White Hmong), Hmong Lenh (Striped, Flower, or Variegated Hmong), and Hmong Njua (Blue or Green Hmong), along with their further subgroups, are Chuanqiandian. The Qiandong sub-branch includes the Hmong Du (Black Hmong), whereas the Hmong Si (Red Hmong) are within the Xiangxi. Yao (Mien) speakers include exclusively the Yao (Mien) and their subgroups. The Lao Sung also includes a small number of ethnic Cham peoples, who belong to the Malayo-Polynesian group of the Austronesian linguistic family. Sino-Tibetan representation within the Lao Sung includes southwestern Mandarin–speaking Haw and ethnic Chinese, as well as Lolo-Burmese speakers like the Akha, Lahu, Phanna, and Si La.[32] It should be noted that some scholars identify a Tibeto-Burman subfamily within the Sino-Tibetan classification. There are an estimated 350 Tibeto-Burman languages, the most spoken of which today is Burmese.

Chinese languages and Vietnamese are spoken in those ethnic communities, but many Lao also understand the latter given the two countries' close economic and political association over the past few decades. A few Lao, most of whom worked with the government or military, also speak Russian, which reflects Laos's strategic alignment during the cold war. Many elderly Lao may also speak French, which remains the official second language in the country and is used widely in government and business. However, English is the common tongue of tourism and international development and is fast supplanting all others as the unofficial second language of Laos.

NOTES

1. Clare Griffiths, ed. *Insight Guides: Laos and Cambodia* (London: Apa Publications, 2005), 43.

2. Ibid., 44–45.

3. Houmphan Rattanavong, "What May Be in Store for the Mekong, Our Great and Sacred Ganges?" *Juth Pakai* 2 (June 2004): 37. See also Nguyen Thi Dieu, *The Mekong River and the Struggle for Indochina: Water, War, and Peace* (Westport, CT: Praeger, 1999).

4. Joe Cummings and Andrew Burke, *Laos* (Footscray, Australia: Lonely Planet, 2005), 45–46.

5. Ibid., 48.

6. U.N. Special Report, *Blue Book of Laos* (Japanese Bank for International Cooperation), www.un.org/special-rep/ohrlls/lde/ldc-rep/LaoDemRep.htm (retrieved February 2008).

7. Cummings and Burke, *Laos,* 46–51.

8. Jeff Cranmer and Steven Martin, *The Rough Guide to Laos* (London: Rough Guides, 2002), 376–383.

9. U.N. Special Report, *Blue Book of Laos* (Japanese Bank for International Cooperation), www.un.org/special-rep/ohrlls/lde/ldc-rep/LaoDemRep.htm (retrieved February 2008).

10. U.N. Common Country Assessment (CCA), *Lao DPR,* June 2006, 4.

11. Vatthana Pholsena and Ruth Banomyong, *Laos: From Buffer State to Crossroads?* (Chiang Mai: Mekong Press, 2004), 70–72.

12. Cummings and Burke, *Laos,* 34.

13. U.N. Conference on Trade and Development (UNCTAD), *Statistical Profiles of Least Developed Countries,* 2005, www.unctad.org (retrieved June 2007).

14. Northeastern Illinois University Center for Southeast Asian Studies, "Resources for Lao Studies," www.seasite.niu.edu/lao (retrieved January 2008).

15. Griffiths, *Insight Guides,* 51.

16. Grant Evans, "What Is Lao Culture and Society?" in *Laos: Culture and Society* (Chiang Mai: Silkworm Books, 1999), 1.

17. Ibid., 1–3; see also Stuart-Fox, *A History of Laos,* chapter 1.

18. Grant Evans, ed. *Laos: Culture and Society* (Chiang Mai, Thailand: Silkworm Books, 1999), 8–9. See also Vatthana Pholsena, "Ethnic Classification and Mapping Nationhood in Contemporary Laos," *Asian Ethnicity* 3, no. 2 (September 2002): 175–197.

19. Vatthana Pholsena, *Post-War Laos: The Politics of Culture, History, and Identity* (Ithaca, NY: Cornell University Press, 2006), 93–95, 173–177.

20. Griffiths, *Insight Guides*, 52–53.

21. Ibid., 54–55.

22. Visiting Arts Culture Profile Project, "Laos Cultural Profile," www.culturalprofiles.org.uk/laos (retrieved September 2007).

23. Cranmer and Martin, *Rough Guide*, 372–373; see also Joachim Schliesinger, *Ethnic Groups of Laos*, vol. 1, *Introduction and Overview* (Bangkok: White Lotus Press, 2003).

24. Cummings and Burke, *Laos*, 36.

25. Schliesinger, *Ethnic Groups of Laos*, vol. 4, *Sino-Tibetan Speaking Peoples* (Bangkok: White Lotus Press, 2003); see also Laurant Chazée, *The Peoples of Laos: Rural and Ethnic Diversities* (Bangkok: White Lotus Press, 1999), 150–160.

26. Si-Ambhaivan Sisombat Souvannavong, "Elites in Exile: The Emergence of a Transnational Lao Culture," in Evans, *Laos*, 180.

27. Chithtalath Seng Ampone, "Education Improvement for Ethnic Children in the Moksuk-Tafa Area," *Juth Pakai* 7 (October 2005): 5.

28. N. J. Enfield, *Linguistic Epidemiology: Semantics and Grammar of Language Contact in Mainland Southeast Asia* (London: RoutledgeCurzon, 2003), 45–72, 365–369.

29. Joe Cummings, *Lao Phrasebook* (Footscray, Australia: Lonely Planet Publications, 2002), 11.

30. Ibid., 17.

31. Northeastern Illinois University Center for Southeast Asian Studies, "Resources for Lao Studies," www.seasite.niu.edu/lao (retrieved January 2008); see also Cummings and Burke, *Laos*, 290.

32. Schliesinger, *Ethnic Groups of Laos*, 1:85–95.

2

A Brief History of Laos

PREHISTORY AND THE TAI MIGRATIONS

THE FIRST PERMANENT settlements in Laos developed approximately forty thousand years ago. Little archaeological evidence of these peoples exists, although it is known that they used stone tools and were primarily hunter-gatherers. By about 10,000 B.C.E. inhabitants of the area were farming and raising livestock. Evidence of agricultural activity near Ban Chiang in northeastern Thailand dates back to 4,000 B.C.E.—one of the oldest finds in the world—pointing to the fact that Southeast Asia was a cradle of human civilization.[1] By 500 B.C.E. people in the Khorat Plateau and Mekong River Valley were using iron. Bronze drums from northern Vietnam suggest that sophisticated metallurgy in the region appeared during the first millennium C.E.

The earliest Iron Age settlements in Laos were found in Xiang Khuang Province on the mysterious Plain of Jars. Here, scattered across a plateau roughly 15 kilometers (10.3 miles) wide are large urns, resembling giant jars, more than two thousand years old. The largest are about 2 meters (6.1 feet) tall and weigh up to ten thousand kilograms (ten tons). Their remote location and decades of conflict made research difficult, but most archaeologists think that they were used to hold the ashes of the deceased. Massive stone pillars and underground chambers discovered more recently support this notion. Although the exact purpose of the urns is unclear, there is no doubt that the Plain of Jars was home to an advanced Iron Age civilization.

Looking down on the Plain of Jars. Courtesy of Martine Duprey.

Broad linguistic and cultural differentiation in Southeast Asia began around 10,000 B.C.E., but it was not until the first millennium C.E. that distinct groups began to emerge. The early inhabitants of Laos spoke Austroasiatic languages, like Mon and Khmer. Tai peoples were still confined to southern China. Confronting more numerous neighbors, between the sixth and eighth centuries C.E. the Tai began to form larger units, called *muang*. These were run by powerful men, called *chao*, who protected the *muang* in return for labor or goods. The *muang* drew Tai peoples together. Gradually pushed out by the Chinese and Vietnamese, the Tai migrated into present-day Laos and Thailand. In turn they displaced indigenous inhabitants, who moved into the mountains. By the ninth and tenth centuries Tai peoples occupied upper Southeast Asia, centered on the kingdom of Nan-Chao in present-day Yunnan, China, and a second state called Yonok in Bokeo Province, northern Laos. However, they were surrounded by larger rivals—the Indianized kingdoms of Champa in Vietnam, the Khmer of Angkor, and the Mon of Burma—all of which had profound effects on the development of Tai identity.

Indian cultures more than Chinese cultures influenced the Tai. As early as the first century C.E. Indian traders crisscrossed the region en route to China by both land and sea. Traders and merchants helped to spread the Hindu religion. Local rulers also likely invited monks and scholars from India to come and help develop new a social structure and belief system. They brought Pali and Sanskrit systems that form the basis of many modern languages in the region. Hindu kingdoms like Funan controlled parts of Laos between the first and sixth centuries C.E. Between the sixth and eighth centuries they were held by Chenla, another Mon-Khmer, Hindu kingdom that stretched into Cambodia.

One of the most important Indianized cultures that shaped the evolution of Laos was the Dvaravati. Although never an empire in the true sense of the word, the Dvaravati had enormous influence in the region, stretching from India through to the Gulf of Thailand. Much of this civilization remains a mystery, but it is clear that between the sixth and ninth centuries it established profitable trade networks in the Chao Phraya River Valley of Thailand. Two kingdoms—one called Sri Gotapura, near Thakhek, and the other known as Muang Sawa, today's Luang Prabang—controlled much of Laos between the eighth and twelfth centuries. It is also known that the Dvaravati were Mon people who converted to Theravada Buddhism. By the eleventh and twelfth centuries Buddhism was solidly entrenched in Laos, as evidenced by relics and statuary.[2] The spread of Buddhism in turn reinforced the sense of uniqueness among Tai peoples and strengthened the *muangs*.

This was especially important given the rise of the Khmer empire toward the end of the ninth century. The Khmer are most famous for the massive temple complex at Angkor in Cambodia, which today is one of the most important ancient sites in the world. The Khmer pushed into southern Laos, northeastern Thailand, and southern Vietnam. They were predominantly Hindus, although under King Jayavarman VII (ruled 1181–1201) the empire adopted Mahayana Buddhism. The Khmer built numerous temples, fortifications, trade posts, and roads. They also controlled a vast trade network between China and India, which brought them into direct contact with the Tai. Most experts agree that by twelfth century the people of Laos were predominantly Khmer, but war and the expansion of the Tai changed this.

Khmer culture dramatically influenced the Tai. Most important was the Khmer political system, which the Tai adopted for themselves. This was based on the *mandala*—a Sanskrit word meaning "essence" or "containing" that underpins Hindu and Buddhist notions of the cosmos. In political terms, the *mandala* is a spatial representation of the state as an organism made up of constituent parts. In this respect, the *mandala* was consistent with the structure of Tai *muangs*. Each could be a separate geopolitical entity while simultaneously part of a larger state. Tribute, in the form of goods and armies, was given to a centralized authority in exchange for defense and support. However, each tributary maintained independence and, theoretically at least, could withdraw support from the *mandala* should the central authority fail. *Mandalas* were designed to minimize warfare and conquest by force.[3]

By absorbing Dvaravati and Khmer cultures, the Tai became increasingly diverse. However, Buddhism provided cohesion while the collapse of Khmer rule provided opportunity for new Tai states to emerge. Khmer power faded in the late thirteenth century as Mongol armies invaded Southeast Asia. Almost simultaneously two major Tai kingdoms developed, both in northern Thailand. One was at Sukhothai, founded between 1279 and 1298 by King Ramkhamhaeng (ruled 1279–1318), while the other was at Lan Na (Lanna), established between 1281 and 1292 under King Mangrai (ruled two kingdoms, 1259–1317). Both were initially tributaries of the Mongol-Chinese Yuan dynasty but quickly expanded their influence. Lan Na incorporated Tai *muangs* in Burma, Laos, and southern China. Sukhothai eventually controlled lands in Thailand and Laos, including Muang Sawa.[4] It was there that the first Lao *muang* began, originally called Xiang Dong Xiang Thong ("City of Flame Trees beside the River Dong"). By the mid-fourteenth century the *mandala* system allowed for the emergence of an even more distinctly Lao-Tai kingdom there known as Lan Xang (Lane Xang).

LAN XANG

Lan Xang, "Kingdom of One Million Elephants," is the historical center of Laos. Legend has it that a young prince from Xiang Dong Xiang Thong named Fa Ngum was exiled from the kingdom after his father attempted to seize power and fled to Angkor to seek Khmer protection. He ended up marrying a Khmer princess and mobilizing an army, first to conquer territories in the Mekong Valley and then to turn against his home. Capturing Xiang Dong Xiang Thong in 1353, Fa Ngum renamed the kingdom Lan Xang Hom Khao ("Kingdom of One Million Elephants and the White Parasol") and ruled through 1368. During his reign the kingdom expanded into northeastern Thailand and southern China.[5]

Although a magnificent general, Fa Ngum was a despotic ruler. He did not tolerate dissent and disregarded the *mandala* system by demanding absolute control of the empire. Fearing insurrections, his top advisers appealed to Fa Ngum's queen, Keo Keng Ya (Kaew Keng Nya), to intervene. She convinced her husband to moderate his ways and seek the counsel of Buddhist monks specially requested from Angkor. They came bearing holy scriptures known as the Tipitaka (see Chapter 3) and one of the most important figures of the Buddha, the Phabang (Prabang), sent by the king of Angkor. Reputedly then already 1,400 years old and crafted in Ceylon (Sri Lanka), the Phabang was

solid gold, weighed 40 kilograms (88 pounds), and was carried by eight at-
tendees. It came in a procession of almost ten thousand people: mostly craftsmen, engineers, and attendants given to Fa Ngum. According to legend, the
Phabang made it as far as Vieng Kham (Phainam), north of Vientiane, but
mysteriously could not be moved further—thus convincing Fa Ngum that it
wanted to stay there. He built a temple to house it and the statue remained
in Vieng Kham and Vientiane for nearly 150 years before finally making the
journey to Xiang Dong Xiang Thong in 1512.

Fa Ngum did not introduce Buddhism to Laos. The religion was established
long before him. However, it is possible that he recognized Theravada Buddhism as the religion of Lan Xang, and thus gave Laos its majority faith today.
Nor is it true that Fa Ngum single-handedly redeveloped the *mandala* system
or secured his kingdom's frontiers. Both were achieved over nearly 150 years
following the establishment of Lan Xang. Nonetheless, Fa Ngum remains an
epic figure in Laotian history. In the search for a uniquely Lao identity today,
he and the kingdom of Lan Xang have become pivotal, leaving some prone
to mythology.[6] Fa Ngum was succeeded by his eldest son, Sam Sen Thai (also
called Oun Heaun or Unheaun; ruled ca. 1373–1416), who was known as
the Lord of Three Hundred Thousand Tai, in reference to the number of men
at his disposal after a census was taken in 1376. He consolidated Lan Xang's
power by strategically marrying into the royal families of both Lan Na and
the increasingly powerful kingdom of Ayutthaya (Ayudhya). He also modeled the administrative, financial, and military systems of Lan Xang on other
Tai states, giving rise to the Tai people as a whole.

However, following his death in about 1416 Lan Xang declined. The fact
that there were eight kings in twenty-two years speaks to internal political
rivalries and a crippling succession crisis. Some scholars contend that during this period a senior queen known as Maha Devi, or Great Goddess,
whose identity remains unclear, dominated Lan Xang.[7] Then, in approximately 1438, the ruler of Vientiane and Sam Sen Thai's only surviving son,
Vangburi, took over the kingdom. Taking the name Sainyachakkapat Phaen
Phaew, or Chakkapat—derived from the Pali term for "universal Buddhist
monarch"—he set about stabilizing Lan Xang. His most important contri-
butions were establishing a clearer line of succession and further entrenching
Theravada Buddhism.[8] However, war with the Vietnamese ended his efforts.
The Vietnamese occupied parts of the kingdom and sacked Xiang Dong Xiang
Thong, forcing Chakkapat to flee.

Over the subsequent twenty years, his successors managed to regain control of the kingdom, force the Vietnamese to withdraw, and secure Lan Xang's
frontiers through close relations with Ayutthaya, which by the early sixteenth century was the most powerful Tai state. This was the golden age of

Lan Xang. Government was reorganized, thus allowing for a centralized and more efficient bureaucracy. Trade networks were expanded, bringing considerable wealth. Buddhist temples, monasteries, and schools were built, making the kingdom a major center not only for religion but also for literature and the arts. The long-delayed arrival of the Phabang in Xiang Dong Xiang Thong during the reign of Vixun (Visoun, Visunurat, Wisunarath; ruled ca. 1501–1520) gave Lan Xang additional prestige. In fact, the Phabang became an even more important religious and political symbol. Everyone was expected to swear loyalty to the king before it, thus making it a representation of sacred power and reinforcing the idea that the monarchy and the faith were inseparable. Successive kings built temples, established elaborate rituals, and dedicated servants to care for the Phabang. Phothisarat (Pothisarath, Phothisarath, or Phothisalarat; ruled ca. 1520–1550) even abolished all other religious symbols in the kingdom, like the *lak muang* (a guardian spirit), issuing a decree against animist spirit shrines (*ho phi*).

Lan Xang also became more important in terms of regional politics. In 1520 Phothisarat took up residence in Vientiane, which was closer to trade networks with Vietnam, Cambodia, and Ayutthaya. It was also closer to the bulk of his people, who had migrated from the Mekong Valley onto the Khorat Plateau. From there Lan Xang exercised more influence, particularly as the Khmer empire receded. Phothisarat also took advantage of rivalries within the Tai world. He was married into the kingdom of Lan Na and, consequently, decided to come to its aid when Ayutthaya invaded it in 1545. Victorious, Phothisarat in effect controlled Lan Na. The following year he arranged for his teenage son, Sethathirat (Sethathirath, Xetthathirat, or Setthathilat), to ascend the throne there. When Phothisarat died shortly thereafter, crushed under his war elephant during a demonstration of his riding skills, Sethathirat returned to rule Lan Xang (ca. 1546–1571). With the new king gone, Lan Na soon rebelled and regained its independence. However, many of its elite families, scholars, and artisans followed Sethathirat, further enriching the cultural development of Lan Xang. Another important Buddhist icon also followed. Before leaving La Na, Sethathirat removed the sacred Pha Keo (Phra Kaew), or Emerald Buddha, which today is the most revered symbol in Thailand. The young king then ordered the construction of the most striking architecture in Laos: Wat Pha Keo in Vientiane to house the Emerald Buddha; the massive That Luang, or Grand Stupa, also in Vientiane, as the symbol of unity; and Wat Xiang Thong in Xiang Dong Xiang Thong to mark his reign. Sethathirat also moved the capital to Vientiane and renamed Xiang Dong Xiang Thong for the venerable Phabang, Luang Prabang, in 1563.

The move was designed to secure a more strategic location for the political center of the kingdom, especially with the rise of the powerful Pegu (Burmese) in the west. Frequent war with the Burmese dramatically effected Lan Xang, and indeed all the Tai peoples, between the sixteenth and eighteenth centuries. By 1560 the Pegu overran Lan Na and threatened both Lan Xang and Ayutthaya, prompting an alliance between the two former enemies. However, even that did not provide security. For almost a decade, war with the Burmese ravaged Tai lands. Luang Prabang was sacked in 1563, and Vientiane fell two years later. The Burmese then lay siege to Ayutthaya between 1568 and 1569. Sethathirat led a rebellion against Pegu, forcing the Burmese to withdraw. For a brief period he ruled the only remaining independent Tai kingdom. The pressures of war had, however, greatly weakened Lan Xang and produced internal revolts. Leading an army south into the mountains to suppress one, Sethathirat mysteriously disappeared in 1571, giving rise to another succession crisis and continuing war.[9] Burmese armies reclaimed Vientiane and through a series of puppet kings extended their control of Lan Xang. For nearly seventy years Lan Xang remained a vassal of Pegu.

The kingdom's revival began under Surinyavongsa (Soulignavongsa or Sourinyavongsa; ruled ca. 1638–1695). As Burmese power declined, he reestablished family ties between Tai kingdoms through marriages. Boundaries with a resurgent Ayutthaya were negotiated, while peace between Lan Xang and its eastern rivals was achieved through Surinyavongsa's taking of a Vietnamese princess as concubine. Trade flourished and the kingdom regained its wealth and influence in the region. During Surinyavongsa's long rule temples and palaces were restored or built anew. Lan Xang once again became a Buddhist cultural and religious center, with, as Dutch merchant Gerritt van Wuysthoff noted, more monks than all the soldiers in Germany.[10]

Indeed, foreign adventurers provide interesting insight on Lan Xang in the sixteenth and seventeenth centuries. The first to arrive were probably Portuguese traders accompanying Burmese envoys in 1545. An epic poem on Portuguese colonies written in 1572 by Luís de Camões mentions the Lao "in their lands and numbers strong," with a "countless throng of tribes whose names a man can scarcely tell." However, van Wuysthoff and Italian missionary Giovanni-Maria Leria are the first Europeans to leave a definitive record of their travels; both arrived in the 1640s and published their work in the 1660s. They were struck not only by the kingdom's prosperity but also by the friendliness and beauty of its people. Writing in 1727, after the division of the kingdom, the Scottish sea captain Alexander Hamilton wrote, "Lao land . . . produces gold, raw silk, and elephant teeth [that] are so plentiful that they stake their fields and gardens about with them." He also noted that with their "lighter complexions" Lao women "were little inferior to Portuguese or Spanish ladies."[11]

By most accounts, seventeenth-century Lan Xang was a multicultural king-dom. Its population included not only Tai but also Khmer, Mon, various mountain people, Vietnamese, Chinese, and Indians. Pali, the ritual language of Theravada Buddhism, was probably the official tongue, but it is likely that many different languages operated in everyday life. Buddhism was the dom-inant, if not exclusive, religion practiced openly. Those who did not follow the faith were considered outsiders, often referred to as *kha*, or "slaves," but there is little evidence that any widespread religious discrimination took place. Most scholars agree that beyond considering themselves Buddhists and Tai, the population of Lan Xang did not have a particular sense of identity, and, despite the contention of nationalist historians, definitely did not consider themselves Lao. There are Western maps of Southeast Asia dating as far back as 1613 that show both Laos and the Regnum Lao ("Lao kingdom"). However, they were likely based on Chinese charts that were generic in their reference, in that they applied to all peoples in the region. Vietnamese traders referred to those Tai who lived Laos as Ailao (or Ai-Lao), although exactly why remains a mystery.[12] Still, as was true throughout the Tai world in the seventeenth cen-tury, Lan Xang did flourish culturally, developing artistic traditions around Indian epics like the Ramayana. In this respect many Lao consider Lan Xang, particularly during its resurgence in the mid to late 1600s, a watershed of Lao identity and the first Lao state.

Ironically, Surinyavongsa himself undid much of Lan Xang's resurrec-tion. Obsessed with maintaining the laws he laid down, Surinyavongsa had his only son executed for adultery, ultimately giving rise to another succes-sion crisis when he died in 1694. Over the subsequent twenty years the Vietnamese and Ayutthaya vied for control of Lan Xang through factions within its courts, producing almost constant conflict. A string of ineffec-tive puppet rulers resulted. The kingdom also suffered from its relative iso-lation. Lacking access to the sea, it could not secure expanded trade net-works in Southeast Asia: an especially vital consideration in an era during which Europeans were bringing new goods and advanced technologies to the region.

By the early eighteenth century Lan Xang was in a steep decline from which it would never recover. Between 1700 and 1713 the kingdom divided into three parts centered on Luang Prabang, Vientiane, and Champasak. Rivalries between them were intense, as each vied for more control by shifting alliances with outside powers. Ayutthaya, which had dramatically recovered in the late seventeenth century, was the most important. By the 1720s it had made all three kingdoms vassal states in a powerful Tai empire. However, war with the Burmese again changed the Tai world. Beginning in 1760, they invaded all the Tai kingdoms. So deep were the animosities between the fragments of Lan Xang that Vientiane sided with the Burmese against Luang Prabang. Ayutthaya sent its forces to repel them but to no avail. After nearly seven years of war on its frontiers Ayutthaya was itself destroyed in 1767. Most of the royal family was killed or carried away, and tens of thousands died or ended up as Burmese slaves.[13] In many respects it appeared that the Tai civilization had come to an end.

Remarkably, that was not the case. Fleeing Ayutthaya, the Tai quickly set up a new capital at Thonburi, near Bangkok. They established a new ruling house, the Chakri dynasty, which is still today the royal family of Thailand. Led by General Taksin (ruled 1767–1782), Thonburi's armies finally defeated the Burmese and forced their retreat. Then they regained lost lands before turning to expansion. With little opposition Taksin took Lan Na in 1776. His armies then swept east into Cambodia and southern Laos, conquering Sikhotabong and Champasak. By 1778 Taksin laid siege to Vientiane. Exacting revenge for Vientiane's support of the Burmese, Luang Prabang joined forces with him in destroying its rival. Thousands, including Vientiane's ruling family, were taken prisoner. From both Vientiane and Luang Prabang, Taksin's armies removed sacred Buddhist icons, including the Phabang and Pha Keo. With this, even the symbolic importance of Lan Xang was gone. As vassals on the periphery of the new empire, the successors of Lan Xang became pale reminders of the first kingdom of Laos.

WAR WITH SIAM

Siam adopted a decentralized *mandala* system that afforded the remnants of Lan Xang considerable autonomy. They maintained independent armies, albeit after declaring their loyalty to the Chakri court, kept the rights to tax, to administer a judicial system, and to conduct a limited foreign policy. Siam insisted on approving succession in the kingdoms and appointing high officials, as well as commanding their armies in time of need. The vassals were also prevented from declaring war. This was in part designed to prevent conflict between the various kingdoms. In fact, the first of the Chakri kings in Siam, Rama I (Phra Phutthayofta or Chaophraya Chakri; ruled 1782–1809), tried hard to heal rifts between them. The king of Vientiane, Nanthasen (ruled 1782–1792), was allowed to take back the Phabang and people whom the Siamese had enslaved. However, when he invaded Luang Prabang in 1792 to exact revenge yet again, Rama I removed Nanthasen from the throne. He replaced him with Inthavong (Inthasom; ruled 1792–1804) who, by fighting off Burmese invasions in both 1797 and 1802, strengthened ties with Bangkok. They were cemented further when Inthavong gave Rama I one of his daughters.[14]

Following Inthavong's death the crown fell to his younger brother, Anu-vong (Anou, ruled 1804–1828), who had distinguished himself as a general in the wars against Burma. He developed Vientiane's standing as a religious and literary center and built some of Laos's most important temples. He was also, at least initially, a loyal ally of Siam, so much so that in 1819 Rama II (Phra Phuttaloetla, ruled 1809–1824) appointed Anuvong's son Yo to rule Champasak. Historians debate whether Anuvong aspired to re-create Lan Xang or some new Lao-Tai kingdom. Some argue that he simply fell under the influence of the Vietnamese, who coveted territories on Siam's periphery. Others contend that by the mid-1820s he had lost faith in the Siamese and resented them for treating the kingdoms of Lan Xang as vassals.[15] Whatever the reason, it is clear that Anuvong did not get along well with Rama III (Phra Nangklao; ruled 1824–1851) and decided to go to war with Siam.

In early 1827 Anuvong and Yo amassed their armies and marched into the Khorat Plateau on the pretext of helping Siam against British encroachments in Burma. Instead they attacked Siamese forces and made their way toward Bangkok. A large army pushed the forces back and within a few weeks violently sacked Vientiane. Yo was taken prisoner, but Anuvong fled to Vietnam, where he raised another army to try to retake his capital the following year. This too failed, ending with Anuvong's capture. Vientiane was destroyed and its population was again forced to leave. The city was abandoned to the jungle and remained in nothing but ruins for several decades.[16] Anuvong was taken in a cage to Bangkok and paraded before its residents as a trophy of war; he died in captivity a short while later. Dreams of rebuilding Lan Xang died with him.

Scholars like Martin Stuart-Fox argue that the story of Anuvong has meaning in the search for Lao identity today, and that different interpretations of the story continue to affect Lao-Thai relations.[17] Although most Thai consider Anuvong nothing more than a traitor who got what he deserved, many Lao see him as a legendary hero who fought against oppressive Siamese rule. They remember that in retribution for Vientiane's rebellion not only the city but also much of the region was depopulated and forcibly relocated to Siam. Thus, the Lao population in northeastern Thailand today can, symbolically at least, connect to the story in a very personal way. Moreover, many Lao see Anuvong as the ultimate nationalist, irrespective of the fact that neither he nor his contemporaries understood the concept of statehood or nationalism as they are known today. Grant Evans points out that it was not until the mass deportations following Anuvong that the Laoization of the Khorat Plateau, and therefore a Lao identity, began, at least in part facilitated by the relative stability Siamese protection afforded. Over the course of the nineteenth century a noticeable differentiation began between the "worldly and sophisticated" Siamese and the increasingly remote and limited Lao.[18]

The destruction of Vientiane completed the collapse of the *muang* system in Laos. Thereafter, only Luang Prabang could claim any degree of autonomy, and at various stages it paid tribute to the Siamese, Vietnamese, and Chinese. Its grandeur had also been significantly reduced. The French explorer Henri Mouhot, famed for introducing the "lost" city of Angkor Wat to Westerners, wrote in 1859 that Luang Prabang was "a delightful little town, covering a square mile of ground" and inhabited by about eight thousand residents.[19] Lao communities flourished on lucrative trade in everything from slaves to spices, but none could regain the status of Lan Xang. There were also demographic shifts beyond the forced depopulation of Vientiane. New migrants like the Hmong, Yao, and other Sino-Tibetan peoples drifted into northern Laos beginning in the 1830s, substantially altering the ethnic and linguistic composition of the area. The collapse of Lao *muang* also changed the diplomatic landscape of the region. The Vietnamese expanded their hold on Siam's eastern vassals, moving soldiers and settlers into the areas depopulated by Rama III's troops. Within a few years they controlled the territory around Vientiane, Champasak, and the semiautonomous kingdom of Xiang Khuang. Luang Prabang, the Mekong Valley, and the Khorat Plateau remained within the Siamese sphere. Tensions between the two empires remained high for several decades, but all-out war was averted, largely because both had to contend with pressures from European colonial powers.

However, neither was spared conflict. During the nineteenth century China endured seemingly endless revolution that affected Southeast Asia. Beginning in the early 1870s, Chinese soldiers fleeing the strife pushed into Laos, leaving paths of destruction wherever they went. Known collectively as the Haw, they were in effect gangs of marauders distinguished only by the color of their battle flags. They defeated Vietnamese armies in Xiang Khuang and sacked what was left of Vientiane before turning their attentions on Luang Prabang. Even before the Haw arrived, some of the city's vassal territories rebelled, like the Kha chiefdom in 1875, prompting Siamese intervention. Rama V (Chulalongkorn; ruled 1868–1910) ordered three separate expeditions against the Haw between 1875 and 1887. The first, in 1875, forced their evacuation of Vientiane but failed to defeat them. The second beginning in 1883 was an almost total disaster. The third, in 1886, was the largest: It aimed not only to crush the Haw but also to expand Siamese territory in northern Laos at Vietnamese expense. The plan nearly worked. However, White Tai tribesmen did not surrender their insurrection as hoped and instead joined the Haw in ravaging Luang Prabang in 1887. Attending the court was the French vice-consul, Auguste Pavie, who was forced to flee.[20] The affair aroused the attention of the newest power in the region and changed the course of Lao history forever.

FRENCH RULE

French penetration of Southeast Asia began in 1858 with a military expedition to Vietnam. Taking advantage of rivalries between Vietnamese kingdoms, the French took Saigon in 1859 and set up a base in Cochin China (South Vietnam). They then began several decades of expansion, establishing military garrisons at Haiphong and Hanoi by 1874. The Haw wars led France to deploy even more soldiers, particularly after its commander in the area was beheaded by the Black Flags in 1882. A large French military expedition forced the surrender of the Haw and their Vietnamese allies at Hué in 1883. The ensuing treaty gave France a protectorate over Vietnam and all its vassal states, which included Laos.

Pavie and other colonial administrators were strong advocates of making Laos a French colony adjacent to possessions in Vietnam. However, Laos itself was never the priority. French interest was focused on Vietnam, a far larger, more accessible, and profitable territory. By the 1880s the French also wanted to push into Siam and build an empire in Southeast Asia similar to the British, who had colonized India, Burma, and Malaya. In all of this Laos was simply a tool. The long record of tribute between Lao–Tai kingdoms and Vietnamese rulers served, in the French mind, as irrefutable evidence of their claim to Laos. Numerous maps, publications, and statements by French officials make it clear that empire was the question, and in this respect, the Haw attack on Luang Prabang in 1887 provided an excellent opportunity to challenge Siamese rule.

Pavie began his second expedition of Laos in 1888, along the way establishing French business interests and military outposts to further claims to the region. Shrewdly, he refused to negotiate with the Siamese on boundary issues, claiming that without proper surveys, the French government could not proceed. Pavie and the governor-general of French Indochina, Jean de Lanessan, pursued an aggressive foreign policy on Laos. In 1892 Pavie was appointed consul general in Bangkok and led discussions with the Siamese aimed either to force them to renounce their claims or to provoke a war. The Siamese argued that natural boundaries, ethnic ties, and the traditional *muang* system gave them claim to Laos. Pavie and Lanessan urged Paris to reject any settlement along the Mekong, thus allowing the French to claim all of Siam. However, the French government was worried about British reaction to their plans. The British were interested in keeping Siam as a buffer between French Indochina and their own colonies, but they were not prepared to fight over it. The Siamese, however, were confident that they had British support and steadfastly refused to back down. A series of small incidents in the contested area was all it took for Paris to respond with force, and in July 1893 French soldiers crossed the Mekong and attacked Siamese positions.[21] While the Siamese held their own along the river, French warships forced their way up the Chao Phraya River and threatened Bangkok. Without British support, the Siamese sued for peace.

An October 1893 treaty recognized all French claims east of the Mekong. Laos was incorporated into French Indochina along with Cambodia and three territorial divisions encompassing Vietnam: Tonkin, Annam, and Cochin China. France also claimed areas that were formerly tributes to Luang Prabang, along with most *muang* elsewhere in northern Laos. That, however, was not the end of French ambitions. Over the subsequent fourteen years Paris pushed for an extension of French rule in Laos and Siam. Through skillful diplomacy the Siamese avoided France's harsher demands, but in general they were forced to accept numerous treaties that reduced their claim to Laos even further. In this fashion, French rule was entrenched and the shape of modern Laos emerged.

Laos was regarded as the most peaceable of French colonies in Indochina because it never witnessed the violence seen in Vietnam or Cambodia. Initially, many in Laos welcomed French rule as liberation from the Siamese. However, the French imposed rules and regulations never before seen in Laos that became the source of discontent. Slavery was abolished and replaced with the corvée, or indebted labor system, which disrupted traditional ideas of status and business among the people, particularly in the south where the slave trade was a major component of the economy. The French decided administrative positions in government, long determined by hereditary rights, on the basis of ability and need. Taxation, though not new, increased and became another focal point for resentment.

However, violent opposition came more from the Lao Theung and Lao Sung. As early as 1895 sporadic rebellions had broken out in the north and south. By 1901 they were increasingly well organized and popular—known collectively as the Holy Man's Revolt in reference to a messianic Alak spiritual leader in Salavan named Bak Mi (better known as Ong Kaeo). Drawing from both Buddhism and local folk beliefs, he claimed to have supernatural powers and to have been chosen by spirits to lead people against the French. Fearing his influence, French authorities tried to arrest him, provoking an insurrection that spread into Siamese territory. Repeated failures to round up the rebels only fed popular support for the revolt. In April 1902 several thousand Lao Lum supporters attacked police and military positions in Savannakhet. Convinced by Ong Kaeo that under his spiritual protection they were immune to bullets, his followers charged French and Lao troops, with several hundred casualties.

For the next three years Ong Kaeo attacked the French throughout the Bolaven Plateau. The French responded with repeated expeditions to round up the rebels. In November 1910 Ong Kaeo was killed. The French beheaded Ong Kaeo's lieutenants and paraded the "holy man's" head on a pike for all his supporters to see. The last holdout in the rebellion was Ong Kommadam, a fearsome Nya Heun tribal leader who escaped assassination during negotiations with the French and kept the resistance alive well into the 1930s.[22]

Smaller rebellions flared up for decades, though none as serious as that of Ong Kaeo. In 1914 Haw raiders from China again descended on Laos, fleeing the republican revolution that overthrew the Qing dynasty. Resenting French domination of the lucrative opium trade, the Haw tried to stir up Lao opposition to foreign rule. This and a simultaneous revolt of the Tai Lue threatened French control of northern Laos and required sizable expeditions to restore calm. Between 1918 and 1922 another rebellion spread from northern Vietnam led by a Hmong spiritual leader named Pachai (Pachay), who envisioned an independent homeland for his people. In some respects the revolt was not so much against the French as it was the Lao Theung and Lao Lum, who were traditional enemies that tried to control the Hmong opium trade.[23] After several years of brutal violence on both sides, support for Pachai waned. French campaigns, employing Lao Theung soldiers, wore down the revolt. In November 1922 Pachai was killed in an ambush, which ended the uprising. However, resistance continued sporadically for decades, illustrating both the depth of opposition to French colonialism and the fragility of any unified Laos.

More than just provoking resistance, the impact of French rule on Laos was immense. To be sure, economic and political development was not a priority. Other than constructing 5,000 kilometers (3,100 miles) of largely inadequate roads, the French did little to stimulate growth. By the end of their rule in 1953, still 90 percent of the population were subsistence farmers. There was almost no industry, no health care, and only a rudimentary primary school education system. Part of the problem was that Laos was not a moneymaking venture for the French and produced only enough wealth to cover the costs of administration. However, the problem was also that France did not consider the colony important. In fact, Laos was a backwater for the French. It was known derisively as the Land of Lotus-Eaters—in reference to the strange, lazy people that Odysseus encounters in Greek mythology—and considered a career-ending appointment in the French civil service. Attentions in the region were always on Vietnam. Yet perhaps because of this ambivalence Laos did not endure the full scope of brutalities that often accompanied European colonialism. The corvée system existed in Laos but never to the same extent that it did in other colonies. There were only ever a few thousand French soldiers and never more than a few dozen French officials garrisoned in the colony. Indeed, by 1940 there were only six hundred French citizens officially in Laos.

French influence was greatest, however, in stimulating a Lao national consciousness. As in all of France's colonies, Lao elites received a French education, and thus were introduced to Western ideas. Many later developed their own notions of nationalism and moved for independence. French designs to Vietnamize Laos also factored into the process. Considering them smarter and harder workers, thousands of Vietnamese were moved to Laos to be merchants and bureaucrats. Many Lao deeply resented the policy and, consequently, developed a sense of their own identity. Following the 1932 revolution against absolute monarchy in Siam (renamed Thailand in 1939), and in response to the rise of extreme nationalism there, the French encouraged the Lao to view themselves as a separate people in an effort to ward off Thai ambitions in the region. National symbols were introduced, such as flags, anthems, ceremonies, and a written language.[24] Through media, education, and the work of revisionist historians, the French promoted the idea of a historical Laos, independent from Thailand. With tremendous changes to the international order after World War II, this process would again fundamentally reshape Laos.

WORLD WAR II AND LAO INDEPENDENCE

The war in Europe broke out in September 1939, but its origins in Asia predate that, with the Japanese conquest of Manchuria in 1931 and invasion of China in 1937. Preoccupied with the impending war in Europe, France could not devote the resources needed to defend its eastern possessions, and Thailand took advantage of the situation to regain its lost possessions in Laos and Cambodia. In June 1940, German armies invaded and defeated France. In Indochina, that meant that the Japanese, allied with the Germans, could control the French government there. Having befriended the Japanese, the Thais pushed their case further. In December 1940 Thai forces attacked French positions in the disputed territories. After a brief war the Japanese intervened and brokered a settlement that returned Lao territories west of the Mekong, Sainyabouli in the north and Champasak in the south, to Thailand.[25] French authorities tried to control the damage by reorganizing the political structure of Laos. In August 1941 they assigned jurisdiction of the Xiang Khuang and Vientiane provinces to the king of Luang Prabang, Sisavangvong, who was a staunch French ally. They also set about modernizing the civil service and putting it under the control of educated, pro-French Lao elites.

Probably the most important Lao figure of the time was Prince Phetsarath (Phetxarat) Rattanavonsga (1890–1959), who held a variety of prominent political appointments before, in 1941, becoming *uparat* (*ouparath, ouparaja,* or *uparaja*), a great deputy king in Buddhist dynasties who served as the king's top adviser. Phetsarath supervised the reorganization himself and was Laos's most popular leader, even more than the king. He was also responsible for the nationalist propaganda aimed to develop a uniquely Lao identity. Although he never actually joined or led it, Phetsarath is credited with sponsoring the Movement for National Renovation, in many respects the first Lao nationalist organization. Some contend that he also saved the Lao language by blocking French attempts to romanize the script. In 1945 he became prime minister just as Japanese forces took over Indochina. Rather than urge unconditional support of the French, as did the king, Phetsarath favored accommodation with the Japanese. When that failed, he redirected Lao nationalism from its anti-Thai and anti-Vietnamese origins toward achieving independence from France.[26] In this respect he became the spiritual leader of several underground movements that opposed both French and Japanese occupation, such as Lao Pen Lao ("Laos for the Lao"), Lao Seri ("Free Laos"), and Lao Issara ("Free Lao").

The Japanese pressured King Sisavangvong to declare independence in April 1945. Phetsarath used the occasion to unify Laos by bringing southern areas into a confederation with Luang Prabang, but pro-French elements in the kingdom who favored a renewed protectorate following Japan's surrender that September challenged the move. Undeterred, Phetsarath declared unification of the Lao kingdom and as a result Sisavangvong dismissed him. Shortly thereafter the Lao Issara led a coalition of nationalist groups in a coup, upheld the declaration of independence, and placed the royal family under house arrest. Laos was in a state of complete confusion. Following the Japanese defeat Chinese nationalist soldiers occupied the north. British forces held the south, while French government officials desperately tried to regain control of their colony. Added to the equation was the Viet Nam Doc Lap Dong Minh ("League for the Independence of Vietnam," or Vietminh), the most powerful movement in Indochina led by the Marxist revolutionary Nguyen Sinh Cung, better known as Ho Chi Minh. Phetsarath hoped that the United States, the world's most important power in 1945, would support Lao independence. Indeed, President Franklin Roosevelt had suggested this for all of Indochina throughout the war. However, with his death in April 1945 and emerging cold war tensions between Western powers and the Soviet Union, U.S. support was not forthcoming. Phetsarath feared that in the confusion the Vietnamese would dominate Laos, but in 1945 the principal enemy was French colonialism, so the Lao Issara and Vietminh formed an uneasy alliance.[27]

Unlike the Vietminh, the Lao Issara was neither a communist nor a communist-led organization, and it was based primarily in urban centers among an educated elite. However, the Vietminh had great influence on the Lao Issara. Vietnamese populations in Laos supported Vietminh nationalist aspirations, if not communism. Moreover, some prominent Lao intellectuals had joined its ranks during the war, including Phetsarath's half brother Prince Souvannaphong (Souphanouvong or Suphanuvong) (1909–1995). Named to the Lao Issara government in 1945, he returned from Vietnam, where he had married, studied, and developed strong communist convictions, which earned him the nickname "Red Prince." With support from the Vietminh, between October 1945 and April 1946 he led Lao Issara forces against French troops. Some bloody engagements ensued, particularly at Thakhek in March 1946, during which Souvannaphong was badly wounded.[28] However, by then the Lao Issara was a spent force. Ho Chi Minh and the Vietnamese abandoned them in pursuit of a temporary diplomatic arrangement with the French. Other prominent Lao, like the Champasak Prince Boun Oum (Bunum) (1912–1980), joined forces with the French. Money and recruitment dried up, and facing arrest, the Lao Issara leadership fled to Thailand, where they were welcomed as anti-French propaganda tools. Phetsarath and Souvannaphong followed to form a government in exile.

In August 1946 France reimplemented a constitutional monarchy in Laos headed by King Sisavangvong. In partial payment for its support of the Japanese during World War II, Bangkok agreed to return territory west of the Mekong. This paved the way for national elections in Laos in December 1946, a new National Assembly, and a new constitution. Between 1947 and 1949 the French granted Laos greater autonomy, and with the offer of a general amnesty many Lao Issara returned home. However, the movement had splintered. One faction, led by Souvannaphong, rejected accommodation with the Thais and French and withdrew from the Lao Issara altogether in 1949. Souvannaphong formed a new group called the Lao People's Progressive Organization, later named the Neo Lao Issara ("Free Lao Front") and then the Neo Lao Hak Xat (NLHX, also the Lao Patriotic Front, or LPF), which sought closer ties with the Vietminh. In 1950 it issued a manifesto calling for a communist revolution in Laos, ending with the notation Pathet Lao ("land of the Lao"), the name by which the group was best known. Wary of the French, Phetsarath remained in Bangkok with a small following. He hoped that by pursuing neutrality in the worsening cold war, an independent Laos could survive internal divisions and avoid domination by either the Vietnamese or Thais.[29] He did not return until 1957, when the king agreed to restore his title as *uparat*. Instead, leadership of the Lao Issara fell to Souvanna Phouma (Suvanna Phuma) (1901–1984), a third half brother who became the country's perennial prime minister over the subsequent twenty-five years.

In February 1950 France surrendered more authority to the new Royal Lao Government (RLG) and provided training and assistance for a national army. In part this was a response to international developments that had significant impact on Laos. First, in October 1949, the communist People's Republic of China (PRC) was proclaimed under Mao Zedong (Tse-tung). Then, in January 1950, the PRC and the Soviet Union recognized the communist Democratic Republic of Vietnam, or North Vietnam, headed by Ho Chi Minh, in the midst of war with the French. In response the United States and Great Britain recognized the independence of Laos and supported the French and the Republic of Vietnam in the south. However, the Soviet Union blocked Laos's membership in the United Nations until 1955. Many nonaligned countries were reluctant to recognize it until full independence was granted. Laos's status took on added importance when, in June 1950, war broke out in Korea. Washington viewed the struggle in Vietnam as part of a broader, international effort to contain the expansion of communism. The war in Korea helped make the link, and within weeks the administration of Harry S. Truman (in office 1945–1953) committed aid to friendly states throughout Asia, including Laos.[30] With French and American tutelage Laos in the 1950s underwent improvements in health care, education, agriculture, and transportation. However, in many respects it was a nation in name only. There was little popular support for any political factions. Aside from Buddhism and a loose sense of Lao history fabricated decades earlier, the people of Laos did not make a nation. Nationhood came nonetheless. By 1954 the French admitted defeat after eight years of war with the Vietminh, capped off by their humiliation at Dien Bien Phu that May. Following the Geneva Conference the French began withdrawing from Indochina. Laos gained full independence that December, whether or not it was ready.

AMERICAN AID AND THE COMMUNIST ADVANCE

The fate of Laos as an independent nation was inextricably linked to Vietnam and the conflict that raged there for decades. Having established a state in North Vietnam, Ho Chi Minh pursued a guerrilla war in the South aimed to unify the country under communism. Laos played a strategic role in this plan as a secret conduit for the movement of troops and provisions. As early as 1953 North Vietnamese troops operated in Phongsali, Hua Phan, and Xiang Khuang provinces against the French. In effect they controlled these areas for the next two decades. North Vietnam sponsored the creation of the Pathet Lao movement and was instrumental in all its operations. The resistance government it established in the jungles of northern Laos included many ethnic Vietnamese or those who, like Souvannaphong, spent the formative years of their lives in Vietnam. Prominent among them was Kaysone Phomvihane (Kaison Phomvihan) (1920–1992), a half-Vietnamese Lao who had studied law in Hanoi. He became one of the first and few Lao members of Ho's Indochinese Communist Party in 1949 and later worked with the Vietminh. In 1955 he became leader of the Lao People's Party, the political wing of the Pathet Lao. He was also the first prime minister and long-serving president of communist Laos. Staunchly pro-Vietnamese, men like Kaysone dominated the Pathet Lao and made it a tool of Hanoi.

Most scholars point out that communism had only a small following among the Lao Lum. Strong religious convictions and support for monarchical rule made many Lao ambivalent at best. The Pathet Lao therefore recruited heavily from ethnic minorities, capitalizing on their resentment toward the RLG and most Lao Lum. Moreover, the Pathet Lao crafted a vision of the communist state that incorporated the Lao Theung and Lao Sung, rather than give them autonomous areas, which perpetuated division and exclusion.[31] Following the Vietnamese model, the Pathet Lao also appealed to the people through good works: building schools, developing rudimentary health-care and education systems, and feeding peasants. Slowly they spread their influence in the Lao countryside throughout the 1950s.

In contrast, the RLG did little to extend its influence beyond the cities and towns of the Lao Lum. It avoided questions about ethnic minorities and focused instead on political consolidation. Government institutions such as the police force and postal service were created. However, the Lao economy remained critically underdeveloped. Nearly two million peasants lived at the subsistence level. Unlike the Thai, Lao farmers were not part of any large-scale agriculture, and food shortages, even in rice, were common. Opium production, a major component of the national economy, curtailed at American insistence, never filtered down to help those most needy. There was a lack of critical infrastructure in transportation and communications and few substantial industries. Laos remained a backwater.

The United States hoped to change this by supporting the RLG in the early 1950s. The primary beneficiary was the fledgling Royal Lao Army (RLA), which the Americans funded, trained, and directed in efforts to control outlying provinces where the Pathet Lao operated. However, there is no question that American intentions were self-interested. The administrations of Dwight Eisenhower (in office 1953–1961) and his successors over the following twenty years pursued the dominant notion in U.S. foreign policy that communist expansion had to be stopped. This was particularly important in the developing world, where many nations achieved independence from colonial masters and underwent profound political changes. Winning the hearts and minds of people became the priority for U.S. foreign policy, especially given communist support for so-called wars of national liberation against colonial empires. In this fashion the United States was gradually drawn into the conflict in Vietnam: first in support of the French and then, as the French withdrew, in defense of noncommunist South Vietnam. Laos was also an important part of the puzzle. During the 1950s observers in Washington saw Laos, not South Vietnam, as the focus of American efforts to contain communism. In this light, Laos was the litmus test for U.S. credibility in the region. It also was an obvious strategic buffer between North Vietnam, the PRC, and the rest of Southeast Asia. Indeed, the Thais considered Laos a potential dagger aimed for their hearts. They feared that, from Laos, Vietnamese and/or Chinese communists could easily launch an offensive, supported by ethnic Lao and Vietnamese in the Northeast.[32]

Strategic concerns, not humanitarian interests, drove U.S. aid to Laos, which dramatically increased in the 1950s. Unfortunately, corruption and government mismanagement meant that assistance often ended up in the hands of black marketers, Chinese tradesmen, or the Lao political and economic elite. Worse yet, the RLG became critically dependent on American aid; by the 1960s, it existed only because of Washington's largesse. In fact, between 1955 and 1963 Laos received more American aid per capita than any other Southeast Asian country, including South Vietnam and Thailand. Most of this was military aid, part of a larger defense program that sent American personnel, equipment, and money throughout Asia. The net effect in Laos was that elites were further reinforced. Family rivalries were entrenched even more, leading to serious internal political problems. The RLA, which profited most from American support, became a prominent player in Lao politics, led by self-interested and notoriously corrupt commanders. In their efforts to combat the activities of the North Vietnamese and their Pathet Lao allies the United States also implemented an extensive network of covert operations, most based in northern Thailand, which made Laos part of a secret war alongside the tragedy that unfolded in Vietnam.[33]

THE ILLUSION OF NEUTRALITY

Elections in December 1955 produced a new government under Souvanna Phouma, who tried to bring all factions in Laos together. As cold war machinations unfolded in his country, Souvanna Phouma was convinced that only neutralism could save Laos. For the next two years he pursued negotiations with his half brother, Souvannaphong, aimed to integrate the Pathet Lao into government. In November 1957 an arrangement was made whereby two

Pathet Lao members, one of them Souvannaphong, joined as ministers in exchange for reassurances that Hua Phan and Phongsali provinces would be returned to government control. Washington viewed this with great concern. Many American officials, along with their Thai allies, considered Souvanna Phouma naive in his dealings with the Pathet Lao, or worse, as a "crypto-communist."[34] They worked first to prevent him from achieving his plan, and then to undermine it once he succeeded. When national elections in 1958 showed surprising support for the NLHX, the Americans withdrew all aid from Souvanna Phouma's government and supported disaffected royalists. The government collapsed, replaced by members of the newly created Committee for the Defence of National Interests (CDNI), a right-wing front sponsored by the U.S. Central Intelligence Agency (CIA).

Headed by Phoui Sananikone, the new government took office in August, quickly declared martial law, and suspended the National Assembly. Behind the scenes the CDNI was run by a CIA-appointed military strongman, Phoumi Nosavan (1920–1985), who was minister of defense. Souvanna Phouma was sent away as Laos's ambassador to France, while Souvannaphong and other Pathet Lao leaders were arrested. Not satisfied with Phoui, in December 1959 Phoumi staged a military coup. He was not able to take power himself, but maintained his hold on government and significantly intensified factional politics in Laos. To make matters worse, in 1959 three of the most respected politicians in the country died in rapid succession, all of natural causes: Phetsarath, King Sisavangvong, and Katay Don Sasorith (Sasorit), an early nationalist who was premier between 1954 and 1956.[35] Hopes for a peaceful resolution to internal conflict in Laos died too.

The Pathet Lao responded to the new government by redoubling efforts among the people in the countryside. By 1960 an estimated 20 percent of the country was under their control. They also managed the escape of Souvannaphong and other detainees, who then made their legendary long march through the jungles back to Pathet Lao headquarters. Other developments also helped their cause. Following notoriously fraudulent elections earlier in the year, in August 1960 a young army captain named Kong Le (Konglae) (born 1934) led a surprising, bloodless takeover of Vientiane. He and his men were angry with the CDNI for derailing neutralism and bringing more violence to the country. With Phoumi in Luang Prabang to discuss funeral ceremonies for King Sisavangvong with his successor, Savangvatthana (ruled 1955–1975), Kong Le forced the government to resign and demanded that Souvanna Phouma be reappointed. No one, including American officials, expected the coup. Moreover, no one expected the enormous support Kong Le received from the Lao public. He became an instant hero, a fact that illustrated the depth of animosity in Laos toward most of its politicians.

The Kong Le coup was another dramatic turning point in Lao history. Souvanna Phouma returned to head a new government, without including the CDNI. Opinions in Washington were mixed. Some feared that communists had inspired the coup. However, others sympathized with Kong Le and doubted the efficacy of supporting right-wing militarists in an attempt to bring about peace. Yet U.S. official policy was only part of the equation. In Thailand, the military government of Sarit Thanarat (Dhanarajata) (in office 1957–1963), himself half Lao and a cousin to Phoumi, responded with an unofficial blockade of Laos, designed to collapse the new government in Vientiane. He also secretly increased support for Phoumi in preparation for a countercoup, aided by the CIA.[36] An airlift of vital supplies into Laos organized by the Soviet Union drew international attention to the crisis and embarrassed Washington. Officially, the Americans tried to broker a deal between factions, resuming aid programs to Souvanna Phouma's government, and distancing U.S. policy from Phoumi. Unofficially, they waited to see the results of Phoumi's attempts to take Laos by force: providing him with munitions, logistical support, and even U.S.-led Thai and Lao Special Forces to get the job done.

Phoumi's return came in December 1960, when CDNI forces clashed with government troops in Vientiane. Over two weeks of fierce fighting nearly six hundred people were killed. The capital was heavily damaged. Souvanna Phouma fled to Cambodia, where he denounced U.S. policy and blamed it for the violence in his country. Other government officials sought refuge in North Vietnam or, like Kong Le, joined forces with the Pathet Lao in the northern provinces. A new government under Boun Oum was formed. However, any hopes that Phoumi could gain control beyond Vientiane were quickly dashed. His troops were themselves divided by factional politics. More important, they were an ineffective fighting force. Even with clandestine U.S. and Thai support they were no match for the Vietnamese-led Pathet Lao, who received help from their Soviet and Chinese allies. By early 1961 a stalemate ensued.

Various suggestions for international negotiations followed, but the real turning point came not in Vientiane but in Washington. In January 1961 John F. Kennedy (in office 1961–1963) took over the U.S. presidency and developed a different approach on Laos. He did not share his predecessor's conviction that Laos was so important to American credibility in Southeast Asia, let alone the world, and, consequently, he threw his support behind the neutralists. However, at exactly the same time Kennedy implemented an unofficial second-track policy aimed to increase covert operations in Laos and Vietnam. He also prepared for a possible escalation of American military involvement in Southeast Asia. Kennedy believed that neutralism in Laos was the best solution to the crisis, but he was not prepared to compromise friendly anticommunist regimes in Thailand or South Vietnam to achieve it.[37]

Anxious to avoid the entrenchment of a large U.S. military presence in the region, the Soviet Union responded positively to the official line. After considerable resistance, it managed to convince the Pathet Lao and North Vietnamese to negotiate, leading to the Geneva Conference on Laos beginning in March 1961. Periodic talks between factions continued for a full year. Then, in March 1962, fighting between Phoumi's men and Pathet Lao units broke out near the town of Luang Nam Tha (Namtha) in northern Laos. Many suspect that Phoumi instigated the fighting, but he and the Thais appealed to Washington that this was a precursor to an invasion of Laos by Vietnamese or even Chinese forces. As Phoumi's troops retreated into Thailand, Sarit, threatening to intervene, ordered Thai soldiers to the Mekong River. Kennedy ordered the 7th Fleet to the Gulf of Thailand and deployed several thousand U.S. soldiers in the northeast close to the Lao-Thai border. It was the first overt deployment of American troops in Southeast Asia since the end of World War II. Even though they were quickly withdrawn, two months later Kennedy pledged support to Thailand beyond their alliance in the Southeast Asia Treaty Organization (SEATO) in the event of communist aggression. For Phoumi, however, this was the end of the road. The Americans saw him as a diplomatic liability and a military failure. With no external support, he reluctantly agreed to the talks and a final arrangement had been devised by July.

Nineteen articles in the 1962 Geneva agreements on Laos specified exactly how neutrality was to be implemented and safeguarded. Unfortunately, it is debatable whether the factions and their foreign sponsors had any intention of honoring them. For example, neither the Americans nor the Vietnamese were anxious to withdraw their soldiers or advisers as required. Although most U.S. military personnel temporarily withdrew in late 1962, an estimated seven thousand North Vietnamese ground troops totally ignored the proviso. Despite agreements on things like prisoner exchange, the sides remained deeply suspicious of one another, and factions continued to jockey for influence almost as the coalition Government of National Union (centered on Souvanna Phouma, Souvannaphong, and Boun Oum) was announced.

Historians debate whether U.S. support for a neutral Laos was genuine. Some argue it was the best that could be achieved given the strategic conditions in the country that favored the communists. Others contend that neutralism worked on flawed assumptions that the Soviet Union, rather than North Vietnam, was the real power broker behind the Pathet Lao, and that the communists had intentions of honoring any accord. Still others quote U.S. General Maxwell Taylor, who characterized the Geneva agreements on Laos as a "tacit understanding" between the two sides that the country would not be the major theater of struggle—that would instead take place in Vietnam.[38]

With such a shaky foundation, the Government of National Union was not long to survive. In early 1963 communists assassinated several prominent figures in the neutralist camp. Fearing reprisals, Souvannaphong fled the capital, in effect dissolving the coalition. In April the Pathet Lao launched an offensive against Kong Le's forces, eliminating them as a military player. For more than a year Souvanna Phouma tried desperately to keep the coalition alive by meeting with Souvannaphong and his supporters in Beijing and Hanoi. Exhausted and frustrated, he announced his intention to resign in April 1964. Phoumi took the opportunity to launch yet another coup and arrest Souvanna Phouma. However, sharp condemnation from the United States, as well as from the Lao king, undermined the move. Souvanna Phouma returned to office with the full support of Washington, but the coalition was shattered. Moreover, by the end of 1964 the fate of Laos rested more with the war in Vietnam than it did with politics in Vientiane.

THE SECRET WAR IN LAOS

President Lyndon B. Johnson (in office 1963–1969) escalated U.S. involvement in Southeast Asia significantly with the bombing of North Vietnam beginning in August 1964 and the deployment of ground troops in the South starting in March 1965. The U.S. military involvement there lasted until 1973, by which point more than fifty-eight thousand Americans and up to five million Vietnamese had been killed, the majority of them civilians. Many of the American bombing missions were flown out of Thailand directly over Laos, which put it in the middle of the conflict. However, most people outside the country did not realize that Laos was also a target. The Americans and their Thai allies had flown covert aerial support for Phoumi's forces for years, and in 1964 they began similar cover for Lao government troops with the blessing of Souvanna Phouma. Confronted with irrefutable evidence that the communists were in violation of the Geneva agreements, he allowed for U.S. combat aircraft to fly in defense of reconnaissance missions. As the operations escalated, the RLG voiced concerns about U.S. planes firing on the Pathet Lao, but in the face of a growing communist threat and periodic coup attempts by the right wing, Souvanna Phouma was critically dependent on the United States. In late 1964 he authorized armed reconnaissance flights over Laos, which in effect gave the U.S. military unlimited authority to prosecute its air war. The principal target was North Vietnamese supply lines crossing into eastern Laos and then into South Vietnam: known as the Ho Chi Minh trail. As fighting intensified in Vietnam, the communists also used Laos as a sanctuary, a training ground, and a logistical base. Washington's solution for this problem was simple: winning the war in Vietnam required the destruction of large parts of Laos.

Over a nearly nine-year period the Americans did exactly that, running an average of 177 sorties a day that dropped a total of nearly 2.1 million tons of bombs on Laos: more than in all of Europe during World War II, or roughly one planeload every eight minutes, every day, for nine years. At that pace, by 1973 more than a half ton of bombs had been dropped per person for everyone living in the country. As a result, Laos has the unfortunate burden of being the most heavily bombed country in the world. Some 260 million cluster bomblets, each the size of a tennis ball, littered Laos. Nearly one-third failed to go off. Known as "bombies" in Laos, today there are an estimated 86 million of them unexploded. They claim lives on a regular basis.[39] Since 1975, an estimated five thousand people have been killed and seven thousand wounded by ordnance in Laos from the Vietnam War era. Given the remoteness of many towns and villages the numbers could be much higher. Experts believe that approximately 40 percent of the victims are children. Chemical defoliants and herbicides, like the famous Agent Orange, were also used in Laos with catastrophic effect on people and the environment. With the support of the American embassy in Vientiane the CIA orchestrated the bulk of the missions, careful to conceal them to the public. Few listened to the North Vietnamese or Pathet Lao radio broadcasts that covered the attacks. In fact, it was not until after secret hearings from the 1969 Senate Foreign Relations Committee were made public that anyone knew about the bombings in supposedly neutral Laos. Still, as the war in Vietnam worsened, Laos remained a principal target for another three years.

Bombing was not the extent of the secret war either. As early as 1959 American trainers were in Laos to develop an effective guerrilla force against the communists. By 1961 the CIA and U.S. Special Forces had assembled a nearly ten-thousand-strong *armée clandestine* that included soldiers from the RLG alongside Thai volunteers and numerous ethnic minorities, nearly half of them Hmong. Fighting for foreigners was nothing new for the Hmong. When Laos was a colony, some had worked with the French to put down rebellions. Others led those rebellions. Similarly, during World War II the Hmong were divided between those who supported the Japanese and those who fought for the Allies. The Vietnam War era was no different. Just as the Pathet Lao and their North Vietnamese sponsors recruited heavily among the Lao Sung, so did the Americans.

However, Washington had an advantage in Vang Pao (born 1931), a Hmong officer in the RLG who began his career as a teenager, fighting with the French against Japanese occupation. By the early 1960s he had distinguished himself with the Americans for his courage and skill fighting the Pathet Lao. The CIA groomed him as the most prominent Hmong commander in the war. Starting with only a few hundred men, by the end of 1960s he led an army of nearly twenty thousand, including Lao regular soldiers, Thai volunteers, Hmong, Khmou, Yao, and other minorities. Most were based in villages scattered in the mountains throughout territory held by the Pathet Lao. His forces were extremely proficient in guerrilla warfare and inflicted serious damage on communist forces. Vang Pao's units also aided the Americans through search-and-rescue operations, communications intelligence, logistical support, transportation, and flying aircraft.[40] By many accounts Vang Pao's forces were the only real obstacle preventing the communists from taking Laos much earlier than they did. Understanding this fact, the CIA developed a massive operation around his secret army that stands today as the largest and most costly covert paramilitary plan that the United States ever implemented. Vang Pao's remote mountain headquarters at Long Cheng, halfway between Vientiane and the Plain of Jars, became a ramshackle city. With all of the flights required for its supply and for missions elsewhere in Laos and Vietnam, most run by the CIA's top-secret Air America, Long Cheng was home to some of the busiest runways in the world. As some scholars contend, it also became the center of a large opium trade used to help fund Vang Pao's army.

Given its importance, the communists targeted Long Cheng, and in early 1968, they launched a major assault as part of the famous Tet Offensive in South Vietnam. Heavy fighting ensued for more than a year, turning the Plain of Jars into a battlefield. An estimated 150,000 refugees fled the area, many dependent on American relief aid for their survival. To sustain Vang Pao in his fight, deemed absolutely essential for the survival of the RLG and the American war effort in Vietnam, Washington dramatically increased bombing. In the first few months of 1969 daily missions over Laos escalated from twenty a day to between two hundred and three hundred. However, seeking shelter in caves and mountain hideouts, the communists continued their advance. Vang Pao's army bore the brunt of it until peace talks in 1973 brought an official end to the American war in Vietnam. An estimated 20 percent of the Hmong population alone died in the process.[41] Tens of thousands of ethnic minorities were made refugees. Perhaps even more tragic and amazing is that some never gave up the fight. Even after the Americans abandoned them, they continued the struggle against the communists. In fact, as discussed subsequently, some still operate today, hopeful that the United States and the rest of the world have not forgotten them.

The legacy of "the Secret War": unexploded bomb. Courtesy of Martine Duprey.

THE COMMUNIST TAKEOVER

In February 1971, South Vietnamese forces invaded southern Laos with U.S. support in another attempt to control the Ho Chi Minh trail. They were forced to retreat within a few months. The U.S. withdrawal from Vietnam beginning in 1973 sealed the fate of the RLG. Negotiations with the Pathet Lao led to the formation of the so-called Provisional Government of National Union that incorporated the communists, but with the departure of the last American "advisers" in June 1974, it was just a matter of time. The fall of Cambodia and South Vietnam to communist forces, both in April 1975, encouraged the Pathet Lao to launch one last military offensive against the RLG, and by August of that year they had occupied Vientiane. Tens of thousands fled in advance of their arrival. However, unlike in Cambodia and South Vietnam, the takeover itself was relatively bloodless, and initially at least, there were few reprisals against the defeated. In November the new Lao People's Democratic Republic (LPDR or Lao PDR) was established, with Kaysone Phomvihane as prime minister (in office 1975–1992) and Souvannaphong as president. Souvanna Phouma was made a special adviser, a job in which his first task was to broker the resignation of King Savangvatthana. All other political parties were abolished as Laos officially became a communist state.

Within a few months the new regime began brutalizing the people. All independent media organizations were closed, businesses were shut down, and schools became the exclusive domain of the Communist Party. Longtime residents of Vientiane noted that the capital appeared as if it had gone back in time; it lost any sense of vibrancy or modernity. In no small way this was because of the flood of people who continued to flee the new regime. Within a few years more than four hundred thousand had left—10 percent of the entire population—first for sprawling refugee camps in Thailand, and then, for some, resettlement abroad. Most of Laos's educated were among the exodus, leaving the country with few professionals to run what little infrastructure there was. Economic collapse followed, made worse by disastrous policies designed to collectivize agriculture and obliterate private enterprise. The cultural revolution, carried out under the auspices of the NLHX, eliminated foreign influences and implemented a host of new standards by which the population was expected to live. Literature, art, and music not authorized by the state were banned. Extravagant clothing, makeup, and even certain hairstyles were prohibited. Given its central place in Lao culture and society, Buddhism also came under communist control. The United Buddhist Association was created to work with government ministries to politicize the clergy (*sangha*) and dictate rituals of the faith.[42] Worst of all, many people were forced into *samana*, political reeducation camps from which some never returned. This included King Savangvatthana and most of his family, sent off in 1977. He, the queen, and the crown prince are believed to have died in detention. Although little is known about the extent of the camps or its victims, approximately forty thousand people are thought to have spent time in them.[43]

The new regime also focused on ethnic minorities. Publicly, the government portrayed the Lao Lum, Lao Theung, or Lao Sung as a united people in support of the communist revolution. Behind the scenes, however, it ruthlessly punished those groups that had fought against the Pathet Lao. It also maintained military campaigns against those who refused to surrender. Although Vang Pao fled the country, eventually seeking exile in the United States, many of his troops remained. Some of them supported the Chao Fa, or "Soldiers of God," who led opposition to the new government in Vientiane. Much like Ong Kaeo at the turn of the twentieth century, Chao Fa's leader Yong Shong Lue developed a religious cult around him, as they were convinced he was a savior of, primarily, the Hmong people. In 1977 the Lao PDR launched an offensive against him with the aid of thirty thousand Vietnamese soldiers, heavy bombing, and rumored use of chemical weapons. Many claim that government soldiers engaged in indiscriminate killing of women and children. Within a year the Chao Fa had been broken, but, remarkably, pockets of armed resistance continue right up to today.

Despite these brutalities, many scholars point out that Laos never witnessed the atrocities seen under communism in Cambodia or Vietnam. Some argue that this is because the Lao people are just not as naturally violent as others in the region. Others point out that after decades of factionalism and the long civil war, the new leaders wanted to put an end to the turmoil short of exterminating their enemy, genuinely believing that communism was the only vehicle that could achieve national unity. It is possible too that some of the communist leadership worried about the prospect of Vietnamese domination, and so it moved to distinguish the Lao PDR through any means, including the extent of state repression. It may also have been different because of Kaysone, who by most accounts was a fairly pragmatic leader.

This can best be seen through his economic and foreign policies beginning in the late 1970s. He acknowledged the failures of collectivization and as early as 1979 implemented changes. Long before the dramatic economic reforms of Soviet leader Mikhail Gorbachev in the Soviet Union or Deng Xiaoping in the PRC, Kaysone abandoned a purely communist model in favor of market socialism. The capstone of this was the unveiling of his *jintannakan mai*, or new thinking policies, in late 1986, which facilitated limited free enterprise. With respect to foreign affairs, Kaysone learned that ideology could be similarly problematic. Although relations with Thailand remained tumultuous, even leading to brief border conflicts in 1977, 1984, and 1988, Kaysone gradually improved bilateral ties. In part this was because of Laos's exclusion from world affairs and its dependency on Vietnam, which, following its invasion of Cambodia in 1978 and subsequent war with the PRC in 1979 and 1980, had become an international pariah. Kaysone also worked on improving Lao-Chinese relations, which reached a dismal low during the Sino-Vietnamese War. After many setbacks, better ties with Bangkok and Beijing ultimately gave the Lao PDR an opportunity to move out from under the shadow of Vietnamese domination and stimulate a near-dead economy through foreign investment.

Corresponding political reforms were not as forthcoming, as Kaysone maintained an iron grip on one-party rule. However, the *samana* were gradually closed and many restrictions had been lifted by the end of the 1980s. Religious controls were loosened, and in fact Buddhism was promoted as the cornerstone of Lao national unity. Kaysone even began clamping down on notorious government inefficiency and corruption. In 1991 a new constitution came into effect, reinstating rights to private property and guaranteeing basic civil liberties. Although the communists retained the only legal political party in the country, Kaysone reduced its control over the state and took away some of its symbolic power by changing national monuments and lessening ideological rhetoric.[44] By the time he died in 1992, Laos was again a fundamentally different place. His successors continued the reforms and oversaw the country's reintegration to the world community. In 1994 the symbolic Friendship Bridge opened over the Mekong near Vientiane linking Laos and Thailand. Then, in 1997, Laos was admitted to the Association of Southeast Asian Nations (ASEAN), finally joining the family of nations in Southeast Asia.

THE LAO PDR TODAY

Unquestionably Laos' opening up has improved its economic situation and, overall, led to a less restrictive regime. However, it remains among the world's poorest nations, heavily dependent on foreign aid. In attempts to move away from the control of Vietnam, Laos has in many respects come to be dominated by Thailand instead. Thailand not only is a major economic player but also is the primary source for all media flowing into Laos. Although some Lao admire and respect the Thais for their progress, after decades of isolation many Lao have a difficult time adapting to Thai cultural influences, which they consider offensive, corrupt, and immoral. Outside influences are also changing the nature of politics and governance in Laos. The need to work within the framework of ASEAN, the United Nations, and a host of aid agencies continues to shape the thinking of Lao leaders, but whether they can keep up with the expectations of people increasingly exposed to foreign ideas remains a question. This is particularly acute given the steady return of Lao and ethnic minorities back into the country, some after decades living abroad, and an increasingly young population that does not remember the revolution with the same enthusiasm as their parents. Communist leaders have responded by trying to shape cultural traditions and historical memory, in effect creating a national identity that reinvents Laos as a kind of hybrid between ancient traditions and more than thirty years of Marxist rule.[45]

Recent developments show that the current regime is still prepared to use force to maintain its control. Although less obvious than they were previously, human rights abuses continue against political opponents and ethnic minorities. Many Lao Sung, and especially the Hmong, face not only routine discrimination and economic marginalization but also directed violence aimed to eliminate a sporadic insurgency that has carried on for three decades. Despite the fact that several thousand desperate Hmong resistance fighters turned themselves in to Lao authorities in 2006 and 2007, the guerrilla campaign continues, and so do violent government reprisals. In June 2007 there were even rumors of Vang Pao's return. A plot to buy nearly US$10 million of illegal guns, rockets, and munitions for Hmong fighters in Laos was uncovered in the United States, implicating Vang Pao. Arrested, indicted, and released on bail, he awaits trial on federal charges that could send him and others accused to prison for life. The Lao PDR has called it great news and portrayed Vang Pao as a terrorist, while Hmong communities, particularly those in the United States, have denounced the whole affair and used it to highlight the abandonment of the Hmong and their continuing ill treatment.[46] The incident reveals how tenuous the notion of a national identity in Laos remains and how a complicated history continues to affect the country today.

NOTES

1. Arne Kislenko, *Culture and Customs of Thailand* (Westport, CT: Greenwood Press, 2004), 33.

2. Peter Simms and Sanda Simms. *The Kingdoms of Laos: Six Hundred Years of History* (Richmond, UK: Curzon Press, 1999), 4–5. See also Jeff Cranmer and Steve Martin, *Rough Guide to Laos* (London: Rough Guides, 2002), 328–329.

3. Martin Stuart-Fox, "On the Writing of Lao History," in *Breaking New Ground in Lao History: Essays on the Seventh to Twentieth Centuries*, ed. Mayoury Ngaosyvathn and Kennon Breazeale (Chiang Mai, Thailand: Silkworm Books, 2002), 2–3. See also Grant Evans, *A Short History of Laos: The Land in Between* (Crows Nest, Australia: Allen and Unwin, 2002), 6.

4. Martin Stuart-Fox, *A History of Laos* (Cambridge: Cambridge University Press, 1997), 9.

5. Cranmer and Martin, *Rough Guide*, 330–331.

6. Stuart-Fox, *History of Laos*, 10.

7. Simms and Simms, *Kingdoms of Laos*, 47–48.

8. Martin Stuart-Fox, *The Lao Kingdom of Lan Xang: Rise and Decline* (Bangkok: White Lotus, 1998), 90–97.

9. Evans, *Short History*, 16.

10. Stuart-Fox, *History of Laos*, 12–13.

11. Mayoury and Pheuiphanh Ngaosyvathn, "Early European Impressions of the Lao," in *Breaking New Ground in Lao History: Essays on the Seventh to Twentieth Centuries*, ed. Mayoury Ngaosyvathn and Kennon Breazeale (Chiang Mai, Thailand: Silkworm Books, 2002), 105–108, 154.

12. Evans, *Short History*, 20–24. See also Mayoury and Pheuiphanh Ngaosyvathn, "Early European Impressions," 108.

13. Evans, *Short History*, 20–24.

14. Rong Syamananda, *A History of Thailand*, 5th ed. (Bangkok: Thai Watana Panich, 1986), 4–9.

15. Stuart-Fox, *History of Laos*, 14–15. See also Evans, *Short History*, 26–29; Simms and Simms, *Kingdoms of Laos*, 129–130.

16. Mayoury Ngaosyvathn, *Paths to Conflagration: Fifty Years of Diplomacy and Warfare in Laos, Thailand, and Vietnam, 1778–1828* (Ithaca, NY: Southeast Asian Program Publications, Cornell University Press, 1998), 190–201.

17. Stuart-Fox, *History of Laos*, 15.

18. Evans, *Short History*, 30–31, 37. See also Grant Evans, "Different Paths: Lao Historiography in Historical Perspective," in *Contesting Visions of the Lao Past: Lao Historiography at the Crossroads*, ed. Christopher Goscha and Soren Ivarsson (Copenhagen: Nordic Institute of Asian Studies, 2003), 103–108.

19. Evans, *Short History*, 34.

20. Clare Griffiths, ed., *Insight Guides: Laos and Cambodia* (London: Apa Publications, 2005), 32–34. See also Tongchai Winichakul, *Siam Mapped: A History of the Geo-Body of a Nation* (Honolulu: University of Hawaii Press, 1994).

21. Volker Grabowsky, "Chiang Kaeng 1893–1896: A Lue Principality in the Upper Mekong Valley at the Centre of the Franco-British Rivalry," in *Contesting Visions of the Lao Past: Lao Historiography at the Crossroads*, ed. Christopher Goscha and Soren Ivarsson (Copenhagen: Nordic Institute of Asian Studies, 2003), 46–50.

22. Stuart-Fox, *History of Laos*, 24–25, 33–37.

23. Evans, *Short History of Laos*, 55–58.

24. Martin Stuart-Fox, "Historiography, Power and Identity: Historical and Political Legitimization in Laos," in *Contesting Visions of the Lao Past: Lao Historiography at the Crossroads*, ed. Christopher Goscha and Soren Ivarsson (Copenhagen: Nordic Institute of Asian Studies, 2003), 82–85. See also Craig J. Reynolds, *Seditious Histories: Contesting Thai and Southeast Asian Pasts* (Seattle: University of Washington Press, 2006), 255–260.

25. See E. Bruce Reynolds, *Thailand and Japan's Southern Advance 1940–1945* (New York: St. Martin's Press, 1994).

26. Vatthana Polsena, *Post-War Laos: The Politics of Culture, History, and Identity*, 66–70. See also Bruce E. Lockhart, "Narrating 1945 in Lao Historiography," in *Contesting Visions of the Lao Past: Lao Historiography at the Crossroads*, ed. Christopher Goscha and Soren Ivarsson (Copenhagen: Nordic Institute of Asian Studies, 2003), 129–164.

27. Evans, *Short History*, 82–86. See also Soren Ivarsson and Christopher E. Goscha, "Nationalism and Royalty in the Making of Modern Laos," *Journal of Southeast Asian Studies* 38, no. 1 (February 2007): 55–81.

28. Geoffrey Gunn, *Political Struggles in Laos 1930–1954* (Bangkok: Editions Duangkamol, 1988), 120–127.

29. Stuart-Fox, *History of Laos*, 66–74.

30. Daniel Fineman, *A Special Relationship: The United States and Military Government in Thailand, 1947–1958* (Honolulu: University of Hawaii Press, 1997), 230–248.

31. Stuart-Fox, *History of Laos*, 74–82.

32. Arne Kislenko, "The Vietnam War, Thailand and the U.S.," in *Trans-Pacific Relations: America, Europe, and Asia in the Twentieth Century*, ed. Yoneyuki Sugita, Jon Davidann, and Richard Jensen (Westport, CT: Praeger Publishers, 2003), 220–222.

33. Arne Kislenko, "A Not So Silent Partner: Thailand's Role in Covert Operations, Counter-Insurgency, and the Wars in Indochina," *Journal of Conflict Studies* 25, no. 1 (Summer 2004): 65–96. See also Timothy N. Castle, *At War in the Shadow of*

Vietnam: U.S. Military Aid to the Royal Lao Government, 1955–1973 (New York: Columbia University Press, 1993), 70–74.

34. Arne Kislenko, "Perhaps Vietnam: John F. Kennedy and Thailand," in *John F. Kennedy and the Thousand Days: New Perspectives on the Foreign and Domestic Policies of the Kennedy Administration*, ed. Manfred Berg and Andreas Etges (Heidelberg: Universitätsverlag Winter Heidelberg, 2007), 122–123.

35. Stuart-Fox, *History of Laos*, chap. 4. See also Evans, *Short History*, 106–120.

36. Norman B. Hannah, *The Key to Failure: Laos and the Vietnam War* (Lanham, MD: Madison Books, 1987), 10–13.

37. Arne Kislenko, "Perhaps Vietnam: John F. Kennedy and Thailand," in *John F. Kennedy and the Thousand Days: New Perspectives on the Foreign and Domestic Policies of the Kennedy Administration*, ed. Manfred Berg and Andreas Etges (Heidelberg: Universitätsverlag Winter Heidelberg, 2007), 121–151. See also Noam Kochavi, "Limited Accommodation, Perpetuated Conflict: Kennedy, China, and the Laos Crisis, 1961–1963," *Diplomatic History* 26, no. 1 (Winter 2002): 95–135.

38. Stuart-Fox, *History of Laos*, 118–126.

39. See Christopher Robbins, *Ravens: The Men Who Flew in America's Secret War in Laos* (New York: Crown Publishers, 1987); Roger Warner, *Backfire: The CIA's Secret War in Laos and Its Links to the War in Vietnam* (New York: Simon and Schuster, 1995).

40. See Timothy N. Castle, *One Day Too Long: Top Secret Site 85 and the Bombing of North Vietnam* (New York: Columbia University Press, 1999).

41. See Keith Quincy, *Harvesting Pa Chay's Wheat: The Hmong and America's Secret War in Laos* (Spokane: Eastern Washington University, 2000); Jane Hamilton-Merritt, *Tragic Mountains: The Hmong, the Americans, and the Secret Wars for Laos, 1942–1992* (Indianapolis: Indiana University Press, 1993).

42. Evans, *Short History*, 174–183. See also Grant Evans, *The Politics of Ritual and Remembrance: Laos Since 1975* (Honolulu: University of Hawaii Press, 1998), 49–70.

43. See Nakhonkham Bouphanouvong. *Sixteen Years in the Land of Death: Revolution and Reeducation in Laos* (Bangkok: White Lotus Press, 2003).

44. Evans, *Short History*, chap. 5; Stuart-Fox, *History of Laos*, chap. 6. See also Ronald Bruce St. John, *Revolution, Reform and Regionalism in Southeast Asia: Cambodia, Laos, and Vietnam* (New York: Routledge, 2005), chaps. 3–4.

45. Evans, *The Politics of Ritual and Remembrance*. See also Martin Stuart-Fox, *Buddhist Kingdom, Marxist State: The Making of Modern Laos* (Bangkok: White Lotus Press, 1996); Shigeharu Tanabe and Charles F. Keyes, eds., *Cultural Crisis and Social Memory: Modernity and Identity in Thailand and Laos* (London: Routledge Curzon, 2002).

46. Kate McGeown, "Laos' Forgotten Hmong," July 2, 2003, BBC News Online, http://news.bbc.co.uk (retrieved January 2007). See also "Hmong Refugees in Thailand: a Population in Danger," Doctors without Borders (Médecins Sans Frontières), June 29, 2007, www.msf.org.uk/news.aspx (retrieved July 2007); Tim Weiner, "General Vang Pao's Last War," *New York Times Magazine*, May 11, 2008, nytimes.com/2008/05/11/magazine (retrieved June 2, 2008).

3

Religion and Thought

BUDDHISM

THE DOMINANT RELIGION in Laos is Buddhism, accounting for roughly 60 percent of the population. Buddhism came to Laos via traders and missionaries from India and spread over the course of several centuries, beginning in the seventh century C.E. By the eleventh and twelfth centuries C.E. it had taken firm root, and by the mid-fourteenth century it had become the dominant religion in Lan Xang. It became the official religion of the kingdom in the early sixteenth century and remained so in the separate divisions of Lan Xang following its collapse. It was also the official faith of Laos under French rule and as an independent country.

Following their takeover in 1975 the communists tried to undermine and control the Buddhist clergy but met with limited success. Whereas in Cambodia Buddhism was ruthlessly suppressed with the destruction of temples and the execution of monks, in Laos the communists opted instead to tolerate and indeed co-opt the faith as part of the Lao national identity. Just one year after coming to power, the communists reversed earlier bans on teaching about Buddhism in school, feeding monks through traditional alms, and forcing the *sangha* to work. Shortly thereafter the government began providing monks with alms itself. In what was seen as a major concession to the religion, in 1992 the Lao DPR changed its national flag by removing the communist hammer and sickle and replacing it with an image of That Luang: one of the most important Buddhist symbols in the country. Today the government's

The Golden Buddha in Vientiane. Courtesy of
Christina Smit.

Department of Religious Affairs oversees monastic training and liturgy but
has allowed more autonomy to the clergy, so long as it continues to "conform" with Marxist principles. There are still prohibitions on the worship of
spirits (discussed in a subsequent section) and certain monastic sects, like the
Thammayut, a sect founded in Thailand and long considered by Lao communists to be a tool of Thai political and cultural influences in Laos. However,
even these are subject to recent changes. Enforcement of the law forbidding
spirit worship is weak, and regulations restricting Thai language religious materials have all but disappeared. Now many Lao monks even go to Thailand
for training.[1] Overall, with the relaxation of communist rule, Buddhism has
flourished and become a major component of everyday life in the country.

Buddhism is the fourth-largest religion in the world, claiming more than
three hundred million adherents. It originated in northern India in the sixth
century B.C.E. as a reform movement within Hinduism when a prince named
Siddhartha Gautama renounced his royalty and began a personal odyssey in
search of the meaning of life. He traveled around India developing a new

philosophy that rejected material possessions, hierarchies, and formalities. He also acquired a following of people who considered him a holy man. According to articles of the faith, he endured many hardships before achieving *nibbana* (nirvana): a state of enlightenment free from worldly demands and desires. Taken from Sanskrit, *nibbana* literally means "to stop blowing" or "to extinguish." Rather than being a heaven, *nibbana* is a state of mind in which all the emotions and passions of human existence are transcended by a pure peace or ultimate happiness. Having achieved this state, Siddhartha Gautama was renamed Buddha, which means "one who has awaken." Following his death in 483 B.C.E. his followers began recording his teachings and spiritual journeys, and they formed the Tipitaka (Tripitaka), or scriptural basis of Buddhism.

Buddhist teachings center on the *dhamma* (*dharma*) or "truth." According to the Buddha there are three dimensions to all life: the *dukkha* (unhappiness, pain, or suffering), *anicca* (impermanence), and *anatta* (a state without ego). Basically *anicca* is the notion that nothing lasts forever. The desire to think that things do last forever and that objects, ideas, or personal experiences can survive leads to *dukkha*. The final realization that nothing is permanent is *anatta*. Buddhists believe that we go through these dimensions in five *skandhas*, a Sanskrit word that means "bundles" or "heaps," which shape the mind and ego. These are form, perception, concept, consciousness, and feeling. When humans are born there is no ego, but because the world around us is so complex, we develop a sense of form, mostly out of feeling threatened. Ideas and experiences that come out of this form are our perceptions, which we try to label, categorize, or otherwise identify through concepts. The consciousness comes when we realize and accept our egos, and this in turn generates emotions or feelings that are the actions of realization.

The *skandhas* lead humans to six realms of thought. First, we try to possess things. Our want becomes addictive and in effect comes to haunt us. This is called the hungry ghost realm. The animal realm is where we act to protect ourselves or get what we want out of fear, ignorance, and ego. The hell realm is one in which confusion and pain torments us because our actions are often frustrated. This is followed by the jealous God realm, in which we develop pride, envy, and mistrust, defining ourselves through competition, external gratification, and the opinion of others. Next comes the God realm, which is in fact a trick, an illusion that forces us back through the other realms to basic existence to begin the journey again. Buddha taught that only in the human realm do people find their true selves and attain liberation.[2]

From the *skandhas* come the four noble truths of Buddhist teachings. First, Buddha taught that all forms of existence have *dukkha*. Second, he identified *tanha* ("want," or more literally "grasping") that caused *dukkha*. Third,

Buddha said that by abandoning the cause or source of one's *dukkha*, the *tanha* will stop. Fourth, Buddha laid out an eightfold path, the Atthangika-Magga or Magga, to achieve this that included having the right understanding, intentions, speech, discipline, livelihood, effort, mindfulness, and concentration; this is often collectively referred to as the Middle Way because the paths avoid emotional extremes. The parts of the path each correspond to pillars of the Buddhist practice: *panna* (wisdom), *sila* (morality), and *samadhi* (concentration). Through these practices Buddhists attempt to rise above a material view of life and transform their characters. Ultimately, if successful in the practice, they will achieve *nibbana*, which is where absolute truth and the end of all suffering is found.[3] More than just being a religion, the adherents of Buddhism consider it a way of life. How it is practiced every day and how one views the world are in fact the faith itself.

Like other major religions Buddhism does have rules. The *sila* contains five major precepts or principles that include prohibitions against killing, stealing, lying, promiscuity, and the consumption of alcohol and drugs. Buddhists believe that only through a moral life can one develop *panna*. *Karma* is the notion that all our actions affect our morality and, consequently, our search for *nibbana*. Because there is no permanence, and in effect no end to time, *karma* is considered to determine not only this life but also all lives; it is based on the idea that enlightenment is not achieved in one lifetime but is possible only after many journeys or reincarnations. Humans must live through many cycles of birth, life, death, and rebirth before shedding all their wants and desires and accepting the truth of existence. With this in mind, Buddhists try to gain merit in their lives by doing good things and living in accordance with the *sila*. However, for them there is no God in the same sense that other religions like Christianity or Islam preach. Buddha never claimed he was a God, and he did not become one when he achieved enlightenment. The fact that he and other important idols are often worshipped as such stems from differing practices of the faith and its blending with local traditions specific to adherents.

Without any real equivalent for heaven or hell concepts, Buddhism instead presumes that only individuals themselves can determine and judge their behavior. There are no absolutely good or bad actions, just actions with different consequences that are part of the journey to enlightenment. Rather than encouraging a blind faith in religion as many other faiths do, Buddhism encourages a constant and critical questioning of everything. In theory at least, it does not allow for discrimination based on other beliefs or condone attempts to convert nonbelievers. The central notion is that people must come to the faith through their own discoveries and that the toleration of other beliefs is essential. In this regard, Buddhists are welcome to experiment with other religions, and many often do. In fact, as discussed subsequently, in Laos Buddhism is intricately interwoven with animistic beliefs, folklore, and mysticism without much contradiction.

Beyond these central elements of the faith there are three major divisions or schools of Buddhism: Theravada (also known as southern Buddhism because of its strong presence in South and Southeast Asia); Mahayana (also known as northern Buddhism because of its following in the more northern reaches of Asia); and Vajrayana (also known as Tantric). The main distinctions among teachings and practices center on how Buddha and his life are interpreted. Theravada Buddhists stress that Buddha was a man, not a God. They recognize only one historical Buddha: the *sakyamuni*, or Siddhartha Gautama. In this perspective icons and temples are designed to praise his teachings, and practitioners demonstrate their gratefulness to his ideas rather than pray to him in the sense familiar to other religions. In the Mahayana strain of Buddhism Buddha is recognized and worshipped in several forms of existence and considered more of a God than a man. Gautama, the "enlightened one," is just one of the many manifestations of Buddha. There are also numerous other Buddhas and bodhisattvas: Beings that having nearly achieved enlightenment deny it to themselves to help others reach *nibbana*. They are all considered gods or demigods and invoked or prayed to for various reasons by the faithful. Moreover, whereas Theravada Buddhism stresses individual enlightenment, the Mahayana school believes that the bodhisattvas are required to help people in their quest. Followers of the Mahayana also believe in numerous world systems based on cosmology.[4] Language defines the two as well. Theravada scriptures are in Pali, whereas those of the Mahayana school are in Sanskrit and then translated into local languages. Vajrayana Buddhism emphasizes that there are certain practices or techniques that can expedite the attainment of enlightenment: paying attention to one's body, the environment in which one lives, acts of altruism, and enjoyment or pleasure free of attachment. All three also follow sutras, or different writings on the faith.

Theravada is the oldest of the three traditions, and indeed claims to follow the pure or original religion based on the teachings of Buddha. In fact, *Theravada* means "way of the elders" in Pali. The Mahayana—or "greater vehicle"—tradition began about five hundred years later in around 250 B.C.E. following a split over interpretations of Buddha's life. Despite being the older of the two divisions, some Mahayana Buddhists derisively refer to Theravada as Hinayana, literally "lesser vehicle," in particular reference to its interpretations of the bodhisattvas. Of the three major schools, Mahayana is the largest, dominating Buddhism in China, Japan, Vietnam, Nepal, and Tibet. Buddhism in Laos draws mostly from the Theravada tradition, which claims about one hundred million, or one-third, of all Buddhists. It is also the majority religion in Thailand, Cambodia, Myanmar (Burma), and Sri Lanka. Buddhism itself reached Southeast Asia around 300 B.C.E., but the Theravada variety did not take full root until more than one thousand years later and has been dominant since. In fact, Thailand claims to have the longest unbroken tradition of Buddhism in the world, being the only country in which the religion was never persecuted or disbanded.

In most Buddhist countries, including Laos, the Theravada and Mahayana traditions operate side by side with no real difficulties. In fact, despite their considerable differences they often draw from each other. Travelers are sometimes confused by the wide variation in Buddhist images, as well as the worship of other idols and even animistic spirits. This speaks primarily to the flexibility of Buddhism and its followers. Especially among ethnic Chinese and Vietnamese adherents of the Mahayana school, also well represented in Laos, divinities from other religions like Taoism or Confucianism are often incorporated with the variations of Buddha and the bodhisattvas to make up a large array of gods and demigods. The "great vehicle" is consistent with both the Taoist concept of individual oneness with the universe and the teachings of the famous Chinese moral philosopher Confucius (551–479 B.C.E.). For many, the three have in effect fused into one, sometimes known as the "triple religion."[5] Theravada Buddhism in Laos and Thailand also adopted many beliefs and customs from the Hinduism of the Khmer empire that remain integral parts of the faith today. Although it is frowned upon by purists and technically illegal in Laos, it is also common to see worshippers of both the Theravada and Mahayana traditions incorporate spirits into their faith from local folklore and animism. This is particularly true in more rural areas, where such beliefs are strong.

OTHER RELIGIONS

If viewed as separate religions, Mahayana Buddhism, Taoism, and Confucianism are the next most prevalent faiths in Laos after Theravada and "spirit cult" worship. However, as discussed previously, they are largely integrated into the dominant national religion. All three are found almost exclusively among ethnic Vietnamese and Chinese populations. Numerous sects within each also exist, such as the Cao Dai, a polytheistic blend of most major religions, spirits, and folklore created in the early 1900s that played an important role in Vietnam's many political conflicts throughout the twentieth century. Catholic missionaries came to Laos with the first explorers and then again with French colonialism, but the faith never took much root. It did have more success in Vietnam, so when ethnic Vietnamese moved into Laos, a Christian presence developed. However, relatively few Lao Lum converted, and the appeal was even less among Lao Theung and Lao Sung. When the communists came to power, all religions, especially those considered foreign, were banned or heavily controlled. All missionaries and clergy were expelled. Today the government has relaxed its control, and there are three officially recognized Christian faiths operating in the country: Catholicism, Seventh-Day Adventists, and the Lao Evangelical Church. The appeal of Catholicism is limited mostly to ethnic Vietnamese populations and urban Lao Lum, specifically in Vientiane, where a large cathedral from the French period remains. Current estimates indicate that about forty-five thousand practicing Catholics live in Laos. Protestantism, however, has spread considerably over the past twenty years and now claims about one hundred thousand followers drawn from all the major ethnic divisions in Laos, but it is particularly prevalent among Lao Theung groups. In more rural areas the religion has again been mixed with local animistic beliefs. Together Catholic and Protestant worshippers make up about 2 percent of Laos' population.

Although the Lao PDR permits the churches to exist, there are rather strict laws governing their actions. All Christians have to technically belong to one of the three. Other sects are illegal, although several, including the Mormons, Jehovah's Witnesses, Lutherans, and Baptists, are known to operate in the country. The Lao constitution also prohibits the distribution of religious materials and bans proselytizing. Several Christian groups allege that their members have been persecuted in Laos, with arrests and illegal detentions making international news as recently as 2007.[6] Some observers argue that the persecutions are aimed especially at Lao Theung and Lao Sung adherents.

Islam has only a very small following in the country, with followers numbering about five hundred, both Shiite and Sunni. The vast majority of these are ethnic South Asians, chiefly from India; some of them trace their ancestry back centuries to traders and missionaries. There is also a small number of Cham from Cambodia who fled the Khmer Rouge regime after 1975. Pockets of Chinese Muslims, most from Yunnan, live in the far north, but their numbers are difficult to gauge. An estimated eight thousand worshippers of the Baha'i faith also reside in Laos, mostly in Vientiane and Pakse; they are closely associated with South Asian groups as well.

ANIMISM

Spirits, known as *phi* (*phii*) are associated with natural elements and phenomena and inhabit specific places like lakes and rivers, forests, and other geographical features. Belief in them predates any organized religion in Southeast Asia, and they are taken very seriously by those who consider them a part of everyday life. Many people in Laos believe that there are thirty-two special *phi*, known as *khwan* (*khouan*), which are guardians that look after one's health and fortunes. Most are associated with elements like water, fire, and the earth. Many special ceremonies are designed to keep the *khwan* happy and watching over people, the most important of which is the *soukhwan* (*sou khouan* or *baci, basi*)—a ritual performed on special occasions, as discussed in later chapters. The *khwan* of those people killed by accident, murder, suicide, or in childbirth are believed to become malevolent spirits; thus special rituals must be performed to prevent them from escaping the dead.[7] The most identifiable symbols of *phi* worship are the *haw phi* (*haw phii*), or "spirit houses," which can be seen in almost all buildings in Laos, and the *lak muang*, or "city pillar shrine," in central Vientiane. Believers in *phi*, often referred to as spirit cults, command the largest non-Buddhist following in Laos.

Phi worship is the central component of animistic belief systems among the Lao Theung and Lao Sung. Almost all the different groups are animists and most also practice some form of ancestor worship as well. Given that most Lao Lum see no inherent contradiction between Buddhism and belief in spirits, it is safe to say that *phi* worship is in fact a common thread among all of Laos' ethnic groups and thus forms a major component of any national identity or culture.[8] Although specific practices differ, most Lao Theung and Lao Sung recognize spirits and their supernatural powers in natural elements and specific locations. Each places special importance in locating structures so as not to disturb the spirits or the ghosts of their ancestors. All groups also have the equivalent of spirit houses and ritual offerings to appease those who reside in them.

Animal sacrifice is still prevalent among many animists, particularly in the more remote areas of Laos. However, some animals are also revered. The Hmong, for example, deeply respect elephants for their strength and intelligence. Some believe that elephants carry dead spirits to the afterlife. Tigers and other predatory animals like bears were traditionally both feared and respected. It was widely believed that, not properly treated, spirits of the dead who could not make the transition to the afterlife took flight and entered the bodies of man-eating tigers. In fact, most animals have specific meanings. For the Hmong butterflies are considered souls of the dead. Frogs bring thunder and live on the moon. Tortoises are the wisest of creatures and bring knowledge. It is considered extremely bad luck for a snake to enter a house, as it means someone who lives there will soon die. Birds that roost in the house are similarly bad omens.[9]

Social hierarchies and practices among Lao Theung and Lao Sung groups reflect the primacy of animistic beliefs. For example, within most Khmou and Hmong communities there are different ranks of spiritual leaders, based on their ability with or responsibility for certain *phi*—called *hrooy* by the Khmou and *neeb* by the Hmong. Only a very select few are allowed to conduct rituals, and there are many prohibitions governing when, where, and why these take place, as well as who can attend. There are also strict taboos in some groups like the Khmou against interaction on different levels with people from certain totems or clan groups. Rites connected to agricultural practices, particularly rice cultivation, are very common throughout all communities, as are rituals governing birth, death, marriage, illness, ill fortune, and traveling. A belief in reincarnation, closely tied to ancestor worship, is prevalent among animists as well.

BUDDHIST RELIGION IN EVERYDAY LIFE

Buddhism is an everyday philosophy and a guideline for living as much as it is a religion. For Buddhists the most important consideration on a daily basis is *het bun,* or "making merit." They believe that individual acts in one's life affect their overall spirituality and ultimately determine *karma* for reincarnations on the path to enlightenment. The most basic and regular form of *het bun* is the giving of alms to monks (*khuu baa*) every morning. This stems from the fact that traditionally monks renounce material possessions and are prohibited from raising livestock or growing food by the *patimokkha*: a set of vows or rules that each must follow (discussed subsequently). Each morning, shortly after sunrise, monks walk in a procession near their temples through most towns and villages in Laos. People line the streets and give the passing monks food, earning merit in return. The ancient practice has even become a tourist attraction, often drawing curious travelers to watch and, in some places, entrepreneurial food vendors to sell rice to give the monks. For men, entering the monkhood (*sangha*) is also a means of merit making. Every man is expected to join the monkhood at least once during his life, and most do so for at least a few months. In fact, one is not considered a true man until he has served in the *sangha*. This is not only for themselves but also their families, which are honored by the service that, according to beliefs, collectively betters their *karma*. For those who are ordained as monks, the merit is even greater. Merit is also achieved through donations to temples and monasteries and by leaving offerings before images of the Buddha: usually food, flowers, incense, candles, or thin pieces of gold leaf, believed to be highly effective at warding off evil spirits, which are applied to the statue.

Monks play an important role in everyday life in Laos. In addition to leading the faithful in prayer, teaching, and administering to various functions at the temple, they preside over many events: everything from blessing new homes to the numerous major Buddhist festivals. The emphasis placed on the monkhood stems from the Theravada belief that the main goal one

Monks receiving morning alms, Thakhek. Courtesy of Jeff Phisanoukanh.

can achieve this to become an *arhat*, in effect, a saint who achieves *nibbana* and is not reborn. The process of becoming an *arhat* is difficult and involves several stages, each requiring great personal discipline. With this in mind, Theravada Buddhism holds that it is extremely difficult, although not impossible, for laypeople to reach the level of an *arhat*. Those who dedicate their lives to the *sangha* have a much better chance of achieving this, which is why Mahayana Buddhists refer to the Theravada school as the "lesser vehicle." Those who enter the monkhood on a temporary basis are known as *samanera*, a Pali word that means "novice," or in Lao as *nehn* (*nen*). Most men join before the age of twenty and are therefore sometimes referred to as *dip*, or "unripe," in reference to their youth.[10] Their service usually lasts only a few months and for most today this coincides with agricultural seasons, when their work on farms is not as required. Those who become fully ordained monks are called *bhikku*. This is from the Pali word that means "beggar," given the prohibitions of the *patimokkha*. Only those over the age of twenty can become fully ordained. In Thailand, one can see monks in both the brown-robed Thammayut and the orange-robed Mananikai orders. However, in Laos only the latter is officially allowed given the government's concern regarding the Thammayut as previously outlined.

As part of their ordination all monks take vows as prescribed by the Vinaya Pintaka, or rules of monastic service. There are 227 in total, most dealing with piety, celibacy, sobriety, and discipline. They are allowed few personal goods in the service other than their robes, alms bowl, a cup for drinking, and hygienic items. There are variations on the daily regiment from temple to temple, but in general their lives are governed by codes of conduct in which almost everything is regulated: meditation, prayers, lessons, eating, and sleeping. Although contact with the outside world is allowed, it is still governed by the vows. For example, monks are permitted to be in the company of women and speak with them, but they (and their robes) are not supposed to have any physical contact whatsoever: including shaking hands. Monks are also not supposed to handle or have money, drink any alcohol, or smoke. However, Theravada monks are not required to be vegetarians. There are differing interpretations of Buddhist scriptures on the subject, but neither the Theravada nor the Mahayana prohibit meat eating. There are restrictions on eating animals killed especially for the monk's consumption, times when meat can be consumed, and on overeating but nothing that bans the practice as a whole. Similarly, monks can watch television, listen to music, and generally have fun, provided that these activities do not interfere with their studies or devotion. In general, monastic life in Laos is more relaxed than in Thailand, in part because of the lack of more conservative Thammayut orders. There is no question that decades of communist control have also undermined some of the more traditional precepts of the religion. In fact, many observers familiar with Theravada Buddhism have noted the lack of discipline and decay of values in Laos among monks.[11] Perhaps in response to this some in the Lao *sangha* have emulated their Thai counterparts and started special, austere retreats in the jungles devoted to meditation, which has earned them the nickname "forest monks."

Theravada Buddhism does not officially recognize any monastic orders for women. Interpretations of the Tipitaka and sutras differ widely on the subject, but most conservative Theravadins believe that the Buddha did not intend for women to become clergy. That said, the scriptures are clear that, however reluctantly, he ordained his stepmother and several other women as *bhikkhuni*, or female monks. Consequently, there is nothing strictly forbidding women from joining, although to date there has been no significant movement in Laos in this regard.[12] Over the past few decades in Thailand there has been a revival in the number of *mae chii*—Buddhist nuns who take vows and live their lives similar to monks—and some discussion about the practice in Laos as well.

For laypeople Buddhism remains largely informal and nonhierarchical. There are few official days of worship, no formal masses or congregations, and nothing that dictates absolutely when and where to pray. Many people go to their local temple, called a *wat*, at least once a day to make merit. They also go on the basis of lunar phases, astrological, and sometimes numerological predictions. The regular visit involves meditation, either privately or in a group, and offerings to the Buddha, such as incense, candles, or lotus buds, which are a symbol of enlightenment representing the passage between darkness and light.[13] Some people, mostly elderly women, bring food to the monks. Donations to the temple, including money, are also received. The monks often conduct lectures or readings, but most worshippers go to the *wat* at their own leisure as part of their own everyday routine. Temples are also the focal point of most Lao communities. In addition to providing religious and spiritual services, they usually serve as centers for education, local events, and even some social services.

The faith is also practiced regularly at home. Spirit houses are found in almost every structure, usually mounted on a pedestal or placed on a shelf. Careful thought goes into planning the size, color, and especially the location of the houses so as not to offend any *phi*. Daily offerings are also made to appease them. The spirits of trees, rocks, and other natural elements are also often honored with small gifts. It is not uncommon to see people affix small clumps of sticky rice or special colored bands of cloth to trees to appease the *phi* they represent. Almost every event in a Buddhist's life, such as birthdays, weddings, and funerals, is directed by his or her beliefs. Monks are usually brought in to preside over ceremonies for these occasions. As in Thailand, most people regularly carry amulets and other images to ward off evil spirits.

As discussed in Chapter 11, Buddhist principles also shape social conduct. Modesty is extremely important to the Lao, and accordingly, overt displays of affection, nudity or revealing dress, and loud or inappropriate behavior are seriously frowned upon. Aggression of any sort, even arguing, is particularly offensive and considered contrary to the Middle Way. In this respect, body posture, gestures, and facial expressions can be critical.[14] Even with these prohibitions Buddhism in Laos is remarkably open and tolerant. Foreigners visiting the country are often welcome to participate in or at least observe religious rituals up close. Most major temples in places like Luang Prabang and Vientiane encourage visitors to attend and even provide opportunities for foreigners to speak with monks so that they can practice their command of other languages and enhance their education.

NOTES

1. Joe Cummings and Andrew Burke, *Laos* (Footscray, Australia: Lonely Planet Publications, 2005), 38.

2. Buddhist Studies Dharma Education Association, "Basic Buddhism Guide," www.buddhanet.net/e-learning/basic-guide.htm (retrieved November 2002).

3. Tom Lowenstein, *The Vision of the Buddha: Buddhism—the Path to Spiritual Enlightenment* (London: Duncan Baird, 2000), 2–32.

4. Robert F. Gombrich, *Theravada Buddhism: A Social History from Ancient Benares to Modern Colombo* (London: Routledge, 2006), 111–114.

5. Clare Griffiths, ed., *Insight Guides: Laos and Cambodia* (London: Apa Publications, 2005), 64–65.

6. U.S. Department of State, *International Religious Freedom Report 2007: Laos*, September 14, 2007, www.state.gov/g/drl/rls/irf/2007/90142.htm (retrieved December 2007).

7. See Minako Sakai, "Reconfiguration of Village Guardian Spirits among the Thai-Lao in Northeast Thailand," in *Founder's Cults in Southeast Asia: Ancestors, Polity, and Identity*, ed. Nicola Tannebaum and Carol Ann Kammerer (New Haven, CT: Yale University Press, 2003), 270–288.

8. Grant Evans, *The Politics of Ritual and Remembrance: Laos since 1975* (Honolulu: University of Hawaii Press, 1998), 77–78.

9. Norma J. Livo, *Folk Stories of the Hmong: Peoples of Laos, Thailand, and Vietnam* (Englewood, CA: Libraries Unlimited, 1991), 4.

10. Jeff Cranmer and Steve Martin, *Rough Guide to Laos* (London: Rough Guides, 2002), 361–362.

11. Evans, *Politics of Ritual*, 68–70.

12. Mayoury Ngaosyvathn, *On the Edge of the Pagoda*, Paper No. 5, York University Working Series, Thai Studies Project, Women in Development Consortium in Thailand, 1990, 10–27.

13. See Robert L. Brown, *The Dvaravati Wheels of Law and the Indianization of Southeast Asia* (Leiden, the Netherlands: E. J. Brill, 1996); Yukio Hayashi, *Practical Buddhism among the Tai-Lao: Religion in the Making of a Region* (Kyoto: Kyoto University Press, 2003).

14. Stephen Mansfield, *Culture Shock! A Guide to Customs and Etiquette, Laos* (Singapore: Times Editions 1997), 114–122.

4

Literature

TRADITIONAL LITERATURE OF THE LAO LUM

As IN THAILAND, the arts in Laos are infused with what some refer to as *khati khong xaoban lao*: a mix of customs, proverbs, songs, rhymes, riddles, and games that might best be described as "folklore."[1] The similarity stems from their common lineage, the near-identical dominant religions, and their interconnected histories. However, there are variations that distinguish Lao arts from those of its neighbor. This is particularly true in the literature of Lan Xang, which, even though based on the same stories as other Tai kingdoms, contained noticeably different interpretations.

Traditionally, literature as a whole in Lan Xang was referred to as "books of search," because to engage in or study writing was a search for meaning. Prose and poetry were considered part of everyday life, ingrained in the religious and philosophical context that Buddhism provides. This differs considerably from the more modern notion of research, which implies some sort of analytical framework and is carried out for more academic purposes. Thus, literature in Lan Xang was not just an art form but also the major intellectual tradition for centuries. It became a primary vehicle for education as well as the predominant form of entertainment. It was inseparable from religion and folklore, and rather than being deemed creative was in fact considered knowledge. The body of work created at the height of Lan Xang is, understandably, often considered the best traditional literature in Laos's history, although new research shows that a large amount was in fact produced after the collapse of the kingdom.[2] For the purposes of discussion here, traditional literature is that produced prior to the establishment of French colonial rule in the late nineteenth century. It is important to note from the outset that today the relevance of traditional folktales in Laos is much greater than in most cultures, especially those of Western societies. The communist government considers them collectively "works of art of the labour class and of the tribal peoples" that represent "the social struggles of the people as well as the instrument for their struggles." More pragmatically, it also considers traditional literature the repository of "culture, customs, history, and everyday life of a people" in the country.[3]

One of the most important cultural cornerstones of all traditional arts in Laos is the Pha Lak Pha Lam (Pharak Pharam). This is the Lao version of the famous Hindu Ramayana ("Rama's Journey," known in Thailand as the Ramakian or Ramakien), which serves as the basis for much of the older literature, music, dance, and art of Theravada Buddhist cultures in Southeast

Wooden carving of Pha Lak Pha Lam in Vientiane. Tibor Bognar/Art Directors & Trip Photo Library.

Asia. Written in India between 700 and 500 B.C.E., the Ramayana is an epic poem that consists of seven books and twenty-four thousand verses. Its major themes are human existence; the search for *dhamma*, or truth; and the classic, universal battle of good against evil. The main plot revolves around the Hindu God Rama and his wife, Sita, whom the demon king Ravana kidnaps. Rama is aided in his quest to get her back by the monkey lord Hanuman, and the poem accounts for their heroic journeys. The Ramayana made its way to the Khmer empire sometime in the eighth century C.E. but did not take root in Laos until much later, by which point it had been infused with uniquely Khmer and Tai traits. It took on other interpretations while popularized at the court of Lan Xang, often blending in references to local places, events, and traditions. Oral and written versions of the Pha Lak Pha Lam had been developed by the fourteenth century, with considerable impact on art, dance, and music, as well as literature, over the next few centuries. Some scholars contend that the Pha Lak Pha Lam was only popular with elites, and thus never really reached "the masses."[4] However, as in Thailand, it is clear that the Ramayana became an important feature of all traditional arts in Laos and remains so today.

In some respects even more important, especially for literature, are the *jataka* tales: a collection of 547 stories from Buddha's previous lives written in India around the fifth century C.E. Known as *satok* (*saa-tok*) in Lao, they appear in the Tipitaka, the central Buddhist canon, and detail moral and ethical lessons through the experiences of Siddhartha Gautama on his journey to enlightenment. The most popular tale in Laos is about Prince Vessantara, the penultimate of Buddha's previous lives, whose charity and humility know no bounds. The heir to the throne of an Indian kingdom, Vessantara is forced into exile after giving away a magic white elephant that ensures rain. Before he leaves, he gives away his worldly possessions: some to the people who made him leave. He and his wife retreat to the wilderness and vow to live in chastity. A wicked old priest looking for servants asks Vessantara for his two small children, and, again in the spirit of absolute charity, he complies while his wife is away. When she returns and learns of the children, she collapses with grief. Fearing that Vessantara may give her away too and be left alone, the god Indra takes the form of a priest and visits the couple. He asks Vessantara for his wife, and when he gives her to him Indra immediately reveals himself and returns her, making it impossible for Vessantara to give away that which a god has given him. In the meantime, the king buys his grandchildren from the evil priest, who then dies, and sets out in the wilderness to invite his son back to the kingdom. Vessantara and his wife return, welcomed by the people, and live happily ever after.[5] As discussed in Chapter 10, today the story is celebrated as a major festival throughout Laos.

An additional fifty tales known as the *panyasa jataka* became particularly important in the development of literature in early Tai kingdoms. Although their origins are unclear, most experts believe that they came to Lan Xang from Lan Na sometime in the late eighth or early ninth century. Of these, twenty-seven are distinct to Laos. Even more than the Pha Lak Pha Lam they merged with local folklore and eventually were revised and expanded in written and oral form to appeal more to the Lao. Read or performed as poetic stories, the *panyasa jataka* changed with every artist, and literally thousands of versions of the same tale emerged. Departing considerably from the generally religious nature of Lan Na's versions, the Lan Xang stories often incorporated sexuality, bawdy language, and humor. Both the *satok* and *panyasa jataka* permeated literature and other arts in Lan Xang until its collapse. In fact, dynastic chronicles from Lan Xang reveal just how important they were. Ostensibly the official records of the kingdom, they often read more like a *jataka* tale. Magic, miracles, and spirits of nature abound. Kings, warriors, and even monks are portrayed as having special powers, including Lan Xang's founder, the legendary Fa Ngum, who had thirty-three magical teeth, a sign of his divinity.[6]

Monks were responsible for acquiring, transcribing, and maintaining literary collections in Lan Xang, as well as for producing and performing creative works of their own. Everything was written by hand on palm leaves and then kept in monastery libraries or in the private homes of nobles and royalty. Remarkably, some of these exist still today in the national museums of Laos and Thailand. The act of writing on the palm leaves was known as *an nangsu*, literally "reading a book," a term that is still used today to describe storytelling.[7] Monks were also responsible for recording laws and important developments in the kingdom, and for writing what, in effect, became the first histories of Lan Xang. With such responsibilities, the prestige of the *sangha* was enhanced, and major temples became politically powerful cultural centers.[8]

Folktales were a far less organized literary tradition in Lan Xang, but in many respects they were even more important. They not only crept into more official interpretations of *satok*, *panyasa jataka*, and even the Pha Lak Pha Lam but also represent an older, more popular voice of the kingdom. Moreover, folktales change—especially in the purely oral context—which makes for almost endless variations and a dynamic, if difficult to catalog, tradition that continues to shape Lao culture today. Many folktales are drawn from the *satok* and deal with both myths and legends, which literary scholars define separately. Myths deal with creation, human relationships with the gods and demigods, and the meaning of existence. They are generally regarded as sacred texts given their implications for religion. By contrast, legends deal with explanations for everyday life: natural phenomenon, animals, and sometimes historical events. Legends are viewed more widely as real or truthful and are secular in nature. Almost all folktales began in the oral tradition but were gradually written down and became an even greater part of the literary culture.

One of the foremost experts on Lao folktales, Wajuppa Tossa, categorizes them into subdivisions that have particular focal points. For example, there are animal tales in which creatures have human traits and serve as allegorical devices to explore our own lives. More serious by design are moral tales, usually involving deities and demons. *Jataka* tales are religious in scope, focusing on the Buddha's past lives. Humorous tales were designed for entertainment purposes but also reinforced social values. Tales of the fool, tall tales, and riddle stories were also for entertainment but often contained Buddhist teachings as well. Some of the more lengthy and complicated folktales include epics ghost stories, tales about god spirits, magic tales, and stories of the trickster, all of which makes for a complex collection.[9]

Probably the best-known myth in Laos is the creation story "Great Gourd from Heaven." It tells the origins of Lao people, made from the god Thaen, and their world Muang Lum. The story begins with Thaen's decision to allow the world to become populated with humans and to allow three lords to rule there. He then sent down a messenger to remind the people to worship him. When there was no response, he sent another messenger and then a third. Finally, an angry Thaen let loose a great flood on Muang Lum. The three lords then built a raft and went to pay their respects. They were allowed to return to the earth with a beautiful buffalo as a gift. When the buffalo died, a vine grew out of its nostrils and from the vine grew three giant gourds. One of the lords pierced a small hole in one with an iron rod and some people started to come out, struggling, sooty, and dark after crawling through the narrow opening. A second lord did the same with an axe, and many more people came out easily, cleaner and whiter than those before them. Other holes revealed animals, forests, lakes and rivers, and jewels. The lords divided them all and taught the people how to live, marry, and respect their elders. When they died, the lords taught them different funeral customs. However, the people were too many and in desperation the lords asked for Thaen's help. Eventually he sent down Khun Bulomrachathirat, or Khun Bulom (Burom), who brought with him many advisers. When that did not solve the problem, Thaen sent down commands on planting crops, weaving, tool making, and other crafts so that the people could manage their own lives. Angered at being so bothered by the lords, he then cut the bridge between Muang Lum and the heavens so that humans could not cross it again. Khun Bulom came to be the people's king. He ruled wisely and divided his kingdom between seven sons, who became the lords of seven cities. He counseled them to be peaceful, helpful, respectful, and content with what they had, to ensure that the kingdom survived.

These and other teachings became known as *kod mai thammasat khun bulom*, or Khun Bulom's law.[10]

The "Great Gourd from Heaven" and other myths like "The Giant Creeper," "Four Marvelous Brothers," and "The Creation of the Mekong" are tales about piety, respect, love, and honor. They seek to explain the origins and meaning of life while reinforcing morality. However, they were also co-opted by various rulers anxious to legitimize their rule and dictate political culture. In the early sixteenth century King Vixun commissioned a written account of Khun Bulom's life to trace the line of Fa Ngum's dynasty back to the mythical lord. Both Phothisarat and Sethathirat supervised the interpretation of *satok* tales and productions of the Pha Lak Pha Lam to ensure that they properly portrayed royalty. Even the French used the popularity of *satok* and *panyasa jataka* in the nineteenth and twentieth centuries to differentiate the Lao from the Siamese, arguing that their unique characteristics suggested that a more Indianized culture had developed in Laos.

Even more important, some scholars point out that myths like that of Khun Bulom also served to separate the Lao Lum from other ethnic groups in Laos. There are several cosmological references in the text that highlight the division of peoples: a universe divided into two (human and deities), two holes in the gourd, and so on. In this respect the myth may have been intended to justify the precarious, often cruel natural order of life between different communities. The first people through the hole had a difficult time and came out fewer, slower, and dark. This may be a reference to indigenous groups that the ethnic Tai—more numerous, cleaner, whiter, and second to pass through the hole—encountered as they moved into Southeast Asia. This would be consistent with the traditional Lao Lum view of Lao Theung as *kha*, or slaves.[11] However, other scholars believe that the myth had more noble intentions, and they see the story as a reminder that, despite our differences, we all ultimately come from the same place.

"Phadaeng Nang Ai" ("King Phadaeng and Princess Aikham") is another well-known myth. It tells the story of the Khmer Princess Aikham, who falls in love with the Lao King Phadaeng. However, their love is unrequited because of Phadaeng's failure to win her hand in marriage in a rocket contest run by her father to appease the rain god and end a long drought. During the contest a *naga* (a mythological serpent) prince named Phangkhi falls in love with the princess and tries to win her affections by turning into a white squirrel with a bell. Aikham orders hunters at the court to shoot the squirrel so she can keep it as a pet, but instead it dies—according to legend, the result of bad *karma* in their previous lives. In his last words Phangkhi asks the gods that the meat be shared with everyone in the kingdom—"about eight oxen carts full and enough for all to eat"—and that "the people who eat my meat will die like me." Aikham shares the meat with all except widows of the kingdom, who had no husbands serving in the army. When the *naga* King Suttho hears of his son's death, he orders his soldiers to kill everyone in the Khmer kingdom who ate the meat. King Phadaeng tries to save his love, but Suttho captures her. Despondent, Phadaeng kills himself but then becomes a ghost king who leads a spirit army against Suttho. The epic battle stops only when the god Indra intervenes and orders them to wait for the next incarnation of Buddha.[12]

Legends of the Lao Lum include love stories like "Bachieng and Malong" and "Phu Phra Phu Nang" ("The Prince and Princess Mountains"), tales about animals like "Dog and Pig," and parables about human desires like "The Blacksmith" and "Crow and Peacock." Many also explain nature, such as "Chakacan" ("The Cicada"). One day a cicada in the forest cried out. Fearing that the cry signaled an attack, an owl shrieked. A startled deer ran away, kicking seeds in a pheasant's eyes. The pheasant tried to eat the seeds, pecking at an ants' nest. The ants ran out and bit a snake, which in turn bit a gourd that fell on a lizard's baby. The lizard went to the king of the forest, the lion, to ask for help and, one by one, he summoned each of the creatures, who recounted what had happened. Blame finally fell on the cicada, from whom the lion demanded tribute in the form of his innards. That is why the cicada's body is hollow.[13] "Maeng Nguan" ("The Singing Cricket") and "The Dog's Urinating Habit" are similar stories about natural phenomena.

"The Tiger Retires" is an animal tale about an old king of the forest who grows weary of chasing other creatures for his food. He asks the animals to volunteer to be eaten because he has been such a good king. When none accepts the invitation, he tells them that he will stop hunting and meditate in his cave until he dies. Rather than miss their king, the animals of the forest rejoice, until the pheasant and the rabbit fight over a hole in the ground. They go to see the tiger to resolve the dispute. After much thought the tiger suddenly grabs the pheasant and eats it. The rabbit is relieved, having won the dispute. Drawing near to the king to extend his thanks, the king eats the rabbit, too.[14] The tale speaks simultaneously to relationships of power and to the particular contexts of our own problems in life, and it simply describes the basic nature of most animals. Other notable animal stories include "Monkey and Crocodile" and "The Sick Deer." Tales about the fool include "Thao Mon Kew" ("The Ignorant Boy Mon Kew"), whereas tales about magic include "The Mango Tree," "The Magic White Swan," and "If It Belongs to Us, It Will Come to Us." Ghost stories like "Phi Ya Wom" ("Grandmother Wom Ghost") and "Phi Kongkoi" ("The Ghost Kongkoi") illustrate the role of spirits in Lao religious beliefs.[15]

Poetry, prose, and even biographical accounts about Xiang Miang (Xiang Mieng) are prime examples of the trickster tradition in Lao folklore; they essentially are spun from the *jataka* tales. In some renditions Xiang Miang is a boy. In others, he is a man. However, he is always portrayed as clever but routinely lazy, selfish, and mischievous—not at all the glorious hero one might expect. A major theme of stories is that he regularly outsmarts elites, including the king, and thus no doubt appealing to more common people. In one story he follows the king everywhere he goes and carries his prized betel nuts. He is ordered to listen to the king's directives and to follow them exactly. On one occasion Xiang Miang is chastised for being too slow behind the king, so on the next trip he speeds up—dropping the nuts in the process. When asked why he has not brought the nuts, he replies that he was simply following the king's orders to be fast, and that stopping to get the nuts would slow him down. He is then ordered to pick up whatever falls behind the king, and, being the trickster, collects droppings from the king's horse and passes them off as betel nuts.[16] In another tale Xiang Miang kidnaps the king's cat and then cruelly trains it to eat rice rather than the fresh fish it was given each day at the court. When the king comes looking for his missing pet, Xiang Miang convinces him that the cat is his when it goes for the rice and not the fish.

Not all Lao folktales are so well known. Many are disappearing from collective memory, in part because they have been passed down only orally and were never fully recorded. Others were in written form but did not survive the test of time or the country's numerous conflicts. Working under the auspices of the Lao PDR government and international agencies, scholars have been working since 1989 to locate, catalog, record, preserve, and promote various works of traditional literature. One of the most important is the Cheuang (Cheung, Thao Chreauang, Khun Cheaung), epic poems based on legends that are generally shared throughout Tai cultures in Southeast Asia. Some are also common to the Mon-Khmer people of the region. To date, very few written examples in the Lao language exist. Most evidence is fragmentary and almost exclusively in the Pali script. The famous Lao scholar Maha Sila Viravong began research on the poems in 1942 with ancient palm-leaf texts, long buried in the Bangkok library, dating between the thirteenth and sixteenth centuries C.E., but there has been little subsequent research. The Cheuang poems recount the life and times of Thao Hung (Cheuang), a Tai ruler from near modern-day Chiang Rai, Thailand. They are part historical chronicle and part legend, infused with Buddhist morality. Some twenty thousand lines of poetry have been translated interpreted to date, but with artifacts from almost every corner of Laos being located, the work is likely to take a long time to finish.[17]

Traditional literature in Laos also includes proverbs, riddles, folk songs, short poems usually put to music (*lam*), and poems meant for song (*mohlam*);

the latter two are discussed in more detail in Chapter 7. Traditional rhymes in Lao literature and song include the *waikhuu*, a means of paying respect to teachers; *kon aan*, epic poems used at special events like births and funerals; *kon phayaa*, one-, two-, or four-line proverbs; *nithaan phayaa*, poems taken from the *satok* tale about Prince Vessantara; *kon lam*, songs with musical accompaniment; *kon hai*, chants for Buddhist monks; *khong*, rhymes based on the number of syllables and lines employed; and *saan*, rhymes in poetic verse or song to send messages.[18]

Any discussion of traditional Lao literature must also reference nonfiction narratives. These include writings about folk medicine, law, and history. Most traditional Lao laws stemmed from two collections, originally transcribed by monks on palm leaves, known as the *khamphi phra thammasat luang* ("Royal Ruling Scriptures") and the *phra khamphi phra thammasat buhan lao* ("Ancient Lao Ruling Scriptures"). Historical chronicles include the Tamnan Phrabang ("The Legend of the Prabang") and the Prawatsat Lao Buhan Sikhotabong ("Ancient Lao History"). There are also didactic chronicles—part proverb and part story—and epistolary chronicles, which were used to send messages of goodwill to readers. Didactic tales like "Puu Son Laan" ("Grandfather Teaches the Children") remind people to know their status in life, show respect, and always be honest.[19] Epistolary chronicles like "Saan Luep Sun" ("The Sun-Blocking Message"), "Saan Som Thi Khud" ("The Message of Wishes"), and "Saan Rak Samoenet" ("The Message of Love") are basically metaphors used to describe love and passion, but they also convey political meanings. For example, "The Sun-Blocking Message" tells about how a giant *garuda* blocks the sun and overshadows the moon. The poem ends with the verse:

> Of these many trees in the forest, dense and thick,
> There is no fragrant sandalwood tree at all.
> Of these many people in the city, crowded and dense,
> No one is my kindred spirit at all. [20]

Far from being a love story, it is in fact a political statement. The *garuda* represents Siam, and the moon and its guardian, the *naga*, stand for Laos. The closing line reflects the alienation of the Lao within the Siamese empire.

Modern Literature in Laos

The division and collapse of Lan Xang was a major threshold not only politically but also with respect to literature. However, it did not produce the definitive end of all ancient traditions. Peter Koret, a renowned expert on Lao literature, points out that although kingdoms became increasingly dominated by foreign powers in the eighteenth and nineteenth centuries, literary traditions survived and indeed flourished. This was particularly true in smaller towns and villages, where outside influences were less pronounced. Monks played a critical role in this by transcribing and safeguarding traditional texts.[21]

Under French rule, traditional Lao culture was largely ignored until colonial administrators decided to encourage a separate identity for Laos in the face of Siamese-Thai nationalism. For the most part the French considered Lao language, religion, and cultural practices backward. They replaced them by imposing French-language education, secularization of the state, and a definitively European culture. Some of the best and brightest minds in Laos during the early twentieth century were in many respects more French than Lao, including major political figures like Souvanna Phouma, who preferred to speak in his adopted language.[22] Elites in Laos were more interested in modern French literary works than in traditional Lao literature. The lack of a public education system and a decline in the influence of the Buddhist *sangha* amplified this erosion of Lao culture. Technology, or the lack thereof, also played an important role. Although printed books first appeared in the 1920s, it was not until the late 1940s that they were commonly available, and the vast majority of those were in French or Thai. Similarly, Lao-language newspapers were not published until the 1940s. In the 1920s and 1930s Siamese publishers printed some accounts of traditional Lao literature in Thai, which monks in Laos then copied onto palm leaves. During the first half of the twentieth century the most prolific literature in Laos was therefore French: poems and prose often penned by or about colonial administrators there that focused on themes like race, sexual liaisons with the Lao, and the clash of cultures.[23]

It took World War II and radical changes in politics and society before modern Lao literature was born. The first novel, titled *Phra Phoutthahoup Saksit* ("The Sacred Buddha Image") by Somchine Nginn, was published in 1944. It was a detective story with a half-Lao, half-French main character. A few other Lao writers emerged in the same period, producing Western-influenced short stories and novels. Newspapers were a major catalyst in this evolution. The first Lao news agency, Agence Lao Presse, was established in the early 1940s. Lao-language papers, *Lao Nhay* ("Great Lao") and *Pathet Lao* ("Land of the Lao"), also hit the presses then. *Lao Nhay* was released in 1941, set up by the French government as a vehicle for Lao nationalism. Although it ran for only five years, the biweekly paper was instrumental in reviving interest in traditional Lao culture by regularly featuring poetry and prose that highlighted connections between Laos and Lan Xang. *Lan Nhay* also fueled new, political prose dubbed "Samay Funfou Xat" ("National Renovation") that inspired Lao nationalists. Through the efforts of scholars like Maha Sila Viravong and

Nhouy Abhay, ancient works were finally classified and standardized rules for poetry introduced. Their *Methods of Composition of the Poetry of the Vientiane People and Kap San Vilasimi* (1942) was a landmark in this respect.[24] Maha Sila Viravong was also an influential historian, becoming the first Lao to write a comprehensive, albeit nationalistic, modern history of the country in 1957.

However, this period was short lived. After World War II a sharp polarization developed within literary circles, again mirroring political developments in the country. Most writers fell into two distinct camps: those who continued to write in the French colonial, and as independence was achieved, Royal Lao government communities, and those who joined more ideological causes such as the Pathet Lao. Writers like Maha Sila Viravong, Thao Ken, Maha Phoumi Chittaphong, and Nouhak Sitthimorada championed the former through work in cultural magazines like *Pheuane Keo* ("Best Friend") and *Khouan Heuane* ("Soul of the House"). Writing under pen names, three children of Maha Sila Viravong—Pakian, Dara, and Duangdueane Viravong—also contributed. Duangdueane married Outhine Bounavong, another author initially in the royalist camp. Many leftist Lao revolutionaries emulated writers in the communist world. The Pathet Lao used anti-imperialist literature, primarily through its newspapers, to win over popular support. Traditional poems and prose were adapted for the communist cause. They warned the RLG of the coming revolution with the proverb, "Elephants do not step on the birds even if you see that their mouths are small. When the birds gather together and collect their strength, they will peck you to death."[25] Important writers in this tradition included Phoumi Vongvichit, the future president of the Lao PDR, who wrote *Pathet Lao Suai Ngam Lae Hang Mee* ("Beautiful and Rich Lao Land"), and Souvanthone Bouphanouvong, who penned *Kong Phan Thisong* ("Second Battalion"), as well as Senthang Sivith, Chanthy Deuansavanh, and Theap Vongpkay.

Many of the same writers also produced fictional short stories, which were a popular form of entertainment in the 1950s and 1960s. However, as late as the mid-1960s Vientiane had only two bookstores: one specializing in Thai-language works and the other specializing in French-language works.[26] Most writing was still circulated through newspapers and magazines. Two of the most influential new publications were *Mittasone* (founded in 1967) and *Phai Nam* (established in 1972), which focused on the many political and social problems Laos faced in the shadow of the Vietnam War. A third periodical, *Nang* (founded in 1972), became the first and only publication in Laos devoted to women writers. All three were also barometers of change in literary circles, as many contributors, formerly advocates of the royalist or Western camp, drifted to the left as conflict further engulfed their country. In the last few years of the RLG collections of short stories and novels began to catch on with the Lao public, many written by Outhine Bounavong, Duangdueane Viravong, and Seri Milamy. Published in 1973, Duangdueane Viravong's "Father Still Isn't Dead" focused on the suffering of women in the war. Originally published in French, Somphavan Inthavong's 1969 poem "Un homme est mort" ("A Man Is Dead") spoke about similar loss and destruction:

> A man is dead, and that is not all.
> Fa Ngum is also dead,
> And Anou and Pangkham too.[27]

New artists like Houmphanh Rattanavong, Phou Phounagsaba, and Soukhy Norasinh also emerged in this period with narratives about feudalism, corruption, foreign influences, and Lao identity.

Not surprisingly, the communist takeover changed the literary scene in Laos once again. Two months after the revolution, papers and magazines like *Phai Nam* were shut down. The new government regulated literature heavily, approving only those stories that illustrated the sacrifice of revolutionaries or the new regime's ideas about ethnic unity and national identity. Many writers fled the country, but some, like Outhine Bounavong and Seri Milamy, stayed on and adjusted their work to conform to communist rule. Outhine eventually became the head of the state publishing house, the chief government translator and editor, and a senior official with the Ministry of Information and Culture. His works like *Death Price*, *What a Beauty*, and *Dic and Daeng*, focus on the negative impact of American culture and the divisions that it caused within Lao society. He helped pen a 1982 compilation of short stories called *Sieng Kong Khong Latthi Vilason Pativat* ("The Echoing Sound of the Doctrine of Revolutionary Heroes"), which celebrated the communist takeover. He also reestablished *Phai Nam* magazine and created a new one called *Vannasin*, which today remains the main voice of government-sanctioned literary culture in Laos. Outhine even created children's fiction like *Pa Kho Lopha* ("The Greedy, Striped, Snake-Headed Fish") designed to promote socialist morality. Reflecting the changes in Laos's political climate, he also wrote about environmental degradation and the disappearance of traditional Lao customs in later works like *Frangipani* (1980) and *Wrapped Ash Delight* (1990).[28] Writing under the pen name Dok Ket, Outhine's widow, Duangdueane Viravong, remains Laos's best-known female literary figure, published collections of traditional folktales like *Kam Pha Phi Noi* ("The Little Orphan and the Spirit"). Writers who had always supported the communist cause, such as Chanthy Deuansavanh, were also prominent after 1975. He was editor of the literary journal *Xiengkhene Lao*, chair of the Lao Writer's Association, and a critically acclaimed author; he won the 1999 Southeast Asian Writer's Award for his novel *Khang Khun Thi Pa Leuk* ("Overnight in the Deep Forest").

The communist takeover also produced a new generation of writers, including Saisuwan Phengphong, Viset Savengseuska, and Bounthanong Somsaiphon. Thongkham Onemanisone was the first Lao to win the prestigious Southeast Asian Writer's Award in 1998 for the novel *Pheua Hak Pheua* ("For Love for Her"). His other works include *Phoum Pannya Sisawat* ("Sisawat's Wisdom") in 1997 and *Dhamma Path Poems* in 2000. Khamlieng Phonsena won numerous awards in the 1980s for novels like *Khwam Hak* ("Love") and *Chai Dieu Hak Dieu* ("One Heart, One Love"). Theap Vongpakay is also a Southeast Asian Writer's Award winner for *Pha Nhou Xivit* ("Storm of Life"), published in 2003. His other works include *Ngao Muon Muang* ("The District Sword") and *Pit Adit* ("Poisoned Past"). One of the youngest contemporary writers in Laos is Thongbay Photisane, whose 2004 novel *Ngua Kap Kien* ("Cows and Carts") also won a Southeast Asian Writer's Award. Other influential writers include Phieu Lavanh, Bounseun Songmany, Othong Khaminsou, and Sengphouxay Inthavikham. However, it is important to note that after 1975 all sanctioned writers in the Lao PDR became civil servants with very limited artistic freedoms. Literature was applicable only to the political designs of the state and in effect became propaganda. Political reforms of the 1980s loosened restrictions, but still today the government continues to control what is released. Some writers living in Laos have evaded this censorship by publishing anonymously in Thailand.[29]

TRADITIONAL LITERATURE OF THE LAO THEUNG AND LAO SUNG

The study of traditional literature among Laos's many ethnic minorities is problematic for a number of reasons. First and foremost, the Lao Theung and Lao Sung groups that developed written scripts did so relatively recently. The Hmong, for example, did not have a writing system until the 1950s, when Catholic missionaries translated and romanized their language. Most ethnicities passed down their culture and customs orally, and they continue to do so today. Second, most groups live on the fringes of Lao Lum society, economically deprived and politically marginalized. Rudimentary services, such as basic education, are severely lacking, let alone things like presses, libraries, archives, and the people needed to manage them. Third, even within the field of Southeast Asian studies, broadly defined, Laos and particularly the literary traditions of the country have received comparatively little attention. This is because of the size and isolation of the country, as well as the closed nature of communist rule since 1975. War and persecution have added to this mix and made it difficult for any written traditional literature to exist among most Lao Theung and Lao Sung.

Fortunately, oral arts do exist, and in the past few decades there have been efforts both within the groups themselves and within academic communities to record, preserve, and study literary traditions. Although scholarship on the topic is still fairly thin, there has been more interest in the past few years. Some of that interest corresponds to a vocal and prominent community of contemporary writers, especially among the Hmong, who borrow from or draw attention to older literary traditions. It also stems from a greater awareness about the plight of Southeast Asia's ethnic minorities. Most of all, the survival of all traditional arts among ethnic minorities depends on the pride and tenacity of the people to make sure their cultures do not die out.

As one of the largest ethnic groups in Laos, the Hmong have probably the best-known traditional oral literatures among ethnic minorities in the country. One of the foremost contemporary Laotian American writers, Bryan Thao Worra, characterizes Hmong literature as "orphaned," like "a ghost that keeps bobbing up to the surface from a deep river."[30] Some Hmong ancient folktales and stories have been recorded through *pa ndau* (*paj ntaub*), elaborate and colorful needlework art. The art also symbolizes animistic religious beliefs, historical events, and family lineages. The folklore of the Hmong and other ethnic groups is not dissimilar to that of the Lao Lum—or any other people in the world—in that it seeks to explain creation, the meaning of life, and the nature of humanity through myths and legends full of spirits, magic, and powerful gods. In fact, there is considerable overlap of folkloric beliefs in the various communities of Laos as a result of interaction over the centuries and, particularly, the prevalence of *phi* worship.

Consider, for example, the Hmong tale explaining the creation of the earth and the origin of the Hmong people, which is very similar to the "Great Gourd from Heaven" in Lao mythology. A brother and sister orphaned by their parents' deaths are left to tend the family farm. They try to clear the fields of weeds only to discover that each night the gods replant them. When they confront one of the gods he tells them that there is no sense working on the fields because a flood is coming. He tells them to instead build large funeral drums and to hide in them. When the flood comes the brother and sister survive in their drum and are the only people left in the world. However, they cannot repopulate the planet because of the taboo about sibling relationships. The brother tries several times to convince his sister to marry him but she declines. After many years she finally agrees, but only if they roll two rocks down opposite sides of the mountain and the rocks came back together again. In the middle of the night the brother cheats and arranges the rocks they had rolled down together on top of the mountain. The sister agrees and a year later they have a child. However, the child is an egg. Not knowing what to do with this they cut the egg up and throw the pieces across their lands. Each of the pieces then grew into many people, representing the different clans of the Hmong.[31]

Other Hmong tales stress the virtues of hard work, respect, and the wisdom of elders in similar fashion to Lao folklore. In one, a dying farmer tells his sons that treasure is hidden on their farm. After he dies, the boys look frantically for the riches by digging up almost all the earth. They cannot find any treasure, but their land does become rich with crops because of all the digging. Most other Hmong folktales incorporate similar morality in stories full of references to the natural world, *phi*, and other devices familiar to the Lao. Groups like the Khmou have very similar traditions, albeit with slightly different interpretations.[32]

CONTEMPORARY LAOTIAN AMERICAN AND HMONG AMERICAN LITERATURE

No discussion of literature with respect to Laos would be complete without reference to expatriate communities, especially in the United States. Almost half of the approximately four hundred thousand people who have fled Laos since 1975 ended up there. There are an estimated three hundred thousand ethnic Hmong alone in the United States, slightly less than the population of Hmong in Laos. About 85 percent of all Laotian Americans and Hmong Americans live in California, Minnesota, and Wisconsin. A young, vibrant body of Laotian American and Hmong American writers has emerged there over the past two decades, and many reflect on questions of identity, the effects of conflict, and the plight of people in Laos today. One of the most gifted is Bryan Thao Worra, whose poem "Burning Eden One Branch at a Time" is a powerful, personal testament to reconcile war in Laos with growing up American:

> My father, a skull before the wars were over,
> Never saw my mother's flight in terror
> ~~As our humbled kingdom fell to flame and shell~~
>
> My mother was stripped to ink among bureaucrats,
> A number for their raw statistics of jungle errors
> ~~Collated into cold ledgers marked "Classified"~~
>
> My feet dangling in the Mississippi have forgotten
> What the mud in the Vientiane feels like between your toes
> While my hands hold foreign leaves and I whisper

"Maple"
"Oak"
"Weeping Willow"

As if saying their names aloud will rebuild my home.[33]

In "A Crime in Xieng Khouang" he details the legacy of the so-called secret war and the tremendous disparities between Lao and Americans today.

Someone stole my boots from
A Phonsavan porch
Around dinner time
In the dark.

I suspect it was my tour guide –
The one who trained to be a diplomat,
Whose future drained away
With the American departure.

When I first bought them,
The box proclaimed they were
"Hard to Kill"
And by extension, I assume,
So was I, though there were no
written words to that effect.
Forty dollars is a good price
But it's nearly a year's pay
In these parts.

I should have known
New American boots
In an Asian size
Don't come by often near
The Plain of Jars.

He stole them from me,
And is now slogging through
The sucking muddy waste
Cluttered with tiny rusting bombies
My America dropped decades ago
For the good of Lao democracy.

His English is exceptional
But he knows he is going to die here
With his dreams
While I return home easily
To get a replacement.

I have to forgive him,
Feeling like a thief
Looking for shiny new boots
Just past the American flags in the aisle.[34]

An excellent range of Hmong American writers can be found in *Bamboo among the Oaks: Contemporary Writing by Hmong Americans.* Published in 2002, this is the first anthology of second- and third-generation Hmong American artists, including the editor Mai Neng Moua, as well as Vayong Moua, Va-Megn Thoj, Bee Cha, May Lee, Kou Vang, Noukou Thao, Pacyinz Lyfoung, Soul Choj Vang, Pa Xiong, Pos Moua, Chachoua Victoria Xiong, and Mayli Vang.[35] Many are the children or grandchildren of refugees who fled during or after the Vietnam War and grew up in the United States. Mai Neng Moua was also one of the founders of *Paj Ntaub Voice,* a Hmong American cultural journal established in 1994.

By no means are Laotian American and Hmong American writers restricted to themes dealing with Laos, the war, or growing up "on the hyphen." For example, Thao Worra also writes dark fiction. It is also important to note that the ethnic divisions seen in Laos do not have the same impact in the United States or elsewhere abroad. There are a number of prominent community organizations in the United States that support the arts among all people from Laos, including the Laotian American Society, the Laotian American National Alliance, and various regional and state Laotian groups. There are also more specific community groups such as the Hmong American Partnership, the Center for Hmong Arts and Talents, the Hmong-American Institute for Learning, and the Hmong Cultural and Resource Center.

NOTES

1. Wajuppa Tossa, "Lao Folk Literature Course," Resources for Lao Studies, Northeastern Illinois University Center for Southeast Asian Studies, www.seasite.niu.edu/lao (retrieved January 2008), chap. 1.

2. Peter Koret, "Books of Search: The Invention of Traditional Literature as a Subject of Study," in Grant Evans, ed., *Laos: Culture and Society* (Chiang Mai, Thailand: Silkworm Books, 1999), 226–257.

3. Wajuppa Tossa, "Lao Folk Literature Course," Resources for Lao Studies, Northeastern Illinois University Center for Southeast Asian Studies, www.seasite.niu.edu/lao (retrieved January 2008), chap. 5.

4. Jeff Cranmer and Steve Martin, *Rough Guide to Laos* (London: Rough Guides, 2002), 385. See also J. M. Cadet, *The Ramakien: The Thai Epic* (Tokyo: Kodansha International 1970), 30–44.

5. Visiting Arts Cultural Profiles Project, "Laos Cultural Profile," www. culturalprofiles.org.uk/laos (retrieved December 2007). See also Sachchidanand Sachai, *The Rama Jataka in Laos: A Study in the Phra Lak Phra Lam* (New Delhi: B. R. Corporation, 1996); Manas Chitakasem, ed., *Thai Literary Traditions* (Bangkok: Chulalongkorn University Press, 1995); Rafe Martin, *The Hungry Tigress: Buddhist Legends and Jataka Tales* (Berkeley, CA: Paralax Press, 1990).

6. Grant Evans, *A Short History of Laos: The Land in Between.* Crows Nest, Australia: Allen and Unwin, 2002), 23. See also John Garrett Jones, *Tales and Teachings of the Buddha: The Jataka Stories in Relation to the Pali Canon* (Boston: Allen and Unwin, 1979).

7. Visiting Arts Cultural Profiles Project, "Laos Cultural Profile," www. culturalprofiles.org.uk/laos (retrieved December 2007).

8. Northeastern Illinois University Center for Southeast Asian Studies, "Resources for Lao Studies," www.seasite.niu.edu/lao (retrieved January 2008).

9. Wajuppa Tossa, "Lao Folk Literature Course," Resources for Lao Studies, Northeastern Illinois University Center for Southeast Asian Studies, www.seasite. niu.edu/lao (retrieved January 2008), introduction.

10. Ibid. See also Xay Kaignavongsa and Hugh Fincher, *Legends of the Lao: A Compilation of Legends and Other Folklore of the Lao People* (Bangkok: Geodata System, 1993).

11. Vatthana Polsena, *Post-War Laos: The Politics of Culture, History, and Identity* (Ithaca, NY: Cornell University Press, 2006), 22–26.

12. Visiting Arts Cultural Profiles Project, "Laos Cultural Profile," www. culturalprofiles.org.uk/laos (retrieved December 2007). See also Wajuppa Tossa, trans. and ed., *Phadaeng Nang Ai: A Translation of a Thai-Isan Folk Epic in Verse* (Lewisburg, PA: Bucknell University, 1990).

13. Wajuppa Tossa, "Lao Folk Literature Course," Resources for Lao Studies, Northeastern Illinois University Center for Southeast Asian Studies, www.seasite. niu.edu/lao (retrieved January 2008), chap. 3.

14. Steven Jay Epstein, *Lao Folktales* (Chiang Mai: Silkworm Books, 1995), 99–103.

15. Peter Koret, "Laos," in *Traveller's Literary Companion to Southeast Asia*, ed. Alastair Dingwall (Brighton, UK: Print Publishing, 1994), 120–157. See also P. B. La-Font, "Laos" in *Southeast Asian Languages and Literatures: A Select Guide*, ed. Patricia Herbert and Anthony Milner (Honolulu: University of Hawaii Press), 67–76.

16. Epstein, *Lao Folktales*, 1–4; see also Herbert and Milner, *Southeast Asian Languages*.

17. Duangduene Nettavong, Foreword to Lao Folk Literature Course, Resources for Lao Studies, Northeastern Illinois University Center for Southeast Asian Studies, www.seasite.niu.edu/lao (retrieved January 2008).

18. Wajuppa Tossa, "Lao Folk Literature Course," Resources for Lao Studies, Northeastern Illinois University Center for Southeast Asian Studies, www.seasite. niu.edu/lao (retrieved January 2008), chap. 11.

19. Wajuppa Tossa, "Lao Folk Literature Course," Resources for Lao Studies, Northeastern Illinois University Center for Southeast Asian Studies, www.seasite.niu.edu/lao (retrieved January 2008), chaps. 8–9.

20. Wajuppa Tossa, "Lao Folk Literature Course," Resources for Lao Studies, Northeastern Illinois University Center for Southeast Asian Studies, www.seasite.niu.edu/lao (retrieved January 2008), chap. 10.

21. Koret, "Books of Search," 226–257.

22. Bounheng Inversin and Daniel Duffy, eds., *Mother's Beloved: Stories from Laos* (Seattle: University of Washington Press, 1997), 7–15.

23. Evans, *Short History*, 65–67.

24. Visiting Arts Cultural Profiles Project, "Laos Cultural Profile," www.culturalprofiles.org.uk/laos (retrieved December 2007).

25. Koret, "Books of Search," 245.

26. Visiting Arts Cultural Profiles Project, "Laos Cultural Profile," www.culturalprofiles.org.uk/laos (retrieved December 2007). See also Bounheng and Duffy, *Mother's Beloved*, 13–15.

27. Evans, *Short History*, 152–153.

28. Bounheng and Duffy, *Mother's Beloved*, 29–33.

29. Peter Koret, "Contemporary Lao Literature," in *Texts and Contexts: Interaction between Literature and Culture in Southeast Asia*, ed. Luisa Mallari-Hall and Lily Rose R. Tope (Quezon City: University of the Philippines Press), 77–103. See also Visiting Arts Cultural Profiles Project, "Laos Cultural Profile," www.culturalprofiles.org.uk/laos (retrieved December 2007).

30. Mai Neng Moua, ed., *Bamboo among the Oaks: Contemporary Writing by Hmong Americans* (St. Paul: Minnesota Historical Society, 2002), 10–11.

31. "Hmong Folk Art Presentation," Hmong Studies Internet Resource Center, www.hmongstudies.org (accessed November 2007).

32. See Norma J. Livo, *Folk Stories of the Hmong: Peoples of Laos, Thailand, and Vietnam* (Englewood, CO: Libraries Unlimited, 1991).

33. Bryan Thao Worra, *Touching Detonations: An E-Chapbook* (Sphinx House Press, 2004), members.aol.com/thaoworra/poetry.htm (retrieved April 2007), 3.

34. Ibid., 12.

35. See Mai Neng Moua, ed., *Bamboo among the Oaks*. See also Shirley Geok-lin and Cheng Lok Chua, eds., *Tilting the Continent: Southeast Asian American Writing* (Minneapolis: New Rivers Press, 2000).

5

Art

TRADITIONAL ARTS

SOME SCHOLARS HAVE said that the arts in Laos are nothing more than an extension of those in Thailand.[1] Unquestionably that is an extreme and pejorative viewpoint. However, most scholars would agree that the traditional arts of Laos never rivaled the quality or quantity of other countries in Southeast Asia. The relative isolation of Laos from major trade routes affected its artistic communities. So too did long periods of war and foreign domination, during which invading armies either destroyed or looted many artifacts. Whereas in Cambodia and Vietnam French colonial administrators made concerted attempts to promote indigenous artistry, chiefly for export, little effort was made in Laos. However, traditional arts did exist in Laos, and examples that survive illustrate characteristics distinct from others in the region. Such works have become important symbols of Laos's past as well as its national identity today.

Buddhism has indelibly shaped all the traditional arts of Laos. Religious influences dominated sculpture, painting, architecture, and many decorative arts. In fact, none of these areas was originally conceived of as art but was rather designed to educate and help inspire people to achieve enlightenment. They were created in part with the belief that both artists and the wealthy patrons who commissioned them earned merit in honoring the Buddha through such images.

Sculpture

The most numerous examples of traditional art in Laos are sculptures, which have survived far better than other works have over time. Sculptures also had particular religious importance, given that just before his death Buddha told disciples anxious to honor him that they could take something from his body and set it in "a mound of dirt."[2] The oldest-known Buddhist statues in Laos are those of the Mon and Khmer, which date to the first millennium C.E. A rock wall at Vangxang, just north of Vientiane, bears carved images of the Buddha that are among the oldest in the country. Despite the legends surrounding it, most scholars believe that the Phabang is in fact Khmer in origin, dating to the thirteenth century. The massive head and torso of the fourteenth-century Buddha at Wat Manorom in Luang Prabang are the best examples of a more indigenous image. Between the fourteenth and sixteenth centuries a distinctly more Lao style evolved in sculptures, most of them stylized versions of the Phabang. This is particularly true of those created during the reign of King Vixun, who was a great patron of the arts. The golden age for traditional sculpture in Laos came between the sixteenth and eighteenth centuries, during the height of Lan Xang. Works from the period can be found in the National Museum in Luang Prabang, or Ho Pha Keo, Wat Sisaket, and Wat Ong Tu in Vientiane.[3]

Most sculptures depicting the Buddha in Laos are not terribly different from those found elsewhere in Southeast Asia given the religious standards that define symbolic representations and the influences of the Khmer, Lan Na, Sukhothai, and Ayutthaya kingdoms. Images of the Buddha, or *lakshanas*, were laid out in ancient texts and Sanskrit poetry. Pali language texts describe 32 *lakshanas*, with 108 characteristics of his feet alone. The position of the Buddha was also derived from religious scripts. Throughout Theravada Buddhist countries there are three types of sitting, or *maravijaya*, Buddhas; one with both soles of the feet upward, one with one leg on top of the sole of the other foot, and one of him sitting on the throne with both feet on the ground. There is also a walking Buddha, unique to the Sukhothai era of ancient Thailand, and a reclining Buddha capturing his last moments on earth before dying. There are also forty hand gestures, or *mudras*; each depicts various meanings or events according to Buddhist philosophy. Six are most commonly seen in Southeast Asia: preaching, bestowing charity, being called to earth, setting in motion the Buddhist faith, meditating, and calming or dispelling fear.[4] The *mudra* known as "defeating Mara" or "victory over Mara" is seen more than any other in Laos. It depicts Buddha sitting in a lotus position with his left hand palm-up on his lap and the right hand pointing down with fingers extended. It symbolizes Buddha's victory over the evil Mara, who tried to distract him from enlightenment.

However, there are two more *mudras* unique to Laos. One shows him with both arms at his sides and fingers pointing downward, often called the "beckoning rain" pose. The other depicts him with arms crossed at the wrists, referred to as the "contemplation" pose. Sculptures of the Buddha from Laos are also distinct in other ways: the ears are usually flatter and longer, the eyebrows are arched, the nose appears thinner, and the bottom of Buddha's robe curls up symmetrically.[5] These characteristics first appeared during the early sixteenth century and became "classically" Lao, even though the variations diminished following the collapse of Lan Xang and were replaced by more Siamese influences.

Bronze was the preferred medium for sculptures in Laos, although sometimes gold, silver, precious stones, or jewels were used. The Phabang is solid gold, whereas the famous Pha Keo that formerly resided in Vientiane and now

Buddha statue at Haw Pha Kaew, Vientiane. Tibor Bognar/Art Directors & Trip Photo Library.

Buddha statue at Wat Xieng Khuan, a Buddha park near Vientiane. Brian Vikander/Art
Directors & Trip Photo Library.

sits in Bangkok as Thailand's holiest image is made of solid jade. Another
famous statue, the Pha (Phra) Phuttha Butsavarat, is made of crystal. It was
crafted and resided in Champasak, but the Siamese took it in the nineteenth
century to Bangkok. Stone, ceramic, and terra-cotta were popular for the
images designed to grace smaller shrines or niches, whereas wooden Buddhas
were put inside caves, such as the spectacular Pak Ou network overlooking
the Mekong River outside of Luang Prabang. Bricks and mortar were used
for giant statues.

Earlier images were often solid bronze, although as Buddhism spread, faster
and more economical means of production were necessary. As a result, most
were made hollow. The sculptor began by making a mold with sand and clay
shaped into a basic image. Shellac and beeswax were then applied as a cover
and medium for carving. Mud or cow dung was used to fill any cracks. The
image was then covered in clay and baked. When it was cooled, the mold was
filled with bronze. The pieces at Wat Manorom suggest that giant images were

Hindu demon at Wat Xieng Khuan, near Vientiane. David Sutton/Art Directors & Trip Photo Library.

constructed in parts rather than as a single whole. As is still true, the image was not a Buddha until monks blessed it. Moving or replacing an image also required blessings, and destroying one was strictly taboo. Even today they are instead repaired, reshaped, or used in other sacred forms.[6]

The importance of sculpture in Laos is underscored in somewhat strange fashion by the popularity of Xiang Khouan (Xieng Khuan), better known as "Buddha Park," just outside of Vientiane. Begun in the 1950s by a self-proclaimed holy man, the riverside park is crowded with giant concrete statues depicting all sorts of figures from Buddhist and Hindu mythology. It is more of a tourist trap than anything else, but it is surprisingly popular with both foreigners and locals.

Painting

With its tropical climate, paintings in Laos did not survive well prior to the development of modern conservation techniques. The best remaining examples of traditional Buddhist painting in Laos can be found on bas-reliefs and prayer or preaching cloths. As in sculpture, strict rules regarding the depiction of the Buddha, colors, forms, and content matter governed painting. The *satok* tales and Pha Lak Pha Lam (Pharak Pharam) were the most common subjects. By today's standards painting was fairly rudimentary, with simple lines and solid blocks of color. Shading and the use of shadow were rare. Unfortunately, the bas-relief works found in Laos today were almost all painted on stucco that was laid over surfaces, which made them more susceptible to damage over the centuries. Many have been restored numerous times. The best examples of bas-relief paintings are found in Wat Sisaket in Vientiane and Wat Pa Heuk in Luang Prabang.[7] There are some examples of painting on other mediums such as furniture or shutters and door frames. Some painters also created illustrations for palm-leaf books. Red and yellow ocher, ground minerals, charcoal, and the dye from vegetable greens were among the materials used to make paint. Brushes were made from animal hairs or fibers and roots from trees.

Scholarship on traditional painting in Laos is thin. Most experts treat the subject as an extension of Thai art history given the preponderant influences of the Lan Na, Sukhothai, and Ayutthaya kingdoms on Lan Xang and then Siamese domination from the early eighteenth century. However, as with sculpture, there were regional variations in painting. By the late eighteenth century art in Laos showed more experimentation in topic matter with the portrayal of nature, everyday life, and even humor. The traditional paintings of northern Thailand and Laos also tend to show brighter colors, blacker outlines, and simpler topics than those found elsewhere.[8]

Other Decorative Arts

The mysterious giant urns found in the Plain of Jars (see Chapter 2) are clear evidence that sophisticated techniques for ceramics existed in Laos at least two thousand years ago. Excavations at Sisattnak, near Vientiane, have uncovered pottery from the second and third centuries C.E. Some scholars contend that kilns found here made between the fifteenth and seventeenth centuries are different from those found elsewhere in Southeast Asia, which suggests that Laos was a major center for glazed ceramics during the height of Lan Xang. Similar excavations at Ban Xang Hai outside of Luang Prabang reinforce this argument, although few definitive archaeological studies have been completed to date. The manufacture of gold and silver wares dates back to between the ninth and thirteenth centuries, when Laos was part of the Khmer empire. However, neither gold nor silver was abundant until the sixteenth century, when skilled craftsmen followed King Sethathirat from Lan Na to Luang Prabang. Gold and silver wares from the Lan Xang era are best seen in jewelry, funeral urns, decorative boxes, and Buddhist votive items.[9]

Wood carving is one of the most recognizable traditional arts in Laos. It predated the spread of Buddhism but became more important as a religious art, used in temples and palaces to adorn door frames, roofs, pillars, and decorative panels. Wood-carvers were also employed to make furniture for the wealthy. The most skilled made the magnificent royal barges, palanquins, and howdahs that royalty used for their transportation. Unfortunately, traditional woodworking skills are dying out in Laos, and in recent years the Lao PDR has implemented programs to preserve and revive them. Woodworking is also a traditional art of many Mon-Khmer and Hmong-Yao groups. Their work is more evident in everyday items like spears, bows, pipes, bowls, spoons, carved figures, and toys. Some groups also make musical instruments from wood, bamboo, and gourds. Bronze drums are particularly artful work in some tribes.

Paper arts are also traditional in Laos, as they are throughout Southeast Asia. Papermaking revolved around the *sa* (*saa*), or mulberry tree, the bark of which was crushed, mixed with water, and made into a paste before being drained and dried into thin sheets. It was then used for sacred texts, gradually replacing palm leaves. It was also used for festive occasions in decorating temples or homes, and in making artistic kites and fans. *Sa* was also originally used in the manufacture of lacquerware, an art closely associated with Thailand and Burma. Woven baskets or dry wood were carved or pressed into various shapes and sizes before being covered in a mix of ash, clay, and rice husks. The latex from rubber trees was then boiled and cooled into a black paste that was then spread over top. After repeated coats, sanding, and polishing, colorful designs were engraved or painted on. There are examples of traditional lacquerware in Laos, but for reasons that are not entirely clear, it never developed into a major center for the craft. Traditionally, and still today, bamboo and rattan were also employed in decorative arts: They are used in making furniture, baskets, containers, and musical instruments. Some of the Lao Theung and Lao Sung also have established histories of basketry.

TEXTILES

Although some people consider them more handicraft than art, textiles represent one of Laos' most important traditions, and one of the few that extends to nearly all ethnic groups. Some of the most recognizable textiles come from the Lao Theung and Lao Sung. This in part stems from the ancient belief that men are considered transitory, as they leave home to build new lives, look for work, or fight wars. Women, on the other hand, traditionally remain and serve as the heart of home life. Consequently, throughout many ethnic groups in Laos, men's dress is simpler, whereas women wear more colorful and elaborate clothes to distinguish where they come from and to represent their tribes or villages. Clothes demonstrate wealth, social standing, and above all, skill.

Weaving and embroidery skills are highly prized by men seeking brides, as well as by traders who exchange other valuable goods for textiles. The Hmong weave elaborate *paj ntaub*, or "story cloths," to record momentous events, such as births, marriages, and deaths. Stitch work is taught to girls as young as five years old and is considered one of the most important skills in a woman's life.

The pattern and color of textiles vary not only between but also within ethnic groups, often right down to villages and individual families. There are, however, more than a dozen clearly identifiable major styles found across Laos, which depend primarily on region, materials used, and the type of loom employed. These are discussed in detail in Chapter 8. Unfortunately, among some groups in the Mon-Khmer language family, the art of traditional textiles has declined. The Lao government has recently implemented various programs to correct this, and together with demand from increased tourism, there are hopes for a revival.[10]

Modern Art

Laos is not known for its modern art or design. Again, the small population, relative isolation, and decades of conflicts factor into this. However, especially before 1975, there was a small but vibrant modern artistic community, especially in painting. Under French rule in the nineteenth century Laos was exposed to Western techniques and styles, and a handful of painters experimented with oil and watercolors. The first Lao school dedicated to modern arts was not established until 1940, when a Frenchman named Marc Leguay (1910–2001) started a small community at Sala in Champasak Province. There he taught drawing, graphic art, and metalwork before the Japanese imprisoned him in 1945. When the war ended, he moved the school to Vientiane and continued teaching. The school was shut down in 1949 for lack of funds, but Leguay remained in Vientiane as an art teacher for nearly three decades. His own work focused on scenes of everyday life in Laos, renowned for its colors and rich textures. He became known as the Gauguin of Laos and achieved considerable local fame. More important, Leguay helped establish the National School of Fine Arts at Vientiane in 1962, which allowed many Lao artists to train at higher levels. Two other provincial schools were established in 1975 at Luang Prabang and Savannakhet. They taught traditional and modern painting, drawing, sculpture, woodwork, metalwork, and pottery.

Decades of conflict and communist rule have seriously affected artistic communities in Laos since then. The persecution of artists in Laos did not reach anywhere near the extent seen in Cambodia, but some still faced internment in political reeducation camps after 1975. The communist government imposed restrictions on all creative arts. Social realism became the mandate, following the same pattern imposed in the Soviet Union, the PRC, and Vietnam. This meant that all arts had to reinforce communist ideology or the revolutionary struggle. Paintings and drawings glorifying the new regime adorned banners, posters, books, newspapers, and virtually all other visual media. Images of healthy, smiling peasants working in fields reaping bountiful harvests became standard, as did pictures of handsome soldiers and government officials protecting the people from foreign threats, and those depicting strong, agile workers building an industrial Laos for the future. Anti-Western and especially anti-American themes were also very common in portrayals of average people fighting against ruthless imperialism.

However, there were also somewhat typically Lao artistic anomalies in the new regime. A prominent example is the giant statue of King Sisavangvong in Vientiane. In other communist states vestiges of the former government were usually destroyed or removed, but not in Laos. The Lao PDR allowed it to remain, although the plaque identifying the statue as Sisavangvong mysteriously disappeared. Some suggest that this is because the sculpture was a gift from the Soviet Union, given following the king's son's state visit there in 1972. Others believe that it remained because the leadership in Laos was more pragmatic than its counterparts elsewhere in the communist world and understood that sympathies for the royal family ran deep. Perhaps with the same nostalgia in mind, the new regime entertained some more traditional arts and co-opted them as part of the "new" Lao socialist identity. For example, artists at the national academy continued reproducing classical or early-modern Western artworks despite their "bourgeois" connotations. Unlike Cambodia, in Laos the academies teaching fine arts were kept open. In fact, the communist government opened a new one, the National Arts Teacher Training School, in 1982, to train educators of art and music at the primary and secondary school levels. However, given their focus on copying rather than creating artistic works, the Lao schools have failed to produce a genuine artistic community in the country. Although political restrictions have been lifted, most artists, even those with elite training, have no market for their talents. Laos has too small and poor a population to support art on any commercial level. Only very recently has the government encouraged a few Lao artists to sell their work overseas.

Prominent Lao artists today include Khamsouk Keomingmuang, whose paintings focus on rural scenes and women in traditional costume, and Kongphat Luangrath, who works in both printmaking and painting. He and his colleagues May Chandavong and Anoulom Souvandouane recently established the Mask Gallery in Vientiane to showcase local art. These artists and others, like Kanha Sikounnavong and Nirad Chounramahy, have had increasing international exposure through exhibitions. There are also several well-known Lao artists working overseas, such as Vong Phaophanit and Phet Cash.[11]

NOTES

1. Jeff Cranmer and Steve Martin, *Rough Guide to Laos* (London: Rough Guides, 2002), 368.

2. Steve Van Beek, *The Arts of Thailand* (London: Thames and Hudson, 1991), 26.

3. Visiting Arts Cultural Profiles Project, "Laos Cultural Profile," www.culturalprofiles.org.uk/laos (retrieved December 2007).

4. Robert E. Fisher, *Buddhist Art and Architecture* (London: Thames and Hudson, 1993), 174–186. See also Philip Rawson, *The Art of Southeast Asia* (London: Thames and Hudson, 1967), 145–153.

5. Cranmer and Martin, *Rough Guide*, 365–366.

6. John Hoskin, "The Subtle Art of Casting Sacred Statues," *Sawasdee Magazine*, June 2002, 29–33. See also Rawson, *Art*, 22–28.

7. Visiting Arts Cultural Profiles Project, "Laos Cultural Profile," www.culturalprofiles.org.uk/laos (retrieved December 2007).

8. Jean Boisseler, *Thai Painting* (Tokyo: Kodansha International, 1976), 110–113. See also Wattana Wattanapun, "The Use of Traditional Tai Images in Contemporary Thai Painting," in *Traditional Tai Arts in Contemporary Perspective*, ed. Michael Howard, Wattana Wattanapun, and Alec Gordon (Bangkok: White Lotus Press, 1998), 193–196.

9. Visiting Arts Cultural Profiles Project, "Laos Cultural Profile," www.culturalprofiles.org.uk/laos (retrieved December 2007).

10. Cranmer and Martin, *Rough Guide*, 368–396. See also; Patricia Cheesman Naenna, "Change as a Method of Identification and Dating Tai Textiles," in *Traditional Tai Arts*, chap. 3.

11. Visiting Arts Cultural Profiles Project, "Laos Cultural Profile," www.culturalprofiles.org.uk/laos (retrieved December 2007).

6

Architecture and Design

HISTORICAL ARCHITECTURE AND ARCHITECTURAL TRADITIONS

TRADITIONAL ARCHITECTURE IN Laos reflects many influences: Indian, Khmer, Burmese, Thai, and Chinese. Unfortunately, much of the country's ancient heritage was lost over the centuries to war and neglect, but there are still sites that illustrate its past grandeur. In particular, Laos has a diverse range of Buddhist temples that rank among the most interesting and important in the world. Considering the mix of more recent French, Vietnamese, communist, and Western influences, the architectural history of Laos is even richer, so much so that Luang Prabang is listed as a United Nations Educational, Scientific and Cultural Organization (UNESCO) world heritage site.

The oldest-known human-made structures in Laos are a series of standing stones dating to between 1000 and 500 B.C.E. found in Hua Phan and Luang Nam Tha provinces. The giant containers on the Plain of Jars date between 300 and 100 B.C.E. Cave and earthworks from the same period suggest rudimentary fortifications made of thatch and wood. The ruins of Hindu and early Buddhist temples indicate that stonework and masonry gradually replaced wood as the primary building material during the first millennium C.E. By the third century C.E. the Mon established a kingdom west of modern-day Bangkok that became the focal point of the Dvaravati empire. By the late eighth century, it stretched into Laos, where the Mon built the original settlements at Luang Prabang and Vientiane. Khmer influences date to the same period, and between the ninth and thirteenth centuries became dominant, particularly in the south. Built between the fifth and seventh centuries, the Hindu and later Buddhist temple Wat Phu Champasak is a good example of Khmer architecture in Laos. Together with other temple complexes in the area, UNESCO designated it a world heritage site in 2002. By the eleventh century the Khmer empire reached Vientiane, where fragments of their temples exist at Pha That Luang and Wat Simuang.

The architectural achievements of Lan Xang are more abundant, although little is intact from the earliest era. Fragments and foundations suggest that there was a vigorous approach to temple construction in the kingdom from its inception. A good example of this was the sanctuary at Viengkham, built in 1359 to house the Phabang during its journey to Fa Ngum's capital. Between the fourteenth and sixteenth centuries, his successors continued the tradition. However, it was not until the sixteenth century that Lan Xang began its architectural golden age. During the reigns of Vixun, Phothisarat, and Sethathirat there was a dramatic expansion, particularly evident in temples such as Wat Vixun in Luang Prabang. Built around 1502 to house the Phabang, it required an estimated four thousand trees. According to legend, the main twelve pillars—each one 30 meters (98 feet) tall—were taken from different forests in the kingdom. Sketches from European travelers show that Wat Vixun was a truly magnificent temple. It held the sacred idol between 1513 and 1707, and again between 1867 and 1887, when Haw raiders destroyed it. It was reconstructed in the late nineteenth century using modern materials but in accordance with the original design. Other temples from this period include Wat May and Wat Pak Khan in Luang Prabang, Wat Phonesay in Vientiane, and Wat Sayasathanh in Vientiane province.[1]

As discussed in Chapter 2, during the reigns of Phothisarat and Sethathirat stronger ties between Lan Xang and Lan Na led to a period of even greater artistic and architectural achievements. A spectacular example is Wat Xiang Thong in Luang Prabang—probably the most famous temple in Laos. Built in 1560, it has remained largely untouched since. It was the only temple in the city that the Haw did not destroy in 1887, owing to the fact that one of their leaders had studied there earlier in his life.[2] In fact, Wat Xiang Thong survived all conquering armies and conflict Laos has endured. It remained the religious centerpiece of the Lao royal family until the communist revolution and today is one of the country's top tourist attractions. So too is Pha That Luang in Vientiane, the most important symbol of national unity in Laos. Originally built between 1565 and 1571, the temple was abandoned following the Siamese conquest of the city in the late 1820s. French explorers found it overgrown with jungle in the 1867, and the Haw raiders destroyed it some twenty years later. The one standing today is a reconstruction made in the 1930s, inspired by the French promotion of a Lao national identity.

Sethathirat also presided over the construction of Wat Mixay, Wat Tay Noi, Wat Tay Yai, Wat Ong Tu, and Ho Pha Keo, all in Vientiane and the latter would house the famous Emerald Buddha. He also built Wat Phia Wat in Xiang Khuang and That Sikhottabong in Khammouane, as well as reconstructing the ancient city of Souvannakhomkham in Sayaburi. However, his death in 1571 put an end to the golden age of Lan Xang. Many of the temples and buildings were destroyed or fell into disrepair during the nearly seventy years of conflict that followed. It was not until the reign of Surinyavongsa in the mid-seventeenth century that Lan Xang regained its glory. During his rule Vientiane was restored and became a major center in the Buddhist world. European accounts attest to the magnificence of its palaces and temples. Unfortunately, the city declined again following his death. Because of the division of Lan Xang, little is known about eighteenth-century architecture in Laos. Several major temples like Wat Nong, Wat Sene, and Wat Xiang Lek were built at Luang Prabang in the early 1700s, while Wat May, Wat Phonesay Sanasongkham, and Wat Pha That Chomsi were constructed late in the century. By the time the Haw invaded, there were sixty-five *wat* in Luang Prabang. Vientiane witnessed less activity until the early nineteenth century when King Anuvong refurbished the city and constructed the famous Wat Sisakhet.[3] It was one of the few major buildings in the city not destroyed during the Siamese invasion of 1828.

The architectural influences of both Siam and France dominated the nineteenth and twentieth centuries prior to the communist revolution. French styles are best seen in Cambodia and Vietnam, where more money was made available for the construction and maintenance of buildings. However, the French did leave their imprint on Laos. The most obvious example is the Royal Palace compound in Luang Prabang, built between 1904 and 1909 for King Sisavangvong. It incorporates traditional Lao and period French designs throughout, even including the three-headed elephant emblem of the royal family alongside the fleur-de-lis. There is also the Résidence Supérieure, built in 1900 as the seat of the colonial government in Vientiane, and the Service des Travaux Publics, constructed in 1907. It now serves as the French embassy. Other examples of French architecture in Vientiane include Bureau de la Résidence (1915), the Lycée Auguste Pavie (1920), the Hôtel du Commissariat (1925), and the Église de Sacré-Coeur (1930). Today most house offices of the Lao PDR government or serve as schools and museums.[4] The former private residences of French colonial officials—multistory brick and stucco villas with large verandas and balconies—still stand out today in centers

Haw Pha Bang, Royal Palace, Luang Prabang. Tibor Bognar/Art Directors & Trip Photo Library.

like Luang Prabang. Some are now refurbished hotels and private residences again.

THE LAO *WAT*

The best-known example of Laos' classical architecture is the *wat* (*vat*). Although the term is interpreted in English as "temples," *wat* can actually refer to a single structure or a complex. There are thousands in the country, and they are very important to every town. Most *wat* are built in fenced-off areas central to the communities they serve, but their exact design is varied. Some *wat* appear crowded and disorganized because of an ad hoc approach in adding to the complexes over time. Building materials and techniques have also changed, producing distinct differences among *wat*. For example, originally wood was used for their construction, but the wood decayed over time. Bricks and plaster make up the majority of *wat* built since the fifteenth century.

The *wat* in Laos are very similar to those elsewhere in Buddhist Southeast Asia. They all contain a consecrated chapel known as a *sim* or *uposatha*, where religious ceremonies take place and the main Buddhist statuary are kept. They also have a *vihara* or *wihann*, where sacred images and texts are kept. Both the *sim* and *vihara* sometimes have verandas, small galleries, or gardens around them. The *sim* is further demarcated by boundary stones, called *sii maa* (*bai sema*), which mark sacred ground at the corners of the building. *Wat* complexes also have *that* (*thaat* or *tat*) or *stupa*: solid cones, bells, or lotus-shaped towers that symbolize the strength of the religion. These designs reflect the Hindu and early Buddhist influences from India and Ceylon that were incorporated by Khmer, Mon, and later Tai builders. *That* function as reliquaries. Many *wat* take their name from the relics the *that* holds. Those holding relics associated with the bodhisattvas are identified by the title Pha That, or "Buddhist relic" in their name. Those from the Buddha himself are called Maha That (Mahathat), or "great relic." Some *wat* also have a *mondop*: a square or cube-shaped building with a pyramidal roof that houses other important objects of the faith. Lectures, meetings, and social functions are held in the *sala* (*saala*), special buildings in the *wat* compound. The monks' residences or *kuti* are also nearby. Larger *wat* may have a library (*haw tai* or *ho tai*), bell towers (*haw rakhang* or *ho rakhang*), drum towers (*haw kawng* or *ho kong*), and buildings that serve as schools, community centers, and even health clinics. Demonstrating the importance of *phi* worship, many *wat* also have spirit houses.[5]

There are different construction styles illustrated in the *wat* throughout Laos, most based on the time they were built, their location, and the materials used. Architectural historians generally identify three schools named after the cities and regions where they originated: the Vientiane, the Luang Prabang, and the Xiang Khuang. The main difference between them is with respect to the roofs of the *sim*. In the Vientiane style front verandas of the *sim* are open with large pillars that support an elongated, overhanging roof. The edges of the roof have high, multitiered peaks that look like flames, often referred to as *dok so fa* ("pointing to the sky") or *jao fa* ("sky hooks"). They represent different levels of Buddhist cosmology and are tipped with dramatic *naga*: the mythical sea serpent that protected Buddha. There is often an ornate decorative screen over the front entrance depicting mythical creatures from Buddhist cosmology or carvings of the Buddha. The Luang Prabang style features *sim* with low sweeping roofs, characteristic of those found in northern Thailand as an illustration of Lan Na influences over the centuries. Wat Xiang Thong is an excellent example. Roofs of the Xiang Khuang school also sweep low but are wider and lack the tiers and ornamentation of the others. The *sim* is also usually raised on a platform. Unfortunately, American bombing during the Vietnam War destroyed most temples in this style—found mainly in the north.[6] Collectively, Lao *wat* can also be distinguished from those in Thailand. Overall they are more modest and restrained. Decorative features like carvings often appear against a background of flames or flowers called *lai lao*: literally, the "Lao pattern." It is also more common in Laos to see Hindu deities and other Khmer influences, particularly carved in the upper lines of the roof.

A QUICK TOUR OF *Wat* IN LAOS

Given the tremendous variety of *wat* in Laos, it is safe to say two things emphatically: No two are exactly alike, and everyone has their own choice as to the best. That said, two *wat* in the country are worth particular mention for their historical significance, unique construction, and religious symbolism. At the top of that list is Wat Pha That Luang, "The Great Sacred Stupa," which now adorns the Lao PDR flag. Officially known as Pha Chedi Lokajulamani, or "World Precious Sacred Stupa," That Luang is the most important religious architecture in the country. King Sethathirat had it built over the site of Khmer ruins, which may have included an even older *that* dating back to the fourth century B.C.E. when, according to legend, monks returned home with a bone from Buddha's body. They convinced the lord of Vientiane to build a massive stone edifice for the faithful to worship around the bone. Today, many Lao believe that the original *that* is encased within the outer shell of the one standing. Covered in gold leaf, the visible structure is surrounded by a square of thirty smaller *that* resembling the guard towers of a fort. The inner sanctuary has high walls with small windows, separated by beautifully made red-lacquer doors.[7] Ornamental *naga*, images of the Buddha, and stylized lotus flowers appear throughout. Four important *wat* were later built around That Luang. The entire complex was restored in 2005 to coincide with the thirtieth anniversary of the Lao PDR. In front of That Luang a giant statue of Sethathirat sits guard with a long, curved sword symbolizing his protection of the heart of the nation. Recently cracks have appeared in the facade of the *that*, caused by the vibrations of heavy traffic all around the complex.

Most visitors to Laos are struck even more by Wat Xiang Thong, the "Golden City" monastery, built by King Sethathirat at the confluence of the Mekong and Nam Khan rivers in the mid-sixteenth century. The sweeping roof represents a bird with graceful, outstretched wings: a mother hen protecting her chicks according to most locals. Gold designs are stenciled onto the black and dark-red walls of the *sim*, most depicting tales from the *satok* or *Pha Lak Pha Lam*. There are also graphic portrayals of people punished for sins against the faith. The rear wall of the *sim* is covered with a beautiful mosaic of animals in the forest, centered on a legendary tree of flames that purportedly

Pha That Luang, Vientiane. Tibor Bognar/Art Directors & Trip Photo Library.

stood there before the temple was constructed. Dubbed the "Red Chapel" because of its red and gold reliefs, a small building directly across from the *sim* houses the sixteenth-century bronze reclining Buddha and unique glass artwork. The funerary hall is adorned with carved teak walls that show more characters from the Pha Lak Pha Lam (Pharak Pharam) along with the carriage used to take King Sisavangvong to his cremation.[8]

TRADITIONAL HOUSES

There is an old saying that a Lao lives in houses built on piles, eats sticky rice, and listens to the *khaen*: a musical instrument made from bamboo. The saying plays on the fact that the Lao Theung and Lao Sung more commonly live in houses on the ground and eat dry rice. Indeed, there is truth to the notion. The traditional Lao house, or *heuan*, sits on stilts raised above the ground to adapt to seasonal rains, which is particularly important for those living along riverbanks. The space underneath is used for storage, cooking, or keeping livestock. Outward-leaning walls and a slightly more rectangular shape distinguish Lao and northern Thai homes. The traditional house is made from wood. Teak is preferred, but now other hardwoods, bamboo, and thatch are more common. Still today, most *heuan* are made by hand, although in larger towns prefabricated wood panels are often used.

The simplest structures have only one room, but many are larger with spaces for cooking and bathing. The roofs of the house are curved, often sharply, to handle heavy rains. A high roof pitch allows for greater room inside, and the openness permits better air circulation, which in a hot climate is an absolute necessity. Sometimes corrugated tin is used as roofing tile, although the traditional design calls for tightly woven bamboo mats or thatch. Tin conducts heat and can make the home very hot, but it is better than other materials for funneling rainwater, used for drinking. It is also more durable and less susceptible to insects, which often nest in thatch. The traditional home has no furniture, only a mat for sitting on the floor and for sleeping. There is usually no running water, no electricity, and no other amenities, especially in rural areas. Kerosene or oil lamps are still widely used today.

Despite its simplicity, the traditional house is constructed with strict adherence to spiritual beliefs and functionality. No construction takes place without the consultation of astrologers, who advise on the location, the timing, and even the materials used. Careful attention must be given to make sure spirits are not disturbed. Rituals and prayers still begin construction of homes in Laos today. The positioning of the house and its internal design revolves around the position of those sleeping, with the direction of the head being particularly important. Buddhists believe that one's feet should not point toward another's head, so homes were set up to have everyone sleep in one direction. In many villages it is common to see neighbors line up their homes in accordance with these principles: back-to-back with the next house so that no one points their feet at anyone's head. This concept also stems from the belief that *phi* can travel only in straight lines, so one can avoid lying parallel under horizontal beams. The notion applies especially for the dead, who must be moved with their feet facing the front gable from the upper part of the house to the lower by a special ladder to ensure that its *phi* does not return.[9] Most Lao homes have altars to honor both Buddha and the *phi*.

Given that many ethnic minorities live in remote, rural communities that are economically disadvantaged, architecture and design among them tends to quite simple and similar to the Lao Lum. Generally speaking, the Tai-Kadai and Mon-Khmer groups live in stilted or partially stilted homes. Those from the Hmong-Yao groups live in houses set squarely on the ground. However, this is not an absolute rule. Some, like the Akha, also employ the use of stilts. Architectural styles have transcended ethnic boundaries, and it is not uncommon to see a fusion of traditions. Some Tai groups, like the Tai Daeng, Tai Dam, and Tai Khao, are noted for larger homes with tortoiseshell-shaped thatched roofs. Some Katuic- and Bahnaric-language family groups construct their homes around a communal house at the center of a village. In areas where access to materials is easier, some traditional homes of the Lao Theung and

Traditional wooden house with leaves in the Bolavan plateau near Thateng. © Alfred Molon–www.molon.de.

Lao Sung have adopted modern buildings materials, whereas those in remote areas continue to reside in houses that have not changed their basic style in hundreds of years. In the more traditional villages of Mon-Khmer groups, a bamboo spirit gate guards the entrance and an area for animal sacrifice is often nearby.

MODERN ARCHITECTURE

Under French rule the construction of houses in urban areas incorporated new materials, such as bricks and stucco, as well as European design influences. However, this was just for the wealthy. Most Lao continued to live in traditional homes. In fact, many French-style homes adopted Lao designs to better deal with the climate. By the mid-twentieth century cities like Luang Prabang and Vientiane had a curious mix of traditional Lao and French neo-colonial architecture, dotted with a few Indian-, Chinese-, and Vietnamese-style buildings.

In the 1950s there was a relative boom in the construction of public buildings, most following Western designs. The National Assembly, now the office of the prime minister, the National Stadium, and the Mahosot Maternity Hospital are a few examples. However, the most recognizable structure from this period is the massive Patuxai Monument in Vientiane. Built in 1957, it was designed to be the Lao equivalent to the Arc de Triomphe in Paris. Indeed, it is situated at a roundabout along the capital's main thoroughfare, Lan Xang Avenue, in exactly the same fashion as the Arc de Triomphe stands along the Champs Elysées. Some refer to the monument as the "vertical runway" because it was made from cement purchased in the United States that was supposed to have been used for the construction of a new airport. The only other major project begun before the revolution was the presidential palace, also in Vientiane: it was started in 1973 and finished in 1986.

The Lao PDR has not considered architecture—old or new—much of a priority, primarily given the country's poverty. However, by the late 1980s monies were freed to create new office buildings in Vientiane. Similarly, a new National Assembly was built in 1990 and Luang Prabang received an international airport terminal in 1997. However, some of the new construction has raised concerns about planning, costs, utility, and the environment. The fourteen-story Don Chan Palace Hotel, built on an island in the Mekong, is an example. Even more pressing is the fact that, with economic reforms, the Lao government has initiated a construction boom that is poorly regulated.[10] It is unlikely to stop any time soon, particularly as the population of Laos grows and becomes more urbanized. With, albeit small, Western-style towers and complexes slowly appearing on Vientiane's skyline, it may be just a matter of time before the traditional *heuan* is relegated to the most remote parts of a modernized Laos.

NOTES

1. Visiting Arts Cultural Profiles Project, "Laos Cultural Profile," www.culturalprofiles.org.uk/laos (retrieved December 2007).

2. Joe Cummings and Andrew Burke, *Laos* (Footscray, Australia: Lonely Planet Publications, 2005), 118–119.

3. Daigero Chihara, *Hindu-Buddhist Architecture in Southeast Asia* (Amsterdam: E. J. Brill, 1996), 220–223.

4. Visiting Arts Cultural Profiles Project, "Laos Cultural Profile," www.culturalprofiles.org.uk/laos (retrieved December 2007).

5. Arne Kislenko, *Culture and Customs of Thailand* (Westport, CT: Greenwood Publishing, 2004), 148–149.

6. Cummings and Burke, *Laos*, 41. See also Clare Griffiths, ed., *Insight Guides: Laos and Cambodia* (London: Apa Publications, 2005), 72–73.

7. Northeastern Illinois University Center for Southeast Asian Studies, "Resources for Lao Studies," www.seasite.niu.edu/lao (retrieved January 2008). See also Cummings and Burke, *Laos*, 70–71, and Griffiths, *Insight Guides*, 75.

8. Jeff Cranmer and Steve Martin, *Rough Guide to Laos* (London: Rough Guides, 2002), 154–157.

9. Northeastern Illinois University Center for Southeast Asian Studies, "Resources for Lao Studies," www.seasite.niu.edu/lao (retrieved January 2008). See also Roxana Waterson, *The Living House: An Anthropology of Architecture in Southeast Asia* (New York: Whitney Library of Design, 1998).

10. Visiting Arts Cultural Profiles Project, "Laos Cultural Profile," www.culturalprofiles.org.uk/laos (retrieved December 2007).

7

Theater, Dance, Music, and Film

TRADITIONAL THEATER, DANCE, AND MUSIC

MUSIC, DANCE, AND theater are closely connected in traditional cultures of Laos. The *lam* or *khap* folk songs and the *lam luang* classical opera are based on traditional music but are theater as well. The *lam* requires audience participation, whereas the *lam luang* is highly theatrical performance art. As is true with most arts in Laos, these forms are ultimately expressions of folktales and/or the *satok* and Pha Lak Pha Lam (Pharak Pharam). The influence of animism is also pronounced, as many songs, dances, and performances involve the *phi*. Probably the best example of this connection is seen during Lao New Year celebrations at Wat Vixun in Luang Prabang. Animistic dances in full costume are performed to honor servants of the mythological Khum Bulom, Phou Nheu, and Nha Nheu, who are the spirit guardians of the city. Many songs, dances, and plays also incorporate myths, legends, cosmological beliefs, and Buddhist morality tales.

KHON AND LAKHON

A traditional, nonmusical theater culture never fully emerged in Laos. Dramatic performances of the *satok*, Pha Lak Pha Lam, and folktales date back to Lan Xang, but outside the preview of royal audiences they never really caught on. Much more commonly, theatrical performances were set to music and dance and known as *khon* and *lakhon*. Both are rooted in the Pha Lak

Pha Lam, but the latter, less formal art, also draws from the *satok* tales. *Khon* and *lakhon* are famous for their colorful and elaborate costuming, especially masks. Made from paper and decorated with gold, lacquer, and imitation jewels, the masks represent traditional monsters, demons, and gods from the Pha Lak Pha Lam. Characters are identified by the colors they wear; the hero Pha Lam (Rama) always wears deep green, whereas Hanuman, his monkey-god ally, wears white. Dance movements are meant to be fluid, delicate expressions of the hands and upper torso, and to communicate emotions.[1] Most scholars believe that both the *khon* and *lakhon* originated during the early stages of Lan Xang, derived from similar performances in Khmer culture. After the collapse of the kingdom Siamese influences took over, and today there is little difference between Thai and Lao renditions of either theater.

LAM AND MOHLAM

Lam is a form of oral literature. The word means to sing, but *lam* is probably best described as a kind of chant. In effect, its performers chant lyrical folk poetry, and the melody or tune comes from intonations in their pronunciation and voice. It is likely that the tradition began long before Buddhism as a means of oral history—passing down tales from generation to generation—and as a way to communicate with *phi*. *Lam* performances are call-and-response in that the performer chants out and the audience replies. There are numerous different styles of *lam* as well as regional variations within Laos and Thailand. For example, *mohlam* (*molam* or *maw lam*) is an expert form of the art, prized for its creativity and precision. Artists in this genre do not work from a memorized script but rather make their *lam* up each time, drawing on folk beliefs, tricks of phrase, and contemporary culture for their material.[2] Training to become a *mohlam* artist is difficult and a lengthy process, but the best are regarded highly in their community and some have star status in Lao society.

There are also subdivisions of *lam* based on the subject matter, the number of performers involved, the poetic form and rhythm used, and the regional variations. *Lam kiaw* is best described as "courting poetry," in that it is traditionally performed by a man and woman and is almost always about romance. *Lam naaw* is "long" poetry because it takes a long time to perform. *Lam pheun* is generally interactive with the audience and employs more humor than drama. There is also *lam khuu* or "paired" poetry, which involves separate dialogues woven together in the same performance. *Lam* employs both formal and informal language, and it seldom takes the shape of a direct conversation between performers. Instead, artists respond to each other indirectly by singing about themes like unrequited love, loss of a loved one, or worry about one's relationships. Buddhist principles about minimizing de-sire have a strong current in *lam*. Most performances end without definitive resolution, but rather are meant to engage the audience's emotions about the impermanence of everything in life. One line from a *lam kiaw* laments, "I will only be satisfied if I can die and be reborn under a tree trunk, blocking the way so that you will walk across it."[3]

Most Lao can identify the region from which the *lam* originates in the first few lines of the performance. *Lam saravane* and *lam siphandone* are among the best known regional variations. There are also numerous styles of *lam* and *khap* performed by ethnic groups of the Lao Theung and Lao Sung, effectively making the art form national. Examples include the *khap Tai Daeng* (Red Tai), *khap Tai Dam* (Black Tai), *lam Meuy* (Tai Meuy), and *lam Phu Tai* (Phu Tai) variations. These employ local instruments or musical accompaniment by hand clapping. It is, of course, almost impossible to accurately gauge all the variations of *lam* and *mohlam* in Laos, although in its recent efforts to showcase the cultural diversity of the country the government has identified at least one hundred major melodies among the different ethnic groups.

LAM LUANG

Lam luang is Lao opera. It originated as a more theatrical way of per-forming *lam* and *mohlam* long ago but did not become popularized until the late nineteenth century. Siamese, Cambodian, Vietnamese, Chinese, and Malaysian theatrical influences also stimulated its development. By the early twentieth century *lam luang* performances involved large troupes—often as many as thirty people—with elaborate sets, costume changes, and orchestral accompaniment. However, it was not until 1972 that a professional *lam luang* organization—the Central Lao Opera—was formed, not by the RLG but by the Pathet Lao. They hoped to promote the tradition as the national art of a communist Laos. In the Lao PDR the troupe has continued and today per-forms about various social issues like HIV-AIDS and drugs as much as it does about more traditional themes. There are also a number of smaller amateur *lam luang* groups in Laos.

TRADITIONAL FOLK DANCE

With such diverse populations it is not surprising that Laos has many tra-ditional folk dances, known collectively as *fon phun muang*. Most are derived from Buddhist teachings or mythologies. They are best known for precise, styl-ized movements of the hand and head, based on the Buddhist *mudra*. One of the most popular Lao Lum dances is the *lam vong*, or "circle dance," in which an individual begins and is then joined by a partner, then by other couples, until the whole crowd forms three connected circles. The *fon uay* is also well known as a welcome dance, as is the *fon dab* men's martial arts dance. Lao Theung and Lao Sung dances include the Hmong *fon bun kin chieng*, or "New Year" dance, the *fon pao bang* Khmou courtship dance, the Red and Black Tai "bamboo pole" dance, and the bell and drum dances of the Yao.[4] There are numerous regional variations in both name and style, particularly among Lao in Isan, but overall there is great continuity in Laos and Thailand with respect to folk dances.

Most tourists to Laos today see folk dances performed with elaborate costumes and staging under the impression that the traditional art is thriving. In fact, dance has declined dramatically over the past few decades. Economic hardship and political repression have undermined the interest of average citizens, and as elders die, the skills involved have not been easily transferred to a new generation. The Lao PDR has tried to revive dance culture in an attempt to "customize tradition" for a new era with the opportunities tourism provides.[5]

TRADITIONAL MUSIC

Music for *lam, lam luang,* and *fon phun muang* is, of course, essential. By far the most important instrument in traditional music in Laos is the *khene* (*khaen*), one of the country's definitive national symbols. Variations can be found among all ethnic groups. This is a large mouth organ made from bamboo tubes specially fitted into a sound box made of wood. Sometimes seven or eight pairs of the tubes are required for each *khene*. Each tube is fitted with a reed, usually made from silver. The player, called a *moh khene*, blows into the box and blocks small holes in the tubes to force the vibration of the reeds and produce a characteristic droning sound. Overall, the *khene* is similar to the Chinese *sheng*, from which it is likely derived. It is used in all traditional theater and dance and has found a home in more modern music in Laos.

There are a range of other instruments used in Lao music. The *pi* is a woodwind instrument similar to a clarinet. The bamboo or wood flute is known as the *khoui*, whereas the *ranaat* is a bamboo xylophone. The *phin* is a small guitar. Specially tuned gongs, called *khong wong yai*, cymbals (*sing*), and hand drums known as *ta phon* are also commonly used. The ensemble used to play for events was traditionally known as *piphat* as it still is in Thailand. After 1975 the Lao government tried to distance the arts of the country from its southern neighbor and renamed traditional musical ensembles *mahori*. Technically, this term applied to smaller groupings in which stringed instruments like the *jakhe*—a kind of zither—dominated.[6] *Mahori* generally played community

Man playing a traditional flute in a village near
Pakse. Courtesy of Jeff Phisanoukanh.

functions and were considered more of a "commoner's" orchestra, which is
why the government favored the name change.

Similar instruments can be found among almost all the ethnic groups of
Laos. There is in fact a wide range of just bamboo flutes, varying in size,
shape, and composition. In more remote areas it is common to see animal
horns or hollowed gourds turned into instruments.[7] Drums and gongs are also
well represented and inventive, as they are made from almost every material
imaginable.

MODERN MUSIC

French colonialism introduced Western-style music to Laos in the early
twentieth century. By the 1920s Vientiane boasted several nightclubs, bars,
restaurants, and dance halls that played contemporary music. Some musicians
experimented and mixed traditional *lam* with French music. Many songs in
the 1920s, 1930s, and 1940s were translated and performed in Lao. New Lao
songs were also produced, most designed to encourage nationalism in the face

of Siamese threats. Popular songs included "Lao Houam Samphan" ("Joining Together the Lao People"), "Lao Houam Vong" ("Unifying the Lao People"), and "Teuan Chay Lao" ("Thoughts of the Lao Heart"). Less politically motivated songs like "Xao Noum" ("Lao Youth"), "Deuane Ngam Nham Nao" ("Moon in Winter"), and "Nay Ta Bok" ("Written in Your Eyes") were also popular during this period.

Independence and increasing American influence in Laos brought even more exposure to modern music. The National School of Music and Dance, established in 1959, introduced voice and instrumental training. A new wave of musicians and popular songs followed. Prominent artists included Bounkhong Pradichit, Phoui Siharath, Nang Kongmi, and Soukanh Vilaysane. In the 1970s Malivanh Voravong, Phomma Phimmasone, Kor Viseth, and Chanthala Outhenesakda were popular. The communists put an end to Western music in the country, deeming it both counterrevolutionary and culturally decadent. In their place patriotic songs were commissioned to celebrate the new Lao PDR. "Pathet Xat" ("Nation Country"), "Thang Lek Kao" ("Road Number 9"), "Hak Muang Lao" ("I Love Laos"), "Sieng Phleng Bontong Nga" ("The Sound of Singing in the Rice Fields"), and "Xom Xeui Kong Pong Kan A Kad" ("Congratulate the Antiaircraft Gunner") were among dozens of revolutionary anthems on the post-1975 music scene.

The relaxation of government restrictions on the arts has led to a more vibrant musical culture. In addition to the resurgence of traditional music, foreign influences have returned. Most evident is the influx of CDs from Thailand. The music industry also has moved in, with companies like Valentine Music, Mega Studio, and Indee Records competing for the new market. Western, Thai, Japanese, Chinese, and Vietnamese music comes into Laos via both legal and illegal means and is particularly accessible in Vientiane. However, local modern music is also popular and played widely on Lao radio. Artists like Alexandra Bounxoui, Pan, Noi Sengsourigna, Sithiphone, and Ting appeal to mainstream audiences, whereas boy bands like Y Power and A Pack are aimed at the teen crowd. Heavy-rock artists include Sapphire, Bohaln, and the Lao-Canadian band Exile. More alternative music can be found with the Cell, Awake, Smile Black Dog, Punky Dolls, and Eighteen.[8] Sysumonk Xayawong, Sopha Thanakone, and Kularp Meaungpiey are popular folk artists.

However, even with globalization and Western influences, *lam* remains the No. 1 music in Laos. Today, the most popular form of *lam* uses satire and comedy, especially bawdy humor. In some parts of Laos variations of *lam kiaw* known as *lam pa nah* (*lam pa nyah*) are especially well received. The courting is more humorous and the performers test one another more with wit. Another variation known as *lam glawn* is highly theatrical, usually staged at large events with many performers, and is the one that foreign tourists most often see. Although *khap* is very similar to *lam*, there is a basic distinction in that it involves a repetitive chorus sung by performers. Over the past few decades both *lam* and *khap* have incorporated Western musical instruments, producing a relatively new hybrid in Laos and Thailand known as *lam luang samay* (*luuk thung*). It is most accurately described as a cross between Western pop music and traditional Lao *lam*, including electric guitars, bass, drums, and keyboards. It is often linked to *lam vong thammada*, a modern hybrid of traditional and Western dance moves.

PUPPETRY

As in Thailand, puppet theater, or *lakhon tukkata*, is an ancient art. It was long associated with the royal family and its court. Traditionally, the large puppets were carved from wood, painted, and costumed to look like characters from *satok* tales and the Pha Lak Pha Lam. Performance artists who did the gestures and voices operated them from below. However, the popularity of puppetry was never widespread in Laos, and outside of Luang Prabang it never quite caught on. In 1978 the Lao PDR government tried to resurrect interest by creating the Central Puppet Troupe, but performances have been rare, owing to a lack of funds and public attention. In recent years a variation of the old art *hun kabong* has been better received. It involves actors in costumes with hand puppets performing similar ancient tales with modern spins from popular culture. A troupe called Théâtre d'Objets Kabong Lao was established with aid from the French government.

MODERN THEATER

The French also have inspired modern theater in Laos. During the 1930s and 1940s Lao productions were put on by the Laotienne Artistique et Sportive, a cultural organization founded with French support. Most of these were Western-style musicals. There were few Lao-language dramatic productions until the communist takeover in 1975. Borrowing from their Vietnamese allies, the Pathet Lao used dramatic theater troupes as a means of propaganda, even employing them at the front during the war. After the revolution the Lao PDR created the Central Spoken Drama Troupe to continue the tradition. Contingent with political reforms in the late 1980s, it also began producing less ideologically driven theater. However, historical and political themes remain very popular. In 2003 the play *King Fa Ngum* was staged to commemorate the seven-hundredth anniversary of a Lao state. Lao legends, folktales, and Buddhist mythology also account for theatrical productions today.

FILM

Aside from some rare documentary footage taken during French rule, there is no real film heritage in Laos of which to speak prior to independence. During the 1950s both the RLG and Pathet Lao produced numerous newsreels and propaganda films. In fact, one of the earliest known films taken in the country is a communist production dating to 1956. The first feature films in Laos were *Khukhak Pheunkhaen* ("The True and Untrue Friend") and *Phaenedin Khong Hao* ("Our Land"), both produced in the early 1960s by the RLG. A small commercial filmmaking industry began shortly thereafter but lacked critical infrastructure. It is believed that only nine feature films were made in the country between 1960 and 1975, about which little other than the titles is known, as most were destroyed.

As with all other arts, after the revolution ideological considerations dictated film. The Ministry of Culture took over all production and established a cinema department to oversee it. Approved propaganda films included the 1980 *Muangkhao Lao Sivithmay* ("New Lives in the Old Town"), *Phoumlamnao Khong Saokhongsang* ("Place of the Elephant Hunters") in 1982, and *Sangsha Pathet Xat* ("Building the Country") in 1987. However, the best-known feature film from the period is the docudrama *Siengpeun Chak Tonghai* ("Sound of Gunfire from the Plain of Jars"), a 1983 coproduction with Vietnam about the escape of a Pathet Lao unit surrounded by RLG forces in 1958. This was followed up in 1988 with *Bouadeng* ("Red Lotus"), directed by the Czech-trained director Som Ok Southiphonh. Set in 1972, the story focuses on a family ravaged by war and the clash of traditional and modern cultures. Neither of the films succeeded and the cinema department was closed in 1988. Shortly thereafter the State Cinematographic Company was opened to manage foreign film distribution, and in 1991 the National Film Archive and Video Centre was established to produce documentary films with the aid of the Japanese government.[9] However, no other feature film was made until the 2007 movie *Sabaidee Luang Prabang* ("Good Morning, Luang Prabang"). It is the first commercial production ever filmed in Laos and the first feature made in twenty years. Directed by the Thai filmmaker Sakchai Deenan, it is a joint Thai–Lao production that stars the Lao-Australian actor Ananda Everingham, already very popular in Thailand, and a Lao actress named Khamly Philavong. The movie is about a Thai photographer who falls in love with a Lao tour guide. It is scheduled to debut in Bangkok in June 2008, although the timing of screenings in Laos are still unclear—especially because the country has only two movie theaters and no film production or distribution company.[10]

Films about or set in Laos are almost as rare as movies made there. American-made action pictures like *Uncommon Valor* (1983), *Missing in*

Action II (1985), and *Bat 21* (1988) center on rescue attempts of downed pilots or prisoners of war held captive in Laos after the U.S. withdrawal from Vietnam. The 1983 movie, part action and part love story, *Love Is Forever* focuses on an Australian journalist deported from Laos and his journey back to reach the love of his life. *Air America* (1990) is a comedic look at clandestine CIA support for the RLG during the 1960s. *Rescue Dawn* (2006) is a dramatic, action film about the real-life story of Dieter Dengler, a German American pilot shot down over Laos during the Vietnam War. It is based on Werner Herzog's 1997 documentary *Little Dieter Needs to Fly*.

The 2006 Thai comedy *Mak Tae Loke Talueng* ("Lucky Losers") originally featured Laos as the setting for a hapless national soccer team commandeered by a Thai superstar player turned coach. However, Lao PDR Foreign Ministry officials strenuously complained about the portrayal of Laos in the movie, forcing the producers to use a fictitious country, Arvee, instead. This followed serious anti-Thai protests in Cambodia after the release of another film, *La-Tha-Pii* ("Ghost Game"), in 2006. The teen-horror flick showed a reality-TV program set in an abandoned military prison that closely resembled Cambodia's infamous Tuol Sleng, the scene of many Khmer Rouge atrocities.

In 2007 the Australian-made documentary *Bomb Harvest* was released to much critical acclaim. It follows Laith Stevens and teams working under the auspices of the Mines Advisory Group and the Lao National Unexploded Ordnance Programme in their efforts to clear the country of unexploded ordnance. It shows the many often-unknown problems of bomb removal, including the dangers of impoverished people trying to dig shells out to sell as scrap metal. Another documentary film about Laos, *Nerakhoon* ("The Betrayal," 2007), has also been well received. Directed by Ellen Kuras and Thavisouk Phrasavath, it follows a family forced to flee Laos in the 1970s and their journeys since. Kuras spent twenty-three years working on the project to highlight the human tragedy of people caught up in the shadows of the Vietnam War.

NOTES

1. Mattana Rutnin, *Dance, Drama, and Theatre in Thailand: The Process of Development and Modernization* (Chiang Mai, Thailand: Silkworm Books, 1996), 12–20.

2. Carol J. Crompton, *Courting Poetry in Laos: A Textual and Linguistic Analysis* (Detroit: Cellar Book Shop, 1979), 95–120.

3. Ibid., 59.

4. Visiting Arts Cultural Profiles Project, "Laos Cultural Profile," www.culturalprofiles.org.uk/laos (retrieved December 2007).

5. For an interesting discussion on this process, see Grant Evans, *The Politics of Ritual and Remembrance: Laos since 1975* (Honolulu: University of Hawaii Press, 1998), 129–140.

    6. Terry E. Miller, *Traditional Music of the Lao: Kaen Playing and Mawlum Singing in Northeast Thailand* (Westport, CT: Greenwood Press, 1985), 131–139.

    7. Visiting Arts Cultural Profiles Project, "Laos Cultural Profile," www. culturalprofiles.org.uk/laos (retrieved December 2007).

    8. See www.laopress.com (retrieved June 2007).

    9. Visiting Arts Cultural Profiles Project, "Laos Cultural Profile," www. culturalprofiles.org.uk/laos (retrieved December 2007).

    10. Australian Broadcasting Corporation, online news, June 9, 2008, www.abc. net.au/news/stories/2008/06/09/2268852.htm.

8

Cuisine and Traditional Dress

LAO CUISINE

ANY DISCUSSION ABOUT Lao cuisine cannot be limited to Laos. There are approximately six times more ethnic Lao in the Isan region of northeastern Thailand than in Laos itself, which makes it necessary to go beyond national boundaries in search of definitively Lao food. In fact, with the recent droves of migrants from Isan further south to Bangkok, the Thai capital has in many respects become the epicenter of Lao cuisine. Some estimate that more Lao are there than in any other city in the world, including Vientiane. There are also sizable expatriate communities in places like the United States and France that make for numerous culinary variations abroad. Moreover, when one speaks about cuisine in Laos, the ethnic and regional diversity of the country must be taken into consideration. Last, it is important to note that Laos does not have the range of markets, stores, or restaurants found in its larger neighbors. The outside world is just now discovering Lao food, which has not transformed or fused with other culinary traditions in the same way that Thai or Vietnamese cooking has. In this respect cuisine in Laos is still a very traditional, simple, and personal art.

Although there are similarities between Lao and Thai food, there are also notable distinctions. The main similarity, one shared with all mainland Southeast Asian cuisines, is the focus on rice. The main difference is that, unlike in the rest of the region, the Lao use sticky rice. Known as *khao niaw* (*klao niaw*), sticky rice is a short-grained, glutinous variety and is usually rolled into small balls and eaten by hand. Long-grained rice, called *khao jao* (*klao jao*), is widely available, but sticky rice remains the Lao staple. Lao Theung and especially the Lao Sung use long-grained rice more. Every Lao meal features rice. Indeed, no meal would be complete without it. It accompanies everything: fresh vegetables, meat or fish dishes, dips, salads, and soups.[1] Rice is usually served as a centerpiece of the meal in a traditional bamboo container called a *tip khao*. It is considered very bad luck to leave off the lid of the *tip khao*. Some believe that it means a divorce will occur, and others think that it signals that hunger will come to the family. Some Lao have smaller portable versions of the basket full or rice and other ingredients that they take with them to work for lunch. Whereas sticky rice is always eaten with the hands, long-grained rice is always eaten with a spoon and fork. Chopsticks are not familiar to the Lao, but they can be found in the ethnic Chinese and Vietnamese communities. Eating rice with chopsticks is considered quite odd, something that foreign travelers often find out quickly.

Another staple of both Thai and particularly Lao cuisine is a strong-tasting fermented fish paste, called *paa daek* (*pa daek*) in Laos. The primary difference is that in Thailand it is often made from saltwater fish, whereas in land-locked Laos it comes from freshwater species. Manufactured versions are also more common in Thailand, whereas many Lao still make theirs from scratch. *Paa daek* is served with every meal as an accompaniment to rice or to flavor the vegetable, meat, or fish dishes served. A thinner, slightly less fishy variation of this, *nam paa*, is also used, particularly in Isan. Even more than in Thai food, Lao cuisine often contains liberal amounts of chilies, known collectively as *maak phet*. Other common ingredients include cilantro (coriander), mint, dill, lemon grass, galangal, ginger, tamarind, sesame seeds, peanuts, soy sauce, lime juice, dried shrimp, vinegar, and garlic. Herbs like dill and mint and spices like galangal are used more commonly in Laos than in Thailand. Special sauces and pastes like *nam phak kaat*, made from fermented lettuce leaves, also are popular.

Lao food is very fresh and generally quite healthful. Most ingredients are obtained on a daily basis at the local market (*talat* or *talad*). Every town has at least one, and they are the best place to learn about Lao food. Most dishes contain some sort of vegetable. Unlike in Thai cuisine, vegetables are often served raw. The Lao also have more of a preference for sour, bitter vegetables than do the Thai. A Lao proverb advises, "Sweet makes you dizzy, bitter makes you healthy."[2] Various kinds of beans, peas, and cabbages are steamed, stir-fried, or served raw either in dishes or on their own. Cauliflower, root vegetables, and gourds also are popular. Numerous greens—spinaches, cresses, and lettuce, as well as some unique to the forests of Laos—appear in many dishes. Foreign travelers may see bamboo shoots, daikon, lotus root, and bitter melon for the first time, but the Lao eat tomatoes, potatoes, eggplants,

Woman selling vegetables at a vegetable market in Pakse. © Alfred Molon—www. molon.de.

cucumbers, corn, onions, and other vegetables more familiar to the Western palette, too.

Meats regularly consumed by the Lao include chicken, duck, pork, beef, and water buffalo. Freshwater fish and prawns are also eaten throughout the country.[3] Goat and lamb are part of the South Asian diet in other places more than in Laos, although some Lao Theung and Lao Sung eat them. Outside of the main towns where hunting is a regular part of life, meat includes deer, wild boar, birds of all sorts, rats, lizards, small jungle cats, and wild dog. Much of it is served raw in salads with vines, leaves, and herbs from the jungle. Not surprisingly, some refer to this as jungle food. As elsewhere in Asia and in other parts of the world, insects are eaten in Laos. It is not uncommon to see them offered, cooked or raw, in markets or being prepared by street vendors. Grasshoppers, cockroaches, ants, and other insects are a good source of protein and many people in Laos consider them quite delicious.

The volume of ingredients makes for enormous variation among dishes in Lao cuisine. Some of the most popular include *som tam* or *tam maak hung*, a green papaya salad made with crab, hot chilies, garlic, tomatoes, peanuts, lime juice, and fish sauce. It often comes with *ping kai*, which is grilled chicken marinated in a mix of coriander root, garlic, pepper, and salt. The national dish of Laos is *laap* (*larb*), spicy minced meat, chicken, or fish mixed with lime juice, garlic, onion, mint, and chilies. Variations known as *laap seau* ("tiger *laap*"), or *laap dip* in Isan, contain raw meat, chicken, or fish.[4] One of the more interesting spins on the dish is found around Pakse. Raw ant eggs are used in place of the meat, sometimes with live ants mixed in. Another favorite is *or lam*, made from dried and salted buffalo meat, chilies, eggplants, lemongrass, and *paa daek*, stewed together and eaten with crispy pork skin and sweet basil. Curries include *khao laat kaeng*—made with long-grained rice—which is especially popular in Isan. Street vendors hawk noodle dishes like *khao pun*—flour noodles with a sweet and spicy coconut-base sauce—as well as barbecued pork meatballs, spring rolls, various stir-fried dishes, and *klao poun*, served with raw chopped vegetables covered in coconut sauce flavored with meat and chilies. *Miang lao* is another popular snack. It is pork fried with garlic, ginger, tamarind, sugar, and fish sauce, served with lemongrass and cilantro in a wrap of pickled cabbage or lettuce leaves.

The Lao are very fond of fish, but an old saying has it that the fish they eat cannot come from the sea because they do not smell like the earth. There are numerous species eaten that come from the Mekong and other rivers in Laos. Carp, eel, stingray, sheatfish, snakefish, and especially the common catfish (*paa duk*) are usually on the menu. The giant Mekong catfish, called *paa beuk* in Lao, is increasingly rare and theoretically protected, but people still fish for it. Known to grow up to nearly 3 meters (9.84 feet) and to weigh 200 kilograms (440 pounds), it is a massive meal. Fish is often served fried crispy (*jeun paa*), grilled (*piing paa*), steamed (*neung paa*), or sweet and sour (*paa som waan*). Prawns, called *kung*, are prepared the same way. Some of the more popular fish dishes are *pa tod kateam* (fried fish with garlic sauce), *ho mook pa* (steamed catfish in banana leaf), and *koy pa* (raw fish salad).[5]

Soups are an important part of Lao cuisine. *Tom khaa kai* is a slightly sour chicken soup made with lime, galangal, coconut milk, and lemongrass. It is also made with fish, called *tom yam paa*, or prawns, known as *tom yam kung*. *Kaeng jeut* is a fairly mild soup made with pork and bitter melon. Other popular soups include *kaeng no may*, made from fresh bamboo shoots, and *kaeng het bot*, with fresh mushrooms.[6] Even more unusual to the Western palate are *kang youk*, made from a young banana tree, and *keang khai mood*, or ant-egg soup. Vietnamese *pho*, or noodle soup, is eaten throughout the country, usually as breakfast or for a snack. *Pho* features vermicelli noodles with beef, mixed in with fresh basil, cilantro, lime juice, bean sprouts, chilies, sugar, shrimp paste, or sesame paste. The Vietnamese influence is also tasted in spring rolls, either the *yaw jeun* deep-fried variety or the *yaw dip* served fresh.

Ethnic Lao widely consume Chinese-style food, usually with chili or other accompaniments. Most of it is Cantonese or Hokkienese, although Yunnanese

Woman selling fish at a market in Pakse. Courtesy of Jeff Phisanoukanh.

food is found in larger centers like Vientiane. Chinese deep-fried dough, *pah thawng ko*, is particularly popular in the north. South Asian food is found almost exclusively in Vientiane, but all the larger towns offer Thai and, to a lesser extent, Italian and French cuisine. A testament to the colonial legacy, pâté, omelets, croissants, and French baguettes, called *khao jii*, are extremely popular in Laos. Other Western food has not fully made its way into Laos yet, although more restaurants and cafés are starting to cater to foreigners. As a sign of economic and political reform, a few top-end restaurants—clearly aimed at tourists—have opened over the past few years in Vientiane and Luang Prabang.

Desserts are not as common or varied in Laos as in the West, although there are some notable sweets, most involving coconut milk or cream. Banana in coconut milk (*nam wan mak kuay*) and coconut pieces in coconut milk are especially popular. So are colored gelatins mixed with ice and coconut and often other ingredients. *Khao niaw mak muang* is mango with coconut milk served over sticky rice. *Khao lam* is sticky rice and coconut milk mixed with red beans and cooked in small sticks of bamboo. Fruit (*mak mai*) is grown primarily in the Mekong Valley, and the best quality and variety is found there. During the hot season it is common to see markets full of fruit familiar to most foreign travelers, like oranges, mangos, bananas, papayas, coconuts, watermelons, and pineapples. However, a more exotic mix can also be found, including durian, rambutan, mangosteen, starfruit, jackfruit, guava, longan, tamarind, rose apple, and lychee.

Drinks in Laos are plentiful and include the standard fare of bottled water and soda pop found almost everywhere. Sugarcane and fresh fruit juices are also widespread. Milk products are less common, given the dearth of dairy production and consumption in Laos, but they can be found in major centers. Coffee is grown in Laos but it came to popularity first with the French. It is found almost everywhere in several styles. The Lao variety, called *kafeh pakxong*, is quite strong. It is usually drunk hot or cold in a glass with condensed milk, similar to the style in Vietnam. Tea is also very common and is a major export. Most restaurants serve it free of charge to their customers. Alcohol is abundant. Imported wines and hard liquors are found in towns and cities, as are the far more potent—and sometimes dangerous—homemade rice whiskies, known as *lao-lao* or *lao-hai*, which are regularly served after meals. Refusing a drink in someone's house is considered rude. Most Lao will pour a drink on the ground or in a special glass for the *phi*.[7]

Beer is also easily found. Particularly popular is the locally made Beer Lao, which many travelers regard as the best beer in Asia. In fact, Beer Lao is today one of the most ubiquitous symbols of the country. Its trademark tiger logo adorns posters and T-shirts, bought mostly by young Westerners as souvenirs of their stay. Far from being simply touristy, Beer Lao speaks to some of the major political transitions in Laos. Established in 1971, the Lao Brewery Company was a French venture originally known as Brasseries et Glaci è Res du Laos. The Lao PDR took it over in 1975 and renamed it. In 1993 the government sold part of its control to two companies: the Chinese-Thai Loxley Co. and Italian-Thai Production Co. Their investment made Beer Lao a sizable venture with three hundred employees and up to thirty million liters of production a year. In 2002 the two companies withdrew and returned Beer Lao to government control. However, in 2004 the major Danish brewer Carlsberg bought 25 percent of the shares in the corporation through its Asian division. Production has risen to 120 million liters, due as a result of Beer Lao's 99 percent control of the domestic market. Its assets are approximately US$60 million.[8]

THE ART OF EATING

The typical Lao kitchen is, by Western standards, extremely basic and may not even have electricity or running water. It is, however, an important part of the home and the center of much activity. The stove, or *tao-lo*, is usually charcoal fired. It resembles a bucket over which a grill or metal plate is put on to cook. A wok (*maw khang*) or pot (*maw nung*) is used for most cooking. Sticky rice is cooked in a bamboo steamer called a *huad*. Everything is served in a common room, usually on a slightly raised wooden or bamboo platform.[9] Family meals are an important part of everyday life in Laos. Few Lao like to eat alone. Meals take a long time to prepare and are seldom planned. The menu depends on whatever is available. Fresh ingredients are absolutely essential, especially considering that most homes lack refrigeration. Typically, the Lao home has a small garden to grow vegetables, fruits, and herbs. Breakfast usually consists of sticky rice, sometimes with pieces of meat, chicken, or fish, and coffee. Lunch involves soup, rice, a meat, chicken, or fish dish, vegetables, and hot sauce. Dinner is often a variation of lunch, but considering the large number of ingredients used in Lao cooking, the variations in flavor are almost endless.

Visitors to a Lao house are rarely asked to eat. Instead, food is offered automatically with the expectation that they will eat no matter what. All dishes are shared and meting out portions is offensive. Everything is served at once. Courses as they exist in the West do not exist. Most food is served at room temperature, stemming from the fact that rice is eaten with the hands. People serve themselves everything, and not eating is considered rude. It is customary to leave a small amount of food on one's plate to avoid appearing gluttonous. Drinks are generally consumed afterward. The whole event is informal and personable: conversation and laughter, as well as a hearty appetite, are encouraged.

CUISINE OF THE ETHNIC MINORITIES

There are just as many variations of cuisine are there are ethnic groups in Laos, which makes it almost impossible to account for all the food habits of the Lao Theung and Lao Sung. Many cuisines are very similar to that of the Lao, both in terms of ingredients and means of preparation. Those living in more remote areas of the country do not, of course, have access to stores or other amenities, and their food reflects that. People in such areas use the forests more than people who live in towns. Needless to say, poverty also plays an important role in this respect. Everything from an animal is used. Innards are considered a delicacy, as they are with the Lao Lum. Dried water buffalo rind, cow placenta, and other things generally considered repulsive to Westerners are commonly eaten upcountry. A traditional northern dish called *luk-andong* is prepared by wrapping a small bird in banana leaves, and then leaving it for a week or more to marinate.[10]

Some ethnic groups have a particular inclination for spicy food, whereas the Hmong have generally milder, even bland, cuisine. Boiled and steamed vegetables are prevalent. All groups use herbs, sauces, and dips, drawing on the influence of Thai, Lao, and Vietnamese cuisine. Few of the ethnic minorities rely on any manufactured or packaged foods; almost everything is grown, raised, or caught. Sweets are extremely rare and not part of the usual diet. The exception for most is a fairly unsweet rice cake, reserved for special occasions. Fruit is a preferred and much healthier alternative. Much like the Lao, in most ethnic groups, all meals are communal and involve several dishes. Unlike the Lao, however, some groups, like the Hmong and Yao, consider eating with your hands rude. This stems from the difference in rice, as they use long-grained rice, eaten with a fork and spoon, rather than the sticky variety.

TRADITIONAL DRESS

Laos does not have an official national dress or costume. However, until the 1975 revolution there were particular styles reserved for the royal court that in effect represented an official dress. For women, this was the *sin* (*sinh*), a wraparound skirt similar to a sarong. For men it was the *sampot*, a wraparound cloth for the lower body pulled up through the legs and tucked in at the back. Both are of Khmer origin and remain today the official dress in Cambodia. Ancient bas-reliefs on the temples at Angkor Wat show intricate *sin* and *sampot* designs dating to the thirteenth century that remain in vogue today. It is likely that the Khmer in turn took the designs from the Indian sarong and dhoti—a kind of billowed trouser—even earlier. Although the names, weaving techniques, color, and design might vary, the basic style of both the *sin* and *sampot* are still found today throughout parts of Asia.

Tai-speaking peoples made changes to production of the garments in several ways. First, they employed a freestanding, framed loom. Second, they cultivated silkworms for silk. Third, they introduced a three-stage design for the *sin*, making it distinct from the sarong. Men's garments were made of thicker silk or cotton than women's garments, but both were crafted from elegant and colorful material, often with block or checked designs. *Sin* in Laos and northern Thailand became noted for their intricate patterns around the edges at the foot of the skirt. A *biang*, or shawl, made from the same material was often added to accompany the *sin*. Longer shawls, or *hom*, were used to wrap around the upper torso in colder climes. More recently the *sin* has been substituted for a *nung*, a tube-style skirt.

Each ethnic group in Laos has its own traditions when it comes to dress. The variations in style and design are incredible and well beyond the scope of any discussion here. However, techniques and patterns are unique not just within groups, but sometimes within villages and even families. Traditions have been passed down for generations. Weaving is a means of identification; designs and colors represent the tribe that the wearer comes from. Groups like the Tai Daeng have numerous variations that experts have not entirely mapped out. Classification, reclassification, and the discovery of different styles continue today.[11] Moreover, some designs and techniques have transferred between groups over time, which makes strict identification difficult. Some scholars focus on twelve major traditional styles of weaving known in Laos, basically divided by region. Those in the South usually use foot looms instead of frame looms and produce intricate designs that show Khmer influences, like temples, elephants, and *apsara* dancers. Most *sin* are one piece and often incorporate beadwork or embroidery. In the Northeast, many Tai tribes use raw silk or cotton, employing a tie-dye style known as *matmii* or *ikat*. Diamond patterns and continuous weft brocade (*khit*) on the skirts are very popular. Central Laos is known for its indigo-dyed cotton *matmii* and minimal weft brocade (*chok*). Typical of the Luang Prabang style is gold and silver brocade with elaborate designs. Most skirts are sewn together from separately woven pieces. Traditionally, dyes throughout Laos are made from indigo, ebony, terra-cotta, tamarind, lacquer, and turmeric, each of which provides a basic color. Bark from trees like the *khaki*, sappanwood, and jackfruit are also used to make other shades.[12]

There are notable distinctions in dress between ethnic groups in each region. For example, Khmou women generally wear a cotton sarong decorated with simple horizontal stripes, accompanied by a long-sleeved black blouse that flares at the waist. It usually has a closure at the side decorated with embroidery, silver coins, or sequins. The Katu and Alak are renowned for their weaving skills, and they make sarongs, blouses, and loincloths for other tribes as well as for themselves. Some textiles have lots of beads—a trademark design of the Alak in particular. Sarongs with horizontal stripes are popular and usually accompanied by two-part sleeveless blouses joined by seams at the side and center. Silver and brass jewelry is also worn.

The Hmong-Yao, Lahu, Akha, and Lisu dress is similar to that of their relatives elsewhere in Southeast Asia, particularly in Thailand. Fine stitch work, elaborate design, and extensive use of silver and other ornamentation are typical of these groups. Blue Hmong women wear pleated skirts with bands of red, white, and blue embroidery on them. They also wear black satin jackets with wide cuffs of orange and yellow embroidery. White Hmong wear black pants with a broad blue slash across the waist and more simple jackets with blue cuffs. Yao women wear a long black jacket with lapels of bright red wool, loose trousers, and a richly embroidered black turban. Black Lahu

Thai Lu tribeswoman in traditional dress in Luang Prabang. Tibor Bognar/Art Directors & Trip Photo Library.

women are known for their distinctive black cloaks with diagonal white stripes and red and yellow decorations on the sleeves. Red Lahu women wear black trousers with white edges and sleeves decorated with red and blue stripes.[13] Akha women wear leggings, short black skirts with a beaded sporrans, and a loose black jacket with decorated cuffs and lapels. They are probably best known for their black caps with silver coins. The Lisu wear very colorful costumes of green and blue tunics embroidered at the cuffs and shoulders with bands of red, blue, and yellow fabric. They are often also adorned with silver ornaments.

Men in the Sino-Tibetan linguistic groups tend to wear long black pants tied at the waist with a plain or embroidered band. On special occasions men wear white shirts with embroidered vests, while women wear a black or multicolored shirt, long pants, striped or white skirts, and a colorful headband. Specific coloration and design depends on the occasion. As evidence of the importance of textiles to traditional peoples in Laos, Hmong groups even took

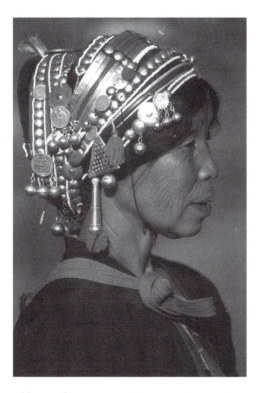

Akha tribeswoman, Muang Long. Jane Sweeney/Art Directors & Trip Photo Library.

their names from the different patterns in clothing. However, many ethnic minorities have increasingly adopted Lao-style *sin* and blouses.

MODERN DRESS

Clothing styles in Laos today reflect the political and social climate of the country, but this is nothing new. Textiles have always illustrated economic, social, and even political changes in Laos. During the Lan Xang era, textiles were used in trade and as tributes received from or paid to other kingdoms. They were also used to reinforce social hierarchies in that only select few were allowed to wear certain garments of particular designs and colors. The court at Luang Prabang commissioned expert weavers to design textiles made from imported European, Chinese, or Vietnamese fabrics. Chinese jackets and shirts were particularly fashionable in the decades just prior to the arrival of the French.[14] By the early twentieth century, French and other Western-style wear became the sign of a new royalty for those who had money, education, privilege, and Western inclinations. In fact, by the 1950s and 1960s Western clothes almost entirely replaced traditional dress among the Lao elites. More traditional voices in the country lamented the decadence of certain fashions, particularly women's pants and skirts above the knee, although traditional weaving continued creating new designs and outside influences changed the nature of Lao textiles.

During the Vietnam War era many people abandoned traditional textiles altogether. Looms were sold or hidden because of the ravages of war, and in some instances the unique skills of families and even tribes were lost over the twenty years of conflict. Many people, even in rural areas, became dependent on foreign textiles, especially from Hong Kong. Fashions from the United States were particularly popular among Lao youths, represented best by tight pants, T-shirts, dark sunglasses, and even cowboy hats. Communism made things even worse by eliminating the export market for locally made textiles and, in some cases, prohibiting the production of silk and the manufacture of clothes.[15] Although traditional *sins* were allowed, colorful ones were considered bourgeois and banned. Blue jeans and other Western clothing were also prohibited, as were long hair for men, short hair for women, and makeup. A standard, solid and dark-colored pants and shirt combination became the official dress for everyone in accordance with the proletarian principles of the new regime. In 1994 the mayor of Vientiane even issued instructions for proper Lao culture, stipulating that "men should wear international suits, or national, ethnic or some other appropriate outfit. Women should wear Lao traditional skirts and wear their hair in a bun or some other proper and appropriate manner."[16]

With the relaxed government of recent years, the Lao PDR has encouraged a resurgence of the indigenous arts, in part to increase self-sufficiency and to attract tourism. However, continuing economic deprivation and government repression of some minorities counteract such attempts. Both traditional and contemporary textiles are sold to local buyers, who in turn retail them to foreign buyers, mainly Thai and Japanese, or tourists. Several shops in Vientiane and Luang Prabang employ local cooperatives to make their products. Increasing international attention over the past few years has driven the price up, so much so that now only foreigners can afford many handmade Lao textiles. Western-style clothes like blue jeans have made a dramatic comeback and are now available in major centers alongside more traditional wear.

NOTES

1. Charmaine Soloman, *The Complete Asian Cookbook* (Vancouver: Raincoast Books, 1992), 320–323. See also Jeffrey Alford and Naomi Duguid, *Hot, Sour,*

Salty, Sweet: A Culinary Journey through Southeast Asia (New York: Artisan, 2000), 13–16.

2. "Lao Cuisine," www.laocuisine.net (accessed October 2006).

3. Daovone Xayavong, *Taste of Laos* (Hong Kong: SLG Books, 2003), 5–12.

4. Clare Griffiths, ed., *Insight Guides: Laos and Cambodia* (London: Apa Publications, 2005), 79–82.

5. Daovone, *Taste of Laos,* 58, 72–90.

6. Soloman, *The Complete Asian Cookbook*, 192–194. See also Alford and Duguid, *Hot, Sour, Salty, Sweet*, 268–269.

7. Joe Cummings and Andrew Burke, *Laos* (Footscray, Australia: Lonely Planet Publications, 2005), 55.

8. Beer Lao, www.beer-lao.com/aboutlbc/.

9. Solomon, *The Complete Asian Cookbook*, 323. See also, Cummings and Burke, *Laos*, 52–57.

10. Mansfield, *Culture Shock*, 150.

11. Patricia Cheesman Naenna, "Change as a Method of Identification and Dating Tai Textiles" in *Traditional Tai Arts in Contemporary Perspective*, ed. Michael C. Howard, Wattana Wattanapun, and Alec Gordon (Bangkok: White Lotus Press, 1998), 47–56.

12. Penny Van Esterik, "Fabricating National Identity: Textiles in Lao PDR," *Museum Anthropology* 23, no. 1 (Spring 1999), 48. See also Cummings and Burke, *Laos*, 43.

13. Virtual Hilltribe Museum, www.hilltribe.org (accessed June 2007).

14. Patricia Cheesman, *Lao Textiles: Ancient Symbols—Living Art* (Bangkok: White Lotus Press, 1988), 44–46.

15. Carol Ireson-Doolittle, *The Lao: Gender, Power, and Livelihood* (Boulder, CO: Westview Press, 2004), 71–72.

16. Grant Evans, *A Short History of Laos: The Land in Between* (Crows Nest, Australia: Allen and Unwin, 2002), 207. See also Grant Evans, *The Politics of Ritual and Remembrance: Laos since 1975* (Honolulu: University of Hawaii Press, 1998), 85–86.

9

Gender, Courtship, Marriage, and Family

TRADITIONAL ROLES OF THE SEXES

ACADEMIC RESEARCH ON women, gender relationships, and family in Laos is very thin. Government restrictions, the physical remoteness of some groups, and various cultural and linguistic barriers continue to present formidable challenges to researchers, especially those from outside the country. What research does exist has been focused mostly on the Lao Lum, leaving out almost half the population of Laos. Even with its relaxation of travel restrictions and increasing freedoms within the state, the Lao PDR remains sensitive about studies of the inequities women face, particularly among ethnic minorities.

Officially, Laos recognizes full gender equality in keeping with its socialist egalitarianism. Shortly after coming to power, the communist government pledged to "realise equality between men and women in all fields, political, economic, cultural and social, and to do away with all acts of contempt or oppression toward women."[1] From a legal standpoint women have equal rights in all respects including labor, land ownership, wealth, and inheritance. They received the right to vote in all elections in 1957, ten years after men. Beyond the legal sphere, women also exercise power in practical, everyday terms. Most Lao families are, in effect, run by women. Not only are they responsible for childrearing, tending the home, cooking, and other domestic duties, but they also usually control the household finances and run the family business. In more traditional communities men engage in the same work as women, including childrearing. Women and men take equal responsibility for farming, animal husbandry, and other daily tasks. However, among those who engage in the practices, hunting is generally the domain of men only, whereas weaving or sewing is exclusively women's work. Moreover, many societies are matrilineal. Lineage, and therefore cultural and social power, is traced through women.[2] Even when they are patrilineal, most ethnic minority groups have similar gender relations. Consequently, in many respects women are the backbone of the country.

Women make up more than half of the labor force and indeed dominate several economic sectors. They constitute approximately 60 percent of workers in agriculture and handicrafts; more than 50 percent in commerce, education, and public health; and nearly 25 percent of those in the public sector and industry. In fact, women are an economic engine in Laos. Recent reforms have enabled some to profit from things like traditional weaving and agriculture, and in turn they have invested in critical infrastructure like irrigation canals, machines, and more tools, not only furthering their own ends but also stimulating the country's economy.[3] Yet as is true in most countries, women generally earn lower incomes than men. They also work longer hours and

Elderly woman and child near Phosavan. © Alfred Molon—www.molon.de.

have fewer avenues for advancement where such opportunities exist. Significant numbers of women work in family-run businesses but do not receive any direct wages. Different from Western countries, it is quite common for women to work alongside men in construction jobs and other strenuous occupations, although they rarely receive the same wages for it. In agriculture, most women (and men) in Laos earn income below basic subsistence levels. Compounding these problems is the fact that women remain the primary child-care givers and attend elderly or sick family members. Considering that, on average, families in Laos number seven people, this is no small task. Perhaps most significant is the fact that women endure dramatically higher illiteracy rates and have lower educational qualifications than men. About 60 percent of the overall population of Laos is literate, but when the sizeable majority is male. Of males over the age of six, nearly 28 percent have never been to school. For females that ratio is 47 percent, and it is even higher in rural areas. Nearly 32 percent of males outside of towns have never attended school, whereas for females the number jumps to 53 percent.[4]

Economics, family dynamics, and gender discrimination all hinder the development of women's education in the country. This is particularly true with respect to ethnic minorities. In almost all groups girls are expected to stay at home and tend to the family. Many girls marry and have children at very young ages, which makes formal education difficult. Some, like the Hmong and Yao, disapprove of female education altogether. Among others there are concerns about the safety of girls traveling long distances between villages and schools. Compounding matters is the fact that the Lao PDR still mandates that all primary education be conducted in Lao, thus presenting ethnic minorities with a language barrier. Poor infrastructure, a lack of properly trained teachers, and poverty contribute to the problem. A host of initiatives undertaken by the Lao PDR in conjunction with the United Nations, the Asian Development Bank, foreign governments, and other international partners have been in place since the early 1990s, but progress is slow. Today, even in urban areas, many women still do not see the advantage of education and consequently either never enroll or drop out early.

Despite its declared intentions, the Lao PDR has not facilitated the political empowerment of women. Although their numbers in the civil service are generally good, few women hold any senior government positions. Those who do hold positions only in sectors deemed suitable for women, like education and health care. Women are well represented in the ranks of the ruling Communist Party, but few can compete for leadership positions given the constraints that their family duties impose. Overcoming the prejudice of male colleagues is another matter. The Lao Women's Union (LWU) is a primary vehicle within the party for the advancement of women, but it suffers from a chronic lack of

Children at a Lao-Chinese school in Pakse. Courtesy of Jeff Phisanoukanh.

funding and expertise. Also, it is focused primarily on women in terms of reproductive and sexual health rather than on the women themselves and their socioeconomic, cultural, and political power.[5]

Women in Laos also confront other serious problems. Desperate poverty and the lure of money in neighboring Thailand have increased prostitution. The industry in Thailand is huge: Some estimates indicate that two million sex workers there generate US$10 billion a year for the criminal enterprises that control them. Anyone familiar with Bangkok or Pattaya knows that they are world famous for prostitution and make Thailand one of the biggest destinations, if not the biggest, for sex tourists. There is big business in teenage wives and in girls who are rented for a few days or weeks. Prices are cheap, and the supply, sadly, is readily available. Most young Thai girls (and boys) in the business are from desperately poor homes. Many, especially from rural areas, are tricked into believing that they can become famous singers or actresses in the big city, or that they will make money working as domestics, nannies, and restaurant workers. Occasionally, girls are even sold into the business by their parents in the hopes of helping the family. Few women in the trade ever really escape it. Notwithstanding Thailand's recent efforts to combat prostitution, it remains a major social problem.[6] In recent years women and even children from Laos have become increasingly involved in the trade; many of them are even poorer and more desperate than the Thais. Experts fear that with government corruption, the lifting of restrictions, and an expanding tourist trade in Laos, it may be just a matter of time before a similarly brisk trade opens within the country itself. To date prostitution remains rare and subject to severe criminal prosecution within Laos. Related to prostitution is the specter of diseases such as HIV/AIDS. Although only a few thousand cases have been documented in Laos, there are serious concerns that infection might expand with increased prostitution. Moreover, there are legitimate worries that most cases go unreported given social stigma, lack of education, and inadequate health care.

WOMEN IN BUDDHISM

As discussed in Chapter 3, traditionally only men join the Buddhist *sangha*. However, on a daily basis it is women who are responsible for many societal functions of the religion. Women give the morning alms to monks. They also attend *wat* more often, volunteering time and labor, bringing food, and taking care of the family's spiritual needs through worship. Women also provide the bulk of health care and other social services that the temples direct. All of these activities are considered means to make merit, and most women take them very seriously. On top of that, even though there are few *bhikkuni* in Laos, women do play an active role in the administration of the faith. Most of the spiritual healers, or shamans, in Buddhist Laos are women.[7] Interestingly, in non-Buddhist communities men usually dominate the ranks of spiritualists.

Buddhism is sometimes seen as the main reason why women in Laos endure inequities, as it serves as a kind of moral framework to perpetuate male domination. Activists in Thailand argue that Buddhism gives women less status by implying in its practices that they are inferior. However, many scholars note that Buddhist texts and rituals are, in fact, more complicated and give paradoxical images of women. In some *jataka* tales, women are heroic and often more virtuous than men. Buddhist scholars also argue that there is no real differentiation between men and women on the path to enlightenment. They contend that women can reach *nibbana* without having first been born as males, and that beliefs to the contrary have nothing to do with the religion.[8] Also, in some Buddhist texts women are presented as full equals of men. Given the concept of *karma*, sexual identity in Buddhism is not fixed for eternity. One can switch genders in different lives. Still, as critics note, in none of Buddha's past lives was he a woman. Many Lao still believe that women have to be reborn first as men to have any chance at reaching *nibbana*. Superstitions

about the effect women have on a man's spirituality also remain strong. Therefore, the role that religion plays in gender issues is convoluted. It is as difficult
to blame Buddhism for the problems women face in Lao society as it is to
blame other religions for the inequalities women confront elsewhere.

SEXUAL ORIENTATION

Homosexuality is illegal in Laos. Until the late 1980s there were reports
of homosexuals being interred in reeducation camps and persecuted. Many
people in the country also consider homosexuality to be an affront to religious practices. However, perhaps surprisingly, most Lao are fairly ambivalent toward homosexuals, bisexuals, transsexuals, and transvestites. As is true
elsewhere in Buddhist Southeast Asia, there is a more private and quiet toleration with respect to sexual orientation. This is consistent with Buddhist beliefs
that individuals should avoid judgment. It also stems from a belief that, related to *karma*, all people have both male and female tendencies, if not past
incarnations. That said, unlike in neighboring Thailand, gay, transsexual, and
transvestite communities in the country are definitely underground. The soft-
ening of government restrictions in Laos has resulted in the recent influx of
fairly open, mostly Lao or Thai homosexuals in Vientiane and Luang Prabang.
Gay travelers are also visiting more given this toleration.

DATING AND MARRIAGE

By Western standards romantic relations between the sexes in Laos are extremely conservative. Dating—particularly multiple partners—is rare. Most
Lao consider casual attitudes toward sexuality to be immoral. Overt acts of affection in public are considered rude, especially between unmarried couples.
Kissing and touching are offensive. Even holding hands is frowned upon. Foreign travelers are shown greater leeway with respect to such matters, but most
people in Laos still consider public acts of affection between tourists insulting.
Relations between foreigners and any Lao citizen are illegal. Special permission
from the government is needed for those who want to get married. It is even illegal to have a Lao in one's hotel room or accommodation late at night. Dating
among Lao is usually a very slow and "innocent" process, in that there is not
much physical contact. It is also frequently public, in that young couples associate with one another within a larger group. Most serious courtship begins
when men are in their early twenties. Women are often teenagers. The legal
age for consent in Laos is fifteen. The average age for both men and women
varies between ethnic groups, but overall many Lao Theung and Lao Sung are
even younger than their Lao Lum counterparts when courtship begins.

Among the Lao Lum there is considerable freedom in selecting partners. When it comes to marriage, it is expected that couples consult their parents and elders. They often propose matches, but formal and binding arranged marriages are rare. Traditionally, a bride-price is required, although since the communist revolution the practice has been officially discouraged. The values vary widely, but generally men are expected to pay their bride's parents for marrying her. The price reflects both the social standing of the groom and the desirability of the bride. It is quite common that the bride's parents return the money to the couple after their wedding as a gift. Bride-price customs are common throughout Asia and stem from the ancient belief that if a man does not spend money on his wife, he will not have the motivation to care for her or his family. They also originated in an even more pragmatic sense as a means of compensating a woman's family for the loss of her labor.

There are considerable distinctions among the Lao Theung and Lao Sung with respect to finding a partner and the bride-price custom. For example, selecting a partner is a fairly independent and open process for the Khmou. Traditionally, Hmong courtship begins at New Year, when young men move between villages to visit relatives. Marriage within one's clan group is strictly forbidden, so going beyond the village is necessary. Everywhere the young men go they are introduced to young women at festivals. The two sexes then line up and play a game called *pov pob* with a fabric ball, during which they come to know each other better and focus their attentions on particular individuals. Sometimes couples attracted to each other play tunes or speak to each other through small mouth harps as a sign of further interest. When the two agree to be together, respected members of different clans negotiate the bride-price to ensure the fairness of the process.[9] Not all unions are successfully negotiated. For Hmong and Yao it usually involves substantial amounts of money or silver. Sometimes the price equates to several hundred U.S. dollars, a considerable sum in Laos. For the Akha and Lahu there is no formal bride-price, although the groom is expected to pay for the wedding and give a gift to his new wife's parents. The bride-price has broken down barriers between some ethnic minorities in Laos by encouraging men to seek wives from those groups that do not require large amounts of money. Intermarriage is increasingly common, especially between Lisu men and Akha women.[10]

Some Lao Sung groups practice a variation of this known as bride capture. By definition bride capture is kidnapping, taking and confining a young woman against her will. Indeed, in the past it was carried out with full seriousness and considered a regular, albeit unfortunate, dimension of rivalry between tribes. Although it is strictly illegal in Laos today, there are occasional reports of the practice continuing. However, for the most part today it is a ceremonial practice, found particularly among the Hmong. If a young couple wishes to marry but fears that either they will not receive their parents' blessings or that the bride-price is too high, they will stage a capture. The young man is aided by friends, who smuggle the girl away and then tell both families what has happened. This leads to negotiations between the fathers of the couple. The usual result is that the young man works for his prospective wife's father to pay off the bride-price.[11]

WEDDINGS

Western-style ceremonies and receptions are becoming common among affluent and urban Lao. However, most still have traditional weddings. The process begins when a community elder or spiritualist is consulted on when to marry. This is done with consideration for the birth dates of the couple, astrological signs, and auspicious times of the Buddhist calendar. Traditionally, among the Lao Lum the prospective groom then takes a present to his bride's parents. On the actual wedding day, he and his male friends form a parade and walk to the bride's parents' house. The groom wears traditional dress and carries a candle and flowers—both important Buddhist symbols—while the rest of the party carries gifts for her family. These are usually determined in advance during bride-price negotiations. Music, song, and laughter are the hallmarks of a good procession. The entourage is met by the bride's parents, who then ask questions of the groom—usually traditional ones about identifying himself and his intentions. The groom is expected to answer them all and show respect for his new family.

After this, a friend of the groom—usually someone older and already married—escorts a special elder, a *phone khuane*, to the door. This is sometimes a Buddhist monk but is more often a spiritualist familiar with both Buddhist and animist rituals. The *phone khuane* performs the wedding ceremony, which involves the recitation of Pali scriptures and, most important, the *baci* (*baasi* or *sukhwan*), an ancient tradition, predating Buddhism, to honor the *phi*. The *baci* usually takes place in the bride's parents' house and revolves around ritual offerings called the *phakhuane*. These are conical-shaped symbols made from banana leaves and flowers, and placed in bowls of rice. Two are brought in, symbolizing the unity of the couple. Guests bring other offerings to lay around them. The *phone khuane* recites blessings and prayers and then takes up two white cotton strings attached to the *phakhuane* to tie around the wrists of the bride and groom. The tying, or *phuk ken*, is then repeated for everyone in the wedding party. It is considered extremely bad luck to remove the string before it falls off of its own accord. When the ceremony is finished everyone yells aloud, "Please come spirit," to call forward and bind the *khwan* spirits to them.

The *baci* is the most common and important ceremony in Laos. It is performed not just at weddings but also on numerous other occasions, including births, deaths, the building of homes, beginning or ending of long trips, and festivals. The idea is that the community, however defined, is strengthened through unity with the *khwan*.[12] With its rooting in animism, non-Buddhists perform the *baci* in similar fashion. Initially banned by the communists, the *baci* was reinstated given how important it is for the Lao people. Now the *baci* is practiced openly, even at state functions. In fact, no event in Laos would be complete without the *baci*.

For Buddhists a wedding also involves a trip to the *wat*, ritual blessings from a monk, prayers, and offerings at a temple. Because a *phone khuane* performs the *baci*, monks may not even be invited to the wedding ceremony. If they are, traditional numerology dictates that an odd number must be present, with nine being especially auspicious. Large dinners, music, and dance follow all ceremonies. Weddings last a full day and sometimes two. In non-Buddhist countries, Laotian communities usually hold traditional ceremonies as well as Western-style weddings, or they go to city hall and get married in accordance with local laws.

SEPARATION AND DIVORCE

Rituals of courtship and marriage are important means of unifying clans and reinforcing communities. They are integral to lineage, and therefore to family, ancestor worship, and the basic concepts of existence. Marriage is an important goal for many in Laos, regardless of their gender or ethnicity. It connects them to their community and, in effect, empowers them. Unmarried people, particularly women, are viewed as having nothing. Among many families they are considered to have failed. Not having children brings a similar shame. Voluntarily childless couples are a great oddity to most people in Laos.

However, there are no such taboos about separation and divorce in Laos. Both are common and allowed under law. Either party can initiate the process. The practice is more prevalent among the Lao Lum and more urban, educated, and wealthier people. Remarriage, including the same rituals of bride-price, is frequent. All ethnic groups strongly discourage divorce, but most allow either party to leave the union. Of course for women this is much more difficult because of their responsibilities to the family and the social stigma attached to divorce in some communities. Many people believe that it is never acceptable for the woman to leave. Others would consider it acceptable only if the husband was especially cruel. For some groups like the Hmong, if a woman was seen to have behaved badly, the husband might demand the bride-price back, thus humiliating her family and making it very difficult for her to marry again. If the husband was seen acting badly, then elders would rule dissolve the union and deny his claim to the bride-price. Rules for divorce vary among the many ethnic groups, but it is common for the party that initiates the dissolution to either pay a fine or forfeit the bride-price.

Custody issues vary from group to group, but generally they follow either the matrilineal or patrilineal traditions of the tribe. Therefore, among the patrilineal Hmong, any children of a divorce would go to the husband. Although it is illegal in Laos, polygamy continues among some groups, including the Hmong. By definition, however, it is restricted to only those who can afford multiple bride-prices, which means that incidences are low. Traditionally, in polygamous households the first wife has higher status than any others and is in charge of the household. Her children are also entitled to special recognition.

THE FAMILY IN LAOS

In most ethnic Lao families a group of related women forms the basis of kinship. The eldest daughter and her husband usually live in her parents' house until their next daughter gets married, when they will move out. It is common for family members to live very close to one another, even when in separate houses and often within the same compound, village, or immediate neighborhood. The youngest daughter is responsible for the care of her parents and inherits their home when they die. Elderly family members almost always live with their children or other relatives. It is not so much a question of economics or that the health-care system of Laos is so poor, but it is rather about respect for the elderly and the sanctity of family. Over time, the daughters within a family form new extended families of their own, but the process remains intact—connecting members through matriarchs to the central family line. Sons generally move away from home and become parts of their wife's family, but they remain connected. They entrust their rights to land or other family possessions through their sisters.[13] Lao Lum lineage is traced through both parents, but aside from ancestor worship, in general, there is no particular emphasis on genealogy.

Among patrilineal groups in Laos brothers are usually the focus of extended families, although in some—particularly in the southern highlands—women again form the connections. Men are recognized as the spiritual head of the family. Inheritance of land and animals is through sons, but daughters are expected to receive dowries as well. Most groups, like the Hmong and Khmou, trace their lineages through men.[14] However, because they marry outside their clans this becomes easily blurred.

Throughout Laos child care is considered a family responsibility in which all members take part. In some communities extended families and even whole villages help look after children. As discussed in Chapter 6, most traditional homes are built with few, if any, individual rooms, so children and parents sleep together. Even in more modern homes, private rooms for children are rare. In this fashion children are incorporated into everyday life and taught at a very early stage about their responsibilities to family. In most homes young children help raise younger children, do household chores, work on farms, or help with small businesses. Western travelers are sometimes surprised to see how independent children in Laos are. Foreigners are also surprised to see how little indulgence is given to children. They are expected to work, play independently, or simply accompany their elders wherever they go. Crying for attention and similar behavior common for children elsewhere is comparatively rare in Laos. Once they have reached an age of understanding, children in Laos are taught about respect for their elders, Buddhist and/or spiritual beliefs, and the rules of good behavior. They are also taught about duty and

Girl with backpack and a baby in a typical village. Courtesy of Rick Madonik.

Young village girls. Courtesy of Rick Madonik.

obligation, concepts that apply not just to the family but to the local village, their community, the country, and its culture as well. The result is that, later in life, children are accustomed to responsibility and more naturally accept the obligation of taking care of their elders.

With Laos' increasingly young population, family planning is an important issue. The lack of adequate education and health care makes this extremely difficult. Premarital sex is on the rise throughout the country, although access to and the use of contraceptives is rare. A major survey in 2004 found that just 3 percent of teenagers aged fifteen to seventeen who had engaged in sex ever used a condom. The number for adolescents aged eighteen and nineteen rose to 6 percent, and for young adults aged twenty to twenty-five it was just 12 percent.[15] Most young people in Laos receive little or no sexual and reproductive health education. Moreover, owing to cultural taboos, concerns for their family or reputation, and a general shyness, few of them, especially women, are willing to discuss such matters when given the opportunity. In recent decades many people in Laos have come to associate the topics with negative cultural influences from Thailand and the West. Abortion is illegal, but it does occur under secretive and usually dangerous conditions. Most abortions are driven by economic conditions or concerns for the family over pregnancies conceived outside of marriage. There are very few studies on sexuality and reproductive health among ethnic groups in the country.

NOTES

1. Sheila Thomson and Sally Baden, "Women and Development in Laos," Report No. 9, prepared for Women, Health and Population Division, Australian International Development Assistance Bureau, February 1993, Institute of Development Studies, University of Sussex, www.bridge.ids.ac.uk/reports/re9c.pdf (retrieved January 2007), 1.

2. See Carol Ireson-Doolittle, *The Lao: Gender, Power, and Livelihood* (Boulder, CO: Westview Press, 2004).

3. Loes Schenk-Sandbergen, "Lao Women: Gender Consequences of Economic Transformation," *International Institute for Asian Studies (IIAS) Newsletter* 9 (Summer 1996), www.iias.nl/iiasn/iiasn9/iiasn9.html.

4. UNESCO Report, "Girls' and Women's Education in Laos," February 1993, www.unescobkk.org/fileadmin/user_upload/appeal/gender/laos.pdf (retrieved October 2007), 2–5. See also Chithtalath Seng Ampone, "Education Improvement for Ethnic Children in the Moksuk-Tafa Area," *Juth Pakai* 7 (October 2006): 4–5; Suksavang Simana, "Ethnic Minority Education," *Juth Pakai* 2 (June 2004): 28–35.

5. Thomson and Baden, "Women and Development," 13–14. See also Ireson-Doolittle, *Lao*, 14–29.

6. Arne Kislenko, *Culture and Customs of Thailand* (Westport, CT: Greenwood Publishing, 2004), 179–180.

7. Mayoury Ngaosyvathn, *On the Edge of the Pagoda*, Paper No. 5, York University Working Series, Thai Studies Project, Women in Development Consortium in Thailand, 1990.

8. Penny Van Esterik, *Materializing Thailand* (Oxford: Berg, 2000), 67–71. See also Chitra Ghosh, *The World of Thai Women* (Calcutta: Best Books, 1990), 24–30.

9. Robert Cooper, *The Hmong: A Guide to Traditional Lifestyles* (New York: Times Editions, 1998), 55–58.

10. Virtual Hilltribe Museum, www.hilltribe.org (accessed June 2007).

11. Robert Cooper, *The Hmong: A Guide to Traditional Lifestyles* (New York: Times Editions, 1998), 61.

12. Mansfield, *Culture Shock!*, 123–124.

13. Mayoury Ngaosyvathn, *Lao Women Yesterday and Today* (Vientiane: Mayoury Ngaosyvathn, 1995), 15–30.

14. See Stephen Mansfield, *Lao Hill Tribes: Traditions and Patterns of Existence* (Oxford: Oxford University Press, 2000).

15. Vanphanom Sychareun, "Meeting the Contraceptive Needs of Unmarried Young People: Attitudes of Formal and Informal Sector Providers in Vientiane Municipality, Lao PDR," in *Reproductive Health Matters* 12, no. 23 (Summer 2004): 155–165, www.rhmjournal.org.uk (retrieved July 2007).

10

Festivals and Fun

TRADITIONAL CELEBRATIONS

FESTIVALS, KNOWN AS *bun* (*boun*), are an important part of culture through-out Laos. As in Thailand, there are numerous holidays and celebrations based primarily on the Buddhist faith and animistic spirituality. In fact, almost every month has a national festival. May, for example, hosts three large national holidays, and there are two each in February, March, and October. Since coming to power in 1975, the communist government of Laos has both influenced the nature of traditional celebrations and invented some new ones in keeping with its ideological beliefs.

All of the major festivals in Laos involve music, dance, singing, theater, parades, games, food, and drink. Most *bun* are similar to those held in Thailand. They coincide with agricultural seasons, the Buddhist calendar, or the lunar calendar, in which December is the first month of the year. Many festivals are aligned with full moons. As a result, precise dates change every year. Some are based on a combination of Buddhist beliefs, Hindu mythology, ancient astrological configurations, and local traditions, which often makes the meaning of the festival unclear to most visitors. Some are centuries old, with uncertain origins, whereas others have been more recently invented.

BUDDHIST CELEBRATIONS

Buddhist celebrations are the biggest and most important in the country. Following the 1975 revolution, the new government tried to ban them for being too closely linked to the monarchy and old elites. However, protests from the public and efforts to reinvent a new Lao national identity conspired to bring them back. Still today the government is anxious to avoid any connection between religion and the old regime, and in this respect Buddhist celebrations in Laos differ considerably from those in Thailand.

Makha Busa (Magha Puja) is marked on the full moon of the third lunar month, in February or March, and marks the gathering of Buddha's disciples to hear him speak without being summoned. It involves prayers and readings from scripture, as well as a communal candle ceremony. The first candle is lit by someone of high rank within the *sangha* on the sacred boundary stones of a *wat*. That candle is then used to light others in the rest of the congregation lined around the *sim*. Special bread made of sticky rice is the traditional gift. The best places to see the ceremony are Vientiane and Wat Phu, near Champasak.

Bun Pha Wet (Bun Mahachaat) is held on different dates throughout the country in March, and it marks the birth of Prince Vessantara, Buddha's second-to-last incarnation, as commemorated in the *satok* tale. The three-day celebration focuses on monks who recite the story in a long chant consisting of one thousand verses, originally recorded on fourteen sets of palm-leaf manuscripts, from morning until night. This begins when a story cloth featuring the tale is paraded through town to the *wat*. The procession also carries one thousand balls of sticky rice to symbolize each verse. Because the festival takes place during one of the hottest months in the region, rain is prayed for to Prince Vessanatara's magical white elephant, which made water in the tale. This is followed by more regular festivities. Lao use the occasion to visit family or friends in other towns and villages, which is why the celebration is staggered throughout the country. Given its importance, many young men choose this time to be ordained as monks.[1]

Visakha Busa (Visakha Puja) is held on the fifteenth day of the sixth lunar month, so May or June, and is regarded as the most important of religious holidays. It represents the birth, death, and enlightenment of Buddha. Prayers, sermons, and chants at the *wat* are accompanied by processions of the faithful, who circle the temple with candles, lotus flowers, and incense. This is followed by Bun Khao Phansa (Khao Watsa), which marks the three months of the rainy season, beginning in July. Monks wander as part of their spiritual discovery, but during this period they stop and reside at particular *wat* so, according to tradition, they do not trample the crops. In practice this is the primary occasion for the ordainment of monks and for them to begin a retreat for study and prayer, representing the period Buddha spent in heaven preaching to his mother, who died when he was just seven days old. Sermons, chants, and prayers again mark the occasion. However, over time this has become more of a festival for everyone, featuring a special candle procession and a large parade accompanied by food, drink, and dance. Bun Awk Phansa (Ok Watsa) ends the three-month retreat in October. People celebrate by making small boats out of banana leaf that carry candles and incense on rivers.[2] For a month between Bun Awk Phansa and the next full moon (October to November) the nation marks Bun Kathin, named for the device used to keep monks' robes tight while they are being made. During this period monks are given robes, bowls, and other items they need in monastic life. Music, dance, and food follow.

Not all Buddhist events are so celebratory. Bun Haw Khao Padabdin (Bun Khao Padap Din), held during the full moon between August and September, commemorates the dead. It coincides with the rainy season, when the land is lush, and is designed to remind the living to be grateful. Over two days people attend *wat* with offerings for monks to pray for their dead ancestors. It is an auspicious time for cremations to take place, and often bones of the dead are exhumed for this purpose.[3] The similar Bun Haw Khao Salak follows in mid-September.

OTHER CELEBRATIONS

New Year's festivities are very big in Laos. Many people consider Bun Pi May (Bun Pi Mai) the biggest party of the year. Even though technically the lunar calendar begins in December, celebrations are not held until April, which is considered more auspicious. The three-day New Year event in mid-April signifies the beginning of the lunar year. Buddhists mark the occasion by cleaning house, buying and wearing new clothes, and making special offerings of fruit and flowers at the local *wat* or by setting up special altars made of sand and stone near their homes. This stems from the ancient belief that ancestors would guarantee someone as much luck as the grains of sand if they were properly honored.[4] As true with all celebrations, prayers and sermons are part of the ritual. However, what makes Bun Pi May unique and fun is water. Water plays an important role throughout Buddhist cultures for its religious significance as well as for its connection to agriculture. It symbolizes purity and cleansing. The New Year signifies a new beginning, and so *Bun Pi May* is a time celebrating the purifying nature of water. Buddhists demonstrate this by ritually washing images of the Buddha. In Luang Prabang, throngs of people bathe the holy Phabang. The guardian spirits of the city, Pu Nyoe and Nya Noe, lead a procession through town. The *baci* follows. The real fun begins after the ceremonies, when people soak one another, symbolically washing away their sins and purifying their spirits. The entire community partakes in good-natured splashing and everyone gets wet. Considering that April is usually the hottest month of

Garuda on Bun Pi May parade, Luang Prabang. Sally Hunt/Art Directors & Trip Photo Library.

the year, the practice is generally welcome. Unwary tourists are a prime target. In some areas of the country water is followed by talcum powder and smears of red lipstick.[5] The festival is accompanied with the usual food and dance, as well as big parades. In Luang Prabang there is also a beauty contest.

The large ethnic Vietnamese and Chinese populations in Laos also mark their own New Year at the end of January or early February. They are best known for large displays of fireworks, special cakes, and large parties, particularly in Vientiane, Thakhek, Pakse, and Savannakhet. Hmong New Year's celebrations, called Nor Chia, come in November. Women wear their best clothes, usually made from green, red, and white silk, along with ornate silver jewelry. Music and food are part of the events, as are ox fighting, archery contests, and other traditional games. Most other ethnic groups in the country commemorate New Year's events in similar fashion. Always looking for a reason to celebrate, many people in Laos also mark the Western New Year on December 31 with big parties.

Festivities centered on agriculture are also prominent in Laos. The annual harvest is marked in late January or early February with Bun Khun Khao (Bun Khoun Lan), during which villagers across the country take part in rituals to thank the spirits who protected the rice crop. A *baci* ceremony is the most important. However, the biggest agricultural celebration is Bun Bang

Bun Pi May festival, Luang Prabang.
© Danny Callcut/stickyrice.co.uk.

Fai (Bun Bangfai), better known as the Rocket Festival, held in May. It marks the beginning of the planting season by calling for rains. As discussed in Chapter 4, the entire event is taken from folklore. Everyone begins by praying in the local *wat* for rain to nourish the year's crops. In the afternoon people then partake in a competition of homemade rockets. Only two types are allowed: one with a tail and one without. In each category there are several variations based on the amount of gunpowder that each rocket contains. Awards are given to those that look the best and travel the highest. In some areas of Laos the Bung Bang Fai is more competitive than fun, with sizable wagers bet on which rocket will go the greatest distance. Men then perform a *lam* dance, dressed as women, with large wooden phalli that are supposed to anger the god Thaen into unleashing the rains.[6]

Other national events include Lai Heau Fai, or the Festival of Lights, held simultaneously with Bun Awk Phansa in October. Large floats replete with many lights are built and then paraded through town to be judged for their color and design. At night they are put on boats and paraded on the river. Smaller individual floats made from banana leaves with candles, flowers, and

Little girl holding flowers in the Little Miss Luang Prabang pagaent. © Danny Call-cut/stickyrice.co.uk.

incense atop are also set loose on the water. The event is most spectacular at Luang Prabang. The Boat-Racing Festival, or Bun Souang Heau (Bun Nam), is held the next day in Vientiane, Savannakhet, and Champasak. One of the most important events in Laos is the weeklong Bun Pha That Luang, held in November to celebrate the national monument in Vientiane. On the first day of the festival hundreds of monks gather at Pha That Luang to receive offerings. A massive procession follows from there to Wat Si Muang. A candlelight ceremony and large *baci* close off events. In between there are parties, fireworks, and games. In recent years the Lao government has used the occasion to host an international trade fair and various culture events.

Local or regional festivals are also common in Laos. In Luang Prabang, a Bun Souang Heua celebration precedes the somber Bun Haw Khao Padabdin with characteristic Lao flare: boat races on the Nam Khan River and a large fair in the city center. A similar boat-racing festival coincides with Bun Haw Khao Salak in Khammuan Province. In late October or early November residents of Luang Nam Tha Province celebrate at Wat That Chieng Theum stupa, just outside the regional capital of Muang Sing. In Savannakhet Province a four-day festival in early December is held to honor Wat That Inhang. In the past few years it has become a sizable sporting event with soccer, boxing, tennis, and more traditional Lao sports. Dancing and drumming competitions are also held. An international trade fair coincides with the celebrations.[7] Other local festivals focus on Wat Sikhottabong in Khammuan and Wat Phou in Champasak.

With so many festivals it is easy to forget that the Lao PDR is a communist state. However, since 1975 it too has gotten into the business of celebration and commemoration. Public holidays have been created to remind the public of the proletarian struggle and communist revolution. These include Pathet Lao Day (January 6), Army Day (January 20), Lao Women's Day (March 8), the Lao People's Revolutionary Party Day (March 22), International Labour Day (May 1), Lao Issara Day (August 13), Liberation Day (August 23), Freedom from the French Day (October 12), and Lao National Day (December 2).[8] Through these events the government has tried to shift public commemorations away from religious and spiritual influences and position itself as the keeper of a national identity.

EVERYDAY FUN

Travelers often feel very relaxed in Laos. Part of this has to do with the fact that it is small, less developed, and relatively untouristy. Indeed, it is often likened to Thailand in the 1960s. However, much of the charm and appeal of Laos rests with its people. They are welcoming, friendly, and easygoing, so much so that foreigners working in Laos joke about how difficult it can be to get anything done. The pace of life and the approach to work are very different from the West. Everyday life in the country revolves around the same basic elements as anywhere else in the world. Work, family, and friends are the pillars for most people. Music, dance, and singing are very popular leisure activities. Widespread access to media, like movies, television, and the Internet, remains restricted by the government and a lack of economic development. Consequently, more traditional exercises, like conversation, storytelling, and games, are still a big part of relaxation and entertainment.

MEDIA

Since 1975 media has been the exclusive domain of the government. Print media and radio have been the principal elements for propaganda and information control. Television is a relative newcomer in this respect, with the first Lao language station launched in 1983. The Internet came even later, with full connectivity established in 1997 and access limited in most areas of the country today. Regulation of the media is the responsibility of the Ministry of Information and Culture, the Ministry of Communications, the Prime Minister's Office, and the Ministry of Public Security. There are laws governing all media and, theoretically, government controls of it. However, final authority rests with the Ministry of Public Security. The licensing, operation, practices, and content of all media are ultimately subject to the ministry.[9] The ministry is also responsible for controlling access to foreign media, which with the lifting of political and economic restrictions and improved technologies has become more problematic in recent years.

The French set up the first radio station in Laos, Radio Nationale Lao, in 1939. It was renamed Royal Lao Radio upon independence in 1953 and Lao National Radio after 1975. Provincial stations were established in the late 1960s and early 1970s, with more added in the 1980s and 1990s. Today, national radio has two channels: one that broadcasts news and entertainment and one that is exclusively dedicated to entertainment. The former carries carefully selected news aimed at target groups within the country, like farmers or youths. English-language news is offered twice daily. Entertainment programs, mostly traditional music, comedy, and drama, are produced and broadcast by Lao National Radio, but in some areas locally scripted material is also aired. In 2003, the station began limited broadcasting through its Web site, following that up in 2004 with English and Hmong language shows. Today there are thirty-one radio stations in Laos, the most important of which is Vientiane Capital Radio. The government has always had difficulty competing with much freer and more diverse Thai radio programming, but in recent years it has combated this influence by broadcasting to the large ethnically Lao population in northeastern Thailand. Other foreign broadcasters in Laos include Voice of Viet Nam, Beijing International Radio, Radio France International, BBC World Service, and Voice of America.

Television in Laos is increasingly important and widespread, but it remains limited outside larger towns and is almost nonexistent in some areas of the country. When first launched in 1983, Lao National Radio and Television aired only three hours a day because of its poor infrastructure. In 1993 Lao National Television was established as a separate entity, with financial and technical support from Japan and Vietnam. Today, it runs two government-controlled stations: TV1, covering mostly news, and TV3, which airs more entertainment. Neither broadcasts around the clock. TV1 airs Lao- and English-language news, whereas TV3 broadcasts entertainment shows and some Western programs, mostly drama and comedy reruns. In 2002 the Lao government contracted a Chinese company to help set up Lao Cable Television. It offers about thirty foreign channels including BBC,

CNN, French TV5, German DW TV, Italy's RAI, MTV, and various others from Thailand, China, and Vietnam. There was a short-lived third station, TV5, which ran French-language broadcasts between 2002 and 2004. There are also plans for a new joint Lao–Chinese channel.

The Lao PDR restricts satellite transmissions by requiring that the Ministry of Information and Culture preauthorize all dishes in the country. However, enforcement of the rules is lax. Those with cable can access signals from Thailand and watch Thai television much more than anything local. In fact, it is estimated that 75 percent of Lao who watch television regularly see only Thai programming. Soap operas, game shows, and Thai movies are particularly popular. Worried about too many negative influences being spread by Thai television, in May 2004 the Lao PDR banned their showing in public venues. Individuals with private access can still watch them, but bar, restaurant, and hotel owners faced jail terms for showing Thai television. There were accusations from the Lao Women's Union that shows from Thailand encouraged incorrect dress and manners. Thai media was blamed for spreading capitalist ideas, which, the Lao government argued, led to crime.

In some respects television, and by extension popular culture, shape the context in which Lao identity is determined today. A Lao journalist noted, "Differences between the Thai and Lao identities are exacerbated during conflicts and periods of tensions, because they boost patriotic feelings. In peaceful times, however, Lao youngsters follow the Thai, because they don't have any idols in the country."[10] The Lao scholar Vatthana Pholsena argues that for many in Laos, especially the government, Thailand serves as a model of what not to become. The Lao PDR compensates for being less developed economically and politically by positioning itself as the more authentic Tai state— and a more moral, virtuous place to live. This plays to the idea that Thailand has become utterly decadent, corrupt, and decidedly un-Buddhist. Even some younger Lao, particularly women, are afraid to go to Thailand. They fear being forced into prostitution, raped, or jailed.

The Lao government has reinforced such beliefs, discouraging Lao from traveling to Thailand and using media to remind citizens about the sex trade, drugs, and other social ills there. An excellent example of this tense cultural relationship came in April 2000, when the Thai pop singer Nicole Theriault allegedly said that Laos was dirty and not worth visiting. The *Vientiane Mai* newspaper retorted that she "intentionally meant to harm Laos' dignity and reputation" and that the Lao, "morally and intellectually, are not inferior to any other people."[11] In 2007 the Lao government lodged formal complaints against Thailand's Channel 7 TV over its soap opera *Pleng Rak Song Fang Khong* ("The Mekong Love Song"). Authorities were offended by scenes that portrayed Laos in unflattering light, particularly one in which a Thai actor dropped the national flower of Laos, a frangipani, in the river. In this light it is not clear what the Lao government thinks of the animated American television show *King of the Hill*, which features as peripheral characters a Lao family in a Texas town. Regularly assumed by ignorant locals to be Chinese or Japanese, the family's father, Khanh, is a fast-talking, acerbic character generally scornful of American culture.

The Lao government's concern about cultural pollution from Thailand and the West is so great that in the 1990s it established "village of culture" and "family of culture" programs designed to combat the ills of foreign influence and promote a uniquely Lao identity. The idea was derived from mass culture movements developed in Vietnam and put in place as early as the 1950s in communist-controlled Laos. Social evils such as drugs, prostitution, and pornography are discouraged, while traditional Lao values in dress, music, dance, and other artistic venues are promoted. In a village of culture, people are supposed to send their children to school, lead a healthful lifestyle, follow traditions, and shun Western influences. Each village has a *wat*, government center, school, and basic health-care facilities. By the mid-1990s there were eighty-five villages and sixteen thousand families throughout the country with these designations.[12]

Recently, the Lao government has also tried to appear more proactive in its approach to combat foreign culture. Magazines like *Update*, *Mahason*, and *Laoteens* carry images of young, attractive, Lao looking very modern and even Western. Some of the articles even include English translations. They are all geared toward teenagers and those in their early twenties. However, they offer stories designed to promote Lao idols rather than foreign ones and to extol the virtues of Lao society in general. There is also more open political content, albeit behind the facade of pop-culture entertainment. For example, the December 2006 issue of *Update* featured an attractive young woman on the cover looking somewhat coy, while running a special report on the National Assembly and changes in the Lao PDR government. Similarly, *Culture* magazine offers tips on traditional clothes, beauty aids, and other issues, often with English-language articles alongside the Lao-language articles. The fact that all the magazines together have a circulation of no more than a few thousand and that the English-speaking population in Laos is extremely small, speculation on the motives behind publishing them is natural. Some observers note that this is a government attempt to make the Lao, and therefore Laos, look important alongside English while simultaneously trying to manage youth culture.[13] Despite their attempts to vilify Western culture, Lao authorities recognize its power and may have decided to manage rather than fight it. After all, many young Lao have generally positive views of the West, even after years of government propaganda.[14] It is also a response to pressures of modernization as seen particularly in Thailand, which some Lao see as a cultural role model.

Although access to foreign newspapers and magazines is restricted, copies of the *Bangkok Post*, *Asiaweek*, and other English-language publications are found in bigger centers. The Lao Ministry of Information and Culture also oversees the only English-language daily newspaper in the country, the *Vientiane Times,* established in 1994. The new frontier for Lao culture in the media will almost certainly play out on the Internet. There are an estimated twenty thousand Internet users in the country, all channeled by government control of just two providers, LaoTel and LaoNet. Some users connect through Internet service providers in Thailand to avoid controls. Although Web access is increasing in keeping with the economic reforms and opening up of Laos, the infrastructure remains very minimal.[15] Moreover, most people in Laos cannot afford personal computers, let alone gain access to the Internet.

SPORTS

Lao love to watch sports of all kinds in public or on television, but few can afford to participate in any organized events themselves. Football (soccer) is gaining appeal in the country, no doubt connected to both increasing media access and the fact that it requires little equipment or training. The infrastructure for all sports in Laos is poor. There is just one major stadium, the Lao National in Vientiane, and no real facilities for development of sports within the country. Most athletes move to Vietnam for access to better coaches, trainers, and athletic facilities. Vietnamese planners are also helping Laos prepare to host the 2009 Southeast Asian games. Recently, some nations have voiced concern about Laos' plans to scale back the number of events to twenty-five from the forty-three offered at the last games in Thailand.

Yet despite these difficult conditions, there are professional sports and athletes in Laos. The country has participated in the Olympics since 1980 in events like the marathon, 100-meter sprint, swimming, and archery, albeit with just a handful of athletes. It has never won any medals. Laos also sent two athletes to the 2000 Paralympics in Sydney. The biggest and best-known professional sport in the Lao PDR is soccer. Founded in 1995, the Lao League has ten teams, including the Lao-American College Football Club (FC), Vientiane FC, the Ministry of Public Safety, the Lao Journalists' Association FC, and the perennial champions Army FC. The Lao Football Federation operates a national team in the Asia division of the Fédération Internationale de Football Association (FIFA). It qualified for the second round of Asian qualifying matches during the 2006 World Cup but did not advance further. As of June

2008 it ranked No. 189 of 199 national teams in the world. There also are national basketball and rugby teams.

Most Lao play traditional sports like *kataw* (*takraw*). Popular in other parts of Southeast Asia, the game is an artistic volleyball for the feet, played with a tightly woven wicker or rattan ball. Played in teams of varying size, the objective is to keep the ball up in the air with the feet and head only. Points are scored for both length of time the ball is kept aloft and the style of acrobatic moves. The game is played both with and without a net, and variations also use a basketball hoop.

Muay Lao, or Lao kickboxing, has not developed into a major sporting industry like its *muay Thai* cousin. It is, however, still popular among amateurs. The sport originated in the fifteenth century as a means of military combat. Fighters (*nak muay*) use their fists, elbows, shins, knees, and feet in an effort to knock opponents down and out. Tripping with the feet and legs and forcing the opponent to his knees are also permitted. However, blows to the head or striking while the opponent is not standing are prohibited. The entire sport is in fact highly ritualized. Apprentices learn from masters only after they have proved that they are committed to the sport. There are ceremonies to mark the maturing of a fighter and to commemorate his first fight. Spirits are regularly consulted and worshipped. Traditionally, before the fight begins, both boxers perform a dance and ceremony to thank their trainers and honor the spirits. The entire fight is accompanied by music, which becomes progressively louder and faster as the match goes along. International boxing (*muay saakhon*) also is fairly popular in Laos.

Much to the dismay of animal rights activists, cockfighting remains one of the country's most popular sports. It originated in Southeast Asia and is found throughout the region. However, unlike in some other countries, the cocks in Laos are not equipped with small knives attached to their feet and consequently last longer in the ring. Everyone wagers on the event and champion roosters command both respect of the audience and sizable revenues for the owner. Fighting between rhinoceros beetles is another spectator sport that involves betting. Large beetles with clawlike horns attack each other and try to push their opponents over. The winner is the last one standing or whichever one does not run away. The beetles are collected while breeding in the rainy season and trained by owners in preparation for fights. They are sometimes seen for sale and trade in town markets. The sport is thought to have originated with Tai peoples centuries ago.[16]

Illustrating the impact of tourism on the country, sporting opportunities for tourists are considerably better developed and growing more rapidly than those for average Lao. Eco-tours in Laos' twenty national parks are a major attraction for tourists. So is trekking, with some of the best opportunities in the world, particularly in the north, to see both pristine natural environments and the lives of relatively untouched ethnic groups. The best infrastructure for organized treks in the area is found in Luang Prabang, Nam Tha, and Muang Sing. Independent trekking is also possible but more dangerous, given the rugged terrain of the country and unexploded ordnance from the Vietnam War era. Rafting, canoeing, and kayaking are quite popular along the Mekong, Nam Tha, Nam Khan, Nam Theun, Se Kong, and other rivers in the country. Whitewater rafting is also big business, with opportunities on the Nam Ou, Nam Xuang, and Nam Ming. Mountain biking and recreational cycling are increasingly popular, although conditions are quite varied and distances between areas with any facilities can be great. Caving and rappelling are posed to be the next major sports catering to tourists, especially as access and infrastructure to remote areas develops.[17]

NOTES

1. Visiting Arts Cultural Profiles Project, "Laos Cultural Profile," www.culturalprofiles.org.uk/laos (retrieved December 2007).

2. Ruth Gerson, *Traditional Festivals in Thailand* (Kuala Lumpur: Oxford University Press, 1996), 1–20. See also Joe Cummings and Andrew Burke, *Laos* (Footscray, Australia: Lonely Planet Publications, 2005), 253–255.

3. Cummings and Burke, *Laos*, 254.

4. www.laopress.com (accessed June 2007).

5. Jeff Cranmer and Steve Martin, *Rough Guide to Laos* (London: Rough Guides, 2002), 55.

6. Visiting Arts Cultural Profiles Project, "Laos Cultural Profile," www.culturalprofiles.org.uk/laos (retrieved December 2007). See also Northeastern Illinois University Center for Southeast Asian Studies, "Resources for Lao Studies," www.seasite.niu.edu/lao (retrieved January 2008).

7. Visiting Arts Cultural Profiles Project, "Laos Cultural Profile," www.culturalprofiles.org.uk/laos (retrieved December 2007).

8. Grant Evans, *The Politics of Ritual and Remembrance: Laos since 1975* (Honolulu: University of Hawaii Press, 1998), 57.

9. Visiting Arts Cultural Profiles Project, "Laos Cultural Profile," www.culturalprofiles.org.uk/laos (retrieved December 2007).

10. Vatthana Polsena, *Post-War Laos: The Politics of Culture, History, and Identity* (Ithaca, NY: Cornell University Press, 2006), 53.

11. *Asiaweek Magazine*, April 28, 2000, www.asiaweek.com/asiaweek/magazine/2000/0428/as.people.html (accessed June 2003). See also Vatthana Polsena, *Post-War Laos*, 73–75.

12. Visiting Arts Cultural Profiles Project, "Laos Cultural Profile," www.culturalprofiles.org.uk/laos (retrieved December 2007).

13. New Mandala: New Perspectives on Mainland Southeast Asia, Australian National University, rspas.anu.edu.au/rmap/newmandala (accessed January 2007). See also Lao Voices, laovoices.com (accessed January 2008).

14. Vatthana Polsena and Ruth Banomyong, *Laos: From Buffer State to Crossroads?* (Chiang Mai, Thailand: Mekong Press, 2004), 49–70, 155–183.

15. Cummings and Burke, *Laos*, 255. See also Visiting Arts Cultural Profiles Project, "Laos Cultural Profile," www.culturalprofiles.org.uk/laos (retrieved December 2007).

16. Cranmer and Martin, *Rough Guide*, 56–57.

17. Ibid., 68–70. See also Cummings and Burke, *Laos*, 247–248.

11

Social Customs

LAO ATTITUDES

MOST TRAVELERS TO the Laos would agree that its people are among the friendliest in the world. They are genuinely interested in foreigners and are usually curious about why they have come to their country. Most people are very relaxed and expect that outsiders do not know much about their customs, so much so that some visitors might be tempted to think that there are no cultural taboos at all. The reality, of course, is that there are many. Some are found throughout Laos, whereas others are specific to certain groups. Most foreigners never encounter these customs, in part because their hosts are unlikely to draw attention to them. That said, an awareness of and respect for attitudes, practices, and taboos in Laos are likely to help open up the various cultures of the country and significantly enrich the traveler's experience.

As the previous chapters have discussed, the people of Laos are generally quite religious, spiritual, and conservative when it comes to social behavior. Public displays of affection, nudity, or lewd behavior are considered rude. As difficult as it may be in a hot country, modest dress to cover the body is important, especially for women. Arrogant or brash behavior also is offensive. Most people will try to avoid confrontation and anger, especially in public. This is consistent with many Asian cultures, which stress the idea of saving face. Shouting, pointing, and posturing aggressively is considered a humiliating affront to one's dignity, particularly in the presence of others. Westerners who expect professional service standards similar to those at home often become frustrated and more demanding. Rather than push someone into action, this has the opposite effect in Laos and people retreat entirely. Many of the ethnic minorities are also sensitive about displays of material wealth. Everyone knows that foreigners who travel to Laos are much wealthier than the average citizen, but those who wear abundant jewelry or fancy clothes are considered condescending.

Overly familiar behavior may also be misconstrued as disrespectful, especially to the elderly and those in authority. Although travelers often are asked questions, joked with, and even invited to participate in events with locals, respect for social hierarchies requires a more detached association. The Lao are renowned for their sense of humor, but joking in return can potentially humiliate someone and cause that person to lose face. Physical contact familiar to Westerners in such circumstances, like slapping people on the back or rubbing their head, is considered rude. The Lao also rarely show surprise, pleasure, or gratitude like Westerners do. Emotional extremes like this are muted, especially in public. For example, opening a surprise gift in front of the giver would be considered a sign of one's greed and expectation. Thanking the giver profusely is uncomfortable for both the giver and the receiver.[1] It also creates a sense of obligation to return the gesture. Similarly, Lao do not feel the need to fill every conversation with talk. Silence is considered respectful and a sign that one is attentive.

The Lao expression *koi koi bai*, or "slowly, slowly," is often cited as evidence of the laid-back attitudes in the country. The pace of life is much slower than most places. The French, Japanese, Vietnamese, and Americans who played such large roles in the history of the country thought the Lao were lazy. Many foreigners who work in Laos today still think that people avoid hard work. There is even a running joke that the acronym PDR stands for "please don't rush." Although this is rather unfair, it is true that the Lao are more concerned with fun—or *muan*. Ambitions related to one's work are not so pressing. Everything must have some sense of *muan*. Hard work is considered bad for the brain. People with high-paying, stressful jobs or advanced education are not necessarily the role models that they might be in other countries. People tend to pity those who have to "think too much" and sacrifice time with friends or family.[2] This feeds directly into the notion of *bo penh ngan*, which loosely translates as "never mind," "no problem," or "forget about it." It is used widely and illustrates the depth of people's fatalism.

Discussions of a personal nature familiar to friends in the West are less common in Laos. Often people relay a matter by invoking third parties, even if everyone knows they are fictitious. Saving face is again the priority. However, many people in Laos routinely ask questions that in the West would be considered overly personal or rude, about age, marital status, children, and

Everyday life on the street—a family on a moped. Courtesy of Rick Madonik.

even income. These are not meant to be intrusive but rather are considered a demonstration of interest. Discussions of a more general nature on things like history, politics, religion, or society are trickier in Laos. Although the government has relaxed its grip over the past few years, people are still acutely aware of censorship. Talk about the royal family, for example, remains controversial, even though nostalgia for the long-deposed monarchy is surfacing.

However, when conversation turns to other countries and people, most Lao will voice strong opinions. The case in point is Thailand, which heavily influences culture and society in Laos. Many people, especially the young, see Thailand as a role model through its music, film, clothes, and other facets of modern culture. Moreover, since the mid-1990s the Thai king, Bhumipol Adulyadej, has emerged as a kind of patron for the Buddhist *Sangha* in Laos as he is in his own country.[3] However, many Lao also see Thailand as decadent, corrupt, and increasingly un-Buddhist. Prostitution, drugs, and crime are seen as the consequences of too much Western culture. Some also point to the depletion of Thai forests, pollution, and other environmental ills as a cautionary tale in economic development modeled on that of their neighbor. An uneasy relationship between the two countries remains: The Thai view the Lao as their little brothers or country bumpkins, whereas the Lao see the Thai as arrogant and condescending.

POWER AND CLASS

Theoretically, the communist revolution put an end to status and hierarchy in Laos. However, in reality it just transferred power to a different elite. Still, with communism came a different code of behavior and language in reference to hierarchies. Honorific titles denoting noble lineage or educational status were abandoned in favor of the more proletariat *comrade*. Today, things are changing again, and increasingly people are reverting to a more traditional recognition of social standing. This is best reflected in language. People are less addressed as *banda sahay* ("all comrades") as they are *banda tan* ("all sirs"). The egalitarian pronoun *hao ni* ("we" or "I") has been replaced by the old *khapachao* (literally, "I, slave of the Buddha").[4] People with wealth, education, and influence are again being distinguished from the masses and afforded special recognition. As discussed in Chapter 3, the same is true of the *Sangha*, which, after initially suffering under the communists, is again the pillar of Lao culture.

Social status is important in Buddhist cultures. It may be based on respect for elders or masculinity and leadership in the traditional family and village unit. It is also based in Buddhist thought, in which a sense of duty and morality are deeply ingrained. Moral goodness is considered a means of spiritual growth that ultimately helps one to achieve wisdom, inner peace, and eventually liberation from *dukkha*. Social standings reinforce respect, obedience, kinship, and community. People in positions of power are considered to have achieved a greater degree of moral goodness, and thus to be wiser. Power and rank are still subject to karma, so that the boss in this life may not be the boss in the next. Many believe that people who abuse their positions will, in turn, be abused by others in another existence. Similarly, some Lao accept their lower position with the belief that in a previous life they may have abused power. Despite socialist ideology, age, rank, and power or influence still influence social hierarchies in Laos.

Among the Lao there is a general acceptance that the individual is insignificant, not so much through any notion of communism but rather because of Buddhist teachings that downplay the self. In fact, Buddhism's emphasis on individual responsibility and its connection to karma on the path to enlightenment contradicts the communist idea of collectivism. Behavior that many outsiders mistake for ideological conformity is in fact rooted in Buddhist acceptance of one's life. As a result, most Lao tend to be deferential, quiet in the face of authority, and anxious to avoid any conflict. The questioning of authority and other obvious challenges are fairly rare. Instead, most Lao work quietly and passively resist when they confront difficulties. Disagreements, particularly in a professional setting, are often resolved subtly and with a minimum of comment. In the workplace volunteerism and other individual initiatives are also far less common than in the West.

BODY LANGUAGE

Like other Buddhists, the Lao are sensitive about physical contact. The head, hands, and feet are off limits, especially in public and in the company of strangers. The head is sacred and used to communicate. Lowering the head slightly in the company of elders, monks, or those deemed to have a higher social standing is a sign of respect. Touching the head, even of children, is considered condescending. Pointing and gesticulating is an insult. When motioning to someone, a palm turned downward is preferable. Both hands should be used in the giving or receiving of items. As is true in many cultures, the left hand is associated with bodily functions. Positioning of the feet is also very important. Feet are considered dirty, so keeping them away from people is important. Pointing of the feet, even accidentally, is taboo. People sitting with their legs stretched out or cross-legged, common among Westerners, are in fact pointing their feet, even if unconsciously. Most Lao will keep their feet tucked under the body or on the ground at all times to avoid inadvertently pointing them at someone. Putting feet up on tables or chairs and touching people with feet is considered extremely rude. Leaving shoes on when entering someone's house or a *wat* also is a grave insult. Many Lao also will avoid direct eye contact, especially when discussing serious matters. Staring is considered aggressive behavior.

Many Lao and ethnic minorities believe that women should never be physically higher than men. Consequently, women are expected to be positioned below men. Visitors traveling on buses, trucks, and boats in Laos often are confused when operators move women from sitting atop the vehicles. It is considered very bad luck. The superstition even extends to things like laundry. Hanging women's clothes above men's clothes on the line to dry is taboo.[5] Under no circumstances is a woman supposed to touch a monk or even his robes. Even when giving alms, great care must be taken to avoid physical contact. When passing items to a monk, male intermediaries are used or the object is placed within the monk's reach.

Touching images of the Buddha is in most cases very rude. An exception is when laying gold leaf during worship. Pointing at the Buddha, surprisingly common among visitors in the *wat*, is also unwelcome. The Lao are understandably upset when the occasional tourist decides to climb large Buddhas or pose for photos with them in unflattering positions. Touching any part of spirit houses, gates, or totems in Lao Theung or Lao Sung villages is similarly offensive. Although most Lao enjoy being photographed and are quick to offer a smile, it is always polite to ask permission first. Among some Lao Theung and Lao Sung photography is viewed with suspicion. Some people consider it a means of capturing their spirit and do not welcome photos of any sort. Taking pictures of spirit houses, gates, and other sacred objects in some areas is taboo.

THE *NOP*

Increasingly, Lao in cities like Vientiane may offer a handshake to foreign tourists as a means of greeting. However, the traditional gesture is the *nop*. Similar to the *wai* in Thailand, the *nop* is an artful, surprisingly complex, all-purpose social action. The hands are held together, palm to palm, as if in prayer and kept close to the body, held in front of the neck, chin, or nose. A slight lowering of the head accompanies the act. It is most commonly a way to say hello and good-bye, but it is also used as deference to show respect for the person being greeted. Age, gender, social rank, and the specific context in

A woman in traditional dress giving the *nop* at Wat Xieng Thong, Luang Prabang. © Danny Callcut/stickyrice.co.uk.

which it is given determine the style of *nop*. Even after decades of communism the *nop* remains distinctly hierarchical. Between equals, or when given to strangers of unclear status, the *nop* is at neck level and the head is kept straight. When directing the *nop* at someone of lower status, the hands are held lower and the head kept straight. When addressing a superior, the *nop* reaches the nose and the head and neck are slightly bent. Before monks the traditional *nop* is supposed to be given by dropping to one's knees, sitting on the heels, and putting the hands ahead as you lower your head to the floor, although this not commonly seen today. Before images of the Buddha this should be done three times.

It is usual for someone junior or "inferior" to be the first to give the *nop*, so the receiver must be careful when responding. Traditionally, it is not used to express thanks and is not given in everyday affairs. It is, therefore, not supposed to be addressed to servants, children, or people who sell you something. Giving a *nop* in these contexts can be seen as insulting, a reminder of the person's lower status. Although this all seems rather daunting, for foreigners the *nop* is in fact a simple act of respect. It is greatly appreciated by the Lao and viewed more as a greeting than a suggestion of rank and class. The origins of the *nop* are not entirely clear, although it probably developed as a *mudra* in India long ago. Some suggest that, like the Western handshake, it evolved as a way of showing one's enemy that no weapon was being carried.

LAO HUMOR

The Lao have an excellent sense of humor, and it is a big part of their everyday culture. A keen wit is highly regarded, especially when in verbal expressions. Clever wordsmiths who can use humor without alienating anyone are considered truly funny. Indeed, humorous verbal exchanges are the basis for *lam* and *mohlam* oral literature and folk songs popular throughout the country. A good storyteller, especially one who uses outrageous tales, bawdy jokes, and even slapstick comedy is always well received in Laos.

FRIENDSHIPS

The Lao consider personal relationships extremely important to both business and family life. Friends are as valuable as any education or wealth and form the fabric of one's community. In fact, when it comes to friendships, the Lao even distinguish between *moo linh* ("play friends") and *moo tai* ("die friends"). The former are more casual acquaintances, and the latter are considered family. Friendships of this nature are expected to be maintained for life. *Moo tai* share in everything and are integral parts of each other's lives.

They share not only their feelings but also their personal possessions, family life, space, and money. Dropping by a friend's house anytime without prior notice, something often considered rude elsewhere, is common among *moo tai* in Laos.[6] Face-to-face communication is considered the only acceptable means of conversation, especially between good friends and about serious issues. Private phones are relatively new in Laos and are considered impersonal. Access to personal computers and e-mail is rare.

BIRTH AND DEATH

As one might expect of a country with so many different cultures, customs with respect to births and deaths vary throughout Laos. However, everywhere they are considered important events and are marked by both ceremony and superstition. Talk about babies is generally muted before their birth, in part because of the high infant mortality rate and folk beliefs that evil spirits may become jealous of the new arrival and mean him or her harm. Names and gifts for the baby are never given before birth. As with other auspicious occasions in Laos, a *baci* ceremony is needed to ensure the new child's fate. Among the Lao Theung and Lao Sung there are other traditions to respect. The Hmong place a leaf at the door of houses to mark a new birth, and everyone is expected to remove their hats before entering. The *hu plig*, or "soul-calling" ceremony, is performed by a shaman to ensure that the new baby has the right spiritual essence and that no other spirits get into it. It is also customary to tell the parents how ugly the child is to dissuade evil spirits lurking nearby from becoming jealous and harming it. A name is not selected for a new child until three days have passed. The placenta is always buried under the house. For girls, it is placed under the parent's bed and for boys it is put under the main pillar. Traditionally, these are then exhumed and buried with the person when he or she dies.

The *baci* is also performed for funerals, along with a host of other rituals designed to honor and release the departed's spirit. Money is often collected for the dead person's family. Silence, rather than condolences or expressions of grief, is the norm. In keeping with Buddhist teachings, death is simply a necessary step on the path to enlightenment, and mourning excessively for the deceased is considered bad for his or her karma. A celebration involving food, drink, and laughter often follows cremation as a means of bringing happiness back into a home. For those who cannot afford festivities, a simple burial or cremation in the woods is standard practice. The dead are never commemorated with plaques or markings in case their spirit becomes angry and uses the site to harass local villages.[7]

Khmou tradition dictates that the deceased is buried the same day that he or she dies. A short ceremony is held during which men wearing only loin-cloths carry the body on a bamboo mat to the gravesite. Poems and folk songs are recited in honor of the dead. The party then walks back to the village in purposely roundabout fashion to confuse any evil spirits that might follow them. Among most Lao Theung and Lao Sung, animals are ritually sacrificed to ensure that the dead are not hungry in the afterlife. Colors play an important role in death and funerals among Laos' many ethnic groups. They are closely tied to the *phi* and are believed to have specific meanings. The Hmong consider red the color of death and wear it only at funerals. Black represents happiness and health. Conversely, the Mien view red as the color of life, much as the Chinese do, and associate black with death. Similarly, the Lisu and Akha see both black and white as colors of loss and do not wear either.

NOTES

1. Mansfield, *Culture Shock!*, 129.

2. Ibid, 174–177. See also Joe Cummings and Andrew Burke, *Laos* (Footscray, Australia: Lonely Planet Publications, 2005), 33.

3. Grant Evans, *The Politics of Ritual and Remembrance: Laos Since 1975* (Honolulu: University of Hawaii Press, 1998), 88–113.

4. Ibid., 88.

5. Joe Cummings, *Lao Phrasebook* (Footscray, Australia: Lonely Planet Publications, 2002), 54.

6. U.N. Development Programme, *Working with Your Lao Partner*, 2003 report, www.seasite.niu.edu/lao/undp/wwyLp.htm (retrieved January 2007).

7. Mansfield, 136.

Glossary

Ailao   term used for a controversial ancient Lao people claimed to have existed in the second and third centuries B.C.E.

an nangsu   storytelling

anatta   in Buddhism, a state of mind without ego

anicca   in Buddhism, the impermanence of all things

arhat   in Buddhism, a kind of saint who achieves nirvana and is not reborn

ASEAN   the Association of Southeast Asian Nations: founded in 1967, and today the most important regional economic and political forum

Atthangika-Magga (or Magga)   in Buddhism, an eightfold path to eliminate *dukkha*

baci (baasi or sukwan)   a very important ceremony used widely to honor the *phi*

bhiang   traditional female shawl

bhikkhu   an ordained monk in the Theravada order

bhikkuni   female monk

bo penh ngan   concept similar to "never mind" in Western cultures

bodhi   the tree of enlightenment in Buddhism

bodhisattva   in Mahayana Buddhism, a being that assists others in achieving enlightenment; in Theravada Buddhism, someone on the path to individual enlightenment

bun (boun)   festivals

Bun Awk Phansa (Ok Watsa)   major Buddhist celebration in October

Bun Bang Fai (Bun Bangfai)   agricultural festival, better known as the "rocket festival," in May

Bun Haw Khao Padabdin (Bun Khao Padap Din)   Buddhist commemoration of the dead in August and September

Bun Haw Khao Salak   Buddhist commemoration of the dead in mid-September

Bun Kathin   Buddhist celebration in October and November

Bun Khao Phansa (Khao Watsa)   major Buddhist celebration in July

Bun Khun Khao (Bun Khoun Lan)   agricultural celebration in January

Bun Pha Wet (Bun Mahachaat)   major Buddhist celebration in March

Bun Pi May (Bun Pi Mai)   Lao New Year

Bun Souang Heau (Bun Nam)   boat-racing festival

CDNI   Committee for the Defence of National interests (CDNI): a right-wing movement supported by the United States

Chakri   the ruling dynasty of Thailand

chao   traditional leader of a *muang*

Chao Fa   "Soldiers of God": an anticommunist guerrilla movement

Cheuang (Cheung, Thao Chreauang, Khun Cheaung)   ancient Lao literary works

Chin Haw   Chinese Muslims

Dhamma   Buddhist teachings about "truth"

dukkha   in Buddhism, pain or suffering from want

fon phun muang   folk dances

Garuda   in Hindu and Buddhist mythology, a giant bird

haw kawng (ho kong)   drum towers of a Buddhist temple

haw phi (haw phii)   spirit houses

haw rakhang (ho rakhang)   bell towers of a Buddhist temple

het bun   the practice of making merit

heuan   traditional Lao house

Hinayana   Sanskrit for "lesser vehicle": a derogatory reference to Theravada Buddhism

hrooy   Khmou equivalent of *phi*

hu plig   soul-calling ceremony of the Hmong

Hua Chiao   ethnic Chinese population in Laos

jao fa   ornamental hooks on buildings

Jataka   547 stories of Buddha's previous lives

karma   the affects of all deeds in life, shaping one's reincarnation and path to enlightenment

kataw (takraw) traditional sport played with a wicker ball

khao jao (klao jao) long-grain rice

khao niaw (klao niaw) short-grain, or sticky, rice

khati khong xaoban lao folklore, proverbs, songs, riddles, games, and other customs

khene (khaen) traditional instrument: a large mouth organ made from bamboo

khon traditional dance theater based on the Pha Lak Pha Lam

Khon Isan the Lao population of northeast Thailand

khwan (khouan) guardian spirits in folkloric beliefs

kuti monks' living quarters

kuu baa Lao word for "monks"

laap (larb) the national dish of Laos: a salad of spicy minced meat or fish

Lai Heau Fai festival of lights in October

lai lao decorative pattern on temples

Lak Muang guardian deity prominent in folkloric beliefs

lakhon traditional dance theater based on the Pha Lak Pha Lam and the *satok*

lakhon tukkata traditional puppetry

lakshanas artistic images of the Buddha

lam (khap) oral literature best known as folk-song performance art

lam luang classical Lao opera

lam luang samay (luuk thung) a blend of traditional *lam* and Western-style pop music

lam vong the most popular folk-dance style

Lao Dhamma ancient Lao script used to translate Pali Buddhist scriptures

Lao Issara the Free Lao nationalist movement during World War II

Lao Lum (Loum) lowland ethnic Lao, making up about 50 percent of the population

Lao PDR acronym for the official name of Laos: the Lao People's Democratic Republic

Lao Sung (Soung) the so-called hill tribes of Laos

Lao Tai ethnic groups closely related to the Lao Lum

Lao Theung (Thoeng) a loose grouping of Mon-Khmer people living at higher elevations

LPF Lao Patriotic Front: a communist political party formed in 1955 and the vehicle for the Pathet Lao (also known as Neo Lao Hak Xat, or NLHX)

LPRP Lao People's Revolutionary Party

maak phet   chilies

Mae Nam Khong   Mekong River in Lao

Mahayana   Sanskrit for "greater vehicle": the largest division of Buddhism

Makha Busa (Magha Puja)   major Buddhist holiday in February

mandala   a Hindu and Buddhist concept that the state is a kind of body

maravijaya   artistic depictions of Buddha sitting

matmii (ikat)   tie-dye pattern used in textiles

mohlam (molam, maw lam)   expert form of *lam*

mondop   square-shaped building in a Buddhist temple complex that houses articles of the faith

moo tai   "die friends": close friends for life

muan   "fun" in Lao

muang   territory, district, or traditional definition of a political entity

muay Lao   Lao kickboxing

muay saakon   boxing

mudra   artistic or symbolic depictions of Buddha's hand gestures

naga (ngeuak or nak)   mythological sea serpent

neeb   Hmong equivalent of *phi*

nibbana (nirvana)   in Buddhism, the state of enlightenment

nop   traditional Lao greeting

Nor Chia   Hmong New Year celebrations in November

pa ndau (paj ntaub)   Hmong needlework art that often depicts folklore and other traditional literature

paa daek (pa daek)   fermented fish paste used in Lao cuisine

panna   in Buddhism, the practice of wisdom

Panyasa Jataka   Fifty "extra" stories of the *jataka*

Pathet Lao   literally "Land of the Lao": a communist group founded in 1950 out of the Lao Issara

Patimokkha   set of rules for monks

Pha Keo (Phra Kaew)   the "Emerald Buddha": one of the most important symbols of the faith and today a national treasure of Thailand

Pha Lak Pha Lam (Pharak Pharam)   Lao version of the Ramayana

Phabang (Prabang)   one of the most important Buddhist icons and a symbol of Lao heritage

Phakhuane   offerings to the spirits given during the *baci*

phi (or phii)   spirits or ghosts important in folkloric beliefs

phone khuane   elder or spiritualist who traditionally performs the *baci*

Phuk ken   tying of symbolic white strings during the *baci*

pov pob   Hmong courtship game played with a fabric ball

Ramayana   epic Indian legend

RLG   Royal Lao Government

Sa (saa)   mulberry tree, used for traditional papermaking

sakyamuni   Theravada Buddhist emphasis on the historical Buddha

sala (saala)   lecture or meeting halls of a Buddhist temple complex

samadha   in Buddhism, the practice of concentration

samana   political "reeducation" camps established under the communists

samanera (nehn or nen)   novice or apprentice monks

sampot   traditional male garment

sangha   Buddhist clergy

sarong   wrap-around skirt

Satok (saa-tok)   Lao word for the *jataka* tales

sii maa (bai sema)   sacred "ordination" stones

sila   in Buddhism, the practice of morality

sim (uposatha)   ordination hall of a Buddhist temple

sin (sinh)   traditional female garment

skandhas   Sanskrit for "bundles" or "heaps": in Buddhism, the dimensions of existence

som tam (tam maak hung)   green papaya salad

soukhwan (sou khuan, baci or basi)   special ceremony to protect individuals by restoring their *khwan*

sutras   traditional writings on Buddhism

talat (talad)   market

tanha   in Buddhism, the "want" that drives *dukkha*

Thai Neua   standardized Thai language system used in Thai regions of southern China

That (Thaat or Tat)   also known as a stupa, large cones, bells, or lotus-shaped constructs in a temple complex

Theravada   Pali for "the way of the elders": a major school of Buddhism and the predominant religion in Laos

tip khao   traditional Lao rice container

Tipitaka (Tripitaka)   collection of sacred Buddhist scriptures

Uparat (Ouparath, Ouparaja, or Uparaja)   "Great Deputy King" in Buddhist dynasties: a principal adviser to the king

Varjayana (Tantric)   a division in Buddhism that emphasizes certain techniques to speed up one's enlightenment

Viet Kieu   ethnic Vietnamese population in Laos

Viet Minh   Viet Nam Doc Lap Dong Minh ("League for the Independence of Vietnam"): a nationalist/communist organization influential throughout Indochina

Vihara (Wihann)   part of the Buddhist temple in which sacred images and texts are kept

Vinaya Pintaka   rules of monastic service

Visakha Busa (Visakha Puja)   major Buddhist celebration in May

wat (vat)   Buddhist temple

Chronology of Lao Kings

This chronology includes only the Lan Xang kingdom and Laos under French rule. In many instances exact dates are unknown or are disputed by scholars. The most commonly agreed-on dates are prefaced by the abbreviation *ca.* The period between about 1427 and 1440 is particularly unclear, given the rapid succession of possibly seven kings: most killed by rivals. In the mid–fifteenth century there was an interregnum during which no king ruled. Most scholars agree that a council of monks and royal officials managed the state. There was another interregnum in the late sixteenth century. Given its isolation and the lack of foreign travelers in the eighteenth century, little is known about the separate kingdoms and their rulers following the decline of Lan Xang. Names with alternative spellings and aliases are given in parentheses.

Kings of Lan Xang

ca. 1353–1368   Fa Ngum

ca. 1368–1416   Sam Sen Thai

ca. 1416–1428   Lan Kham Deng

ca. 1427–1429   Phommathat (Phommathad)

ca. 1429–1430   Mun Sai

ca. 1430–1432   Fa Khai

ca. 1433–1434   Khon Kham

ca. 1434–1435	Yukhon
ca. 1435–1437	Khai Bua Ban
ca. 1437–1438	Kham Keut
ca. 1438–1479	Chakkaphat (also Sao Tiakaphat)
ca. 1479–1485	Souvanna Banlang (Suvama Banlang, also Theng Kham)
ca. 1485–1495	La Sen Thai (Lahsaenthai)
ca. 1495–1500	Som Phou (Sompou)
ca. 1500–1520	Vixun (Visoun, Visunurat, or Wisunarath)
1520–1550	Phothisarat (Pothisarath, Phothisarath, or Phothisalarat)
1550–1571	Sethathirat (Setthatirath, Xetthatirath, or Setthathilat)
1571–1574	Sen Soulintha (also Saensurin)
1574–1580	Mahaupahat (under Burmese rule)
1580–1582	Sen Soulintha (also Saensurin)
1582–1583	Nakhon Noi (under Burmese rule)
1583–1591	interregnum
1591–1596	Nokeo Koumane (Koumone)
ca. 1596–1622	Thammikarath
1622–1623	Upanyuvarat (Oupagnouvarath)
1623–1627	Phothisarat II
ca. 1627	Mone Keo
ca. 1627	Tone Kham
ca. 1627–1638	Vichai
ca. 1638–1694	Surinyavongsa (Soulignavongsa, Sourinyavongsa)
ca. 1694	Tian Thala (usurper)
ca. 1694–1695	Ong Lo
ca. 1695	Nantharat
ca. 1695–1707	Sai Ong Hue
ca. 1707–1713	division of Lan Xang into kingdoms of Luang Prabang, Vientiane, and Champasak; all vassals to Ayutthaya
ca. 1713–1893	individual kingdoms under Burmese, Vietnamese, Siamese, and French rule

Kings of Laos (since 1893)

1893–1904*	Unkham
1904–1959*	Sisavangvong
1959–1975	Savangvatthana

*King of Luang Prabang and (after 1945) Laos.

Suggested Readings

GENERAL INFORMATION

Chazeé, Laurant. *The Peoples of Laos: Rural and Ethnic Diversities*. Bangkok: White Lotus Press, 1999.

Cranmer, Jeff, and Steve Martin. *Rough Guide to Laos*. London: Rough Guides, 2002.

Cummings, Joe, and Andrew Burke. *Laos*. Footscray, Australia: Lonely Planet Publications, 2005.

Dakin, Brett. *Another Quiet American: Stories of Life in Laos*. Bangkok: Asia Books, 2003.

Evans, Grant, ed. *Laos: Culture and Society*. Chiang Mai, Thailand: Silkworm Books, 1999.

Griffiths, Clare, ed. *Insight Guides: Laos and Cambodia*. London: Apa Publications, 2005.

Hmong Studies Internet Resource Center, www.hmongstudies.org.

Karber, Phil. *The Indochina Chronicles: Travels in Laos, Cambodia, and Vietnam*. Singapore: Marshall Cavendish, 2005.

Kremmer, Christopher. *Bamboo Palace: Discovering the Lost Dynasty of Laos*. Sydney: Harper Collins Australia, 2003.

Mansfield, Stephen. *Lao Hill Tribes: Traditions and Patterns of Existence*. Oxford: Oxford University Press, 2000.

Northeastern Illinois University, Center for Southeast Asian Studies. "Resources for Lao Studies," www.seasite.niu.edu.

Rehbein, Boike. *Globalization, Culture, and Society in Laos*. London: Routledge, 2007.

Schliesinger, Joachim. *Ethnic Groups of Laos*, 4 vols. Bangkok: White Lotus, 2003.

Stieglitz, Perry. *In a Little Kingdom*. Armonk, NY: M. E. Sharpe, 1990.

Vatthana Polsena and Ruth Banomyong. *Laos: From Buffer State to Crossroads?* Chiang Mai, Thailand: Mekong Press, 2004.

Virtual Hilltribe Museum, www.hilltribe.org.

Visiting Arts Cultural Profiles Project, "Laos Cultural Profile," www.culturalprofiles. org.uk/laos.

History

Castle, Timothy N. *At War in the Shadow of Vietnam: U.S. Military Aid to the Royal Lao Government, 1955–73*. New York: Columbia University Press, 1993.

———. *One Day Too Long: Top Secret Site 85 and the Bombing of North Vietnam*. New York: Columbia University Press, 1999.

Daum, Andreas, Wilfried Mausbach, and Lloyd C. Gardner, eds. *America, the Vietnam War, and the World: Comparative and International Perspectives*. New York: Cambridge University Press, 2003.

Evans, Grant. *A Short History of Laos: The Land in Between*. Crows Nest, Australia: Allen and Unwin, 2002.

———. *The Politics of Ritual and Remembrance: Laos since 1975*. Honolulu: University of Hawaii Press, 1998.

Goscha, Christopher E., and Soren Ivarsson, eds. *Contesting Visions of the Lao Past: Lao Historiography at the Crossroads*. Copenhagen: Nordic Institute of Asian Studies, 2003.

Gunn, Geoffrey C. *Political Struggles in Laos, 1930–54*. Bangkok: Editions Duang Kamol, 1988.

Hamilton-Merritt, Jane. *Tragic Mountains: The Hmong, the Americans, and the Secret Wars for Laos, 1942–1992*. Indianapolis: Indiana University Press, 1993.

Hannah, Norman B. *The Key to Failure: Laos and the Vietnam War*. Lanham, MD: Madison Books, 1987.

Maha Sila Viravong. *History of Laos*. New York: Paragon Book Reprint, 1964.

Mayoury Ngaosyvathn and Kennon Breazeale, eds. *Breaking New Ground in Lao History: Essays on the Seventh to Twentieth Centuries*. Chiang Mai, Thailand: Silkworm Books, 2002.

Nakhonkham Bouphanouvong. *Sixteen Years in the Land of Death: Revolution and Reeducation in Laos*. Bangkok: White Lotus Press, 2003.

Quincy, Keith. *Harvesting Pa Chay's Wheat: The Hmong and America's Secret War in Laos*. Spokane: Eastern Washington University, 2000.

Robbins, Christopher. *The Ravens: The Men Who Flew in America's Secret War in Laos*. New York: Crown Publishers, 1987.

Stuart-Fox, Martin. *A History of Laos*. Cambridge: Cambridge University Press, 1997.

———. *Buddhist Kingdom, Marxist State: The Making of Modern Laos*. Bangkok: White Lotus Press, 1996.

————. *The Lao Kingdom of Lan Xang: Rise and Decline*. Bangkok: White Lotus, 1998.

Vatthana Polsena. *Post-War Laos: The Politics of Culture, History, and Identity*. Ithaca, NY: Cornell University Press, 2006.

Warner, Roger. *Backfire: The CIA's Secret War in Laos and its Links to the War in Vietnam*. New York: Simon and Schuster, 1995.

RELIGION AND THOUGHT

Brown, Robert L. *The Dvaravati Wheels of Law and the Indianization of Southeast Asia*. Leiden, the Netherlands: E. J. Brill, 1996.

Buddhist Studies Dharma Education Association, www.buddhanet.net/e-learning/basic-guide.htm (accessed November 2002).

Gombrich, Richard F. *Theravada Buddhism: A Social History from Ancient Benares to Modern Colombo*. London: Routledge, 2006.

Harris, Ian Charles, ed. *Buddhism, Power, and Political Order*. London: Routledge, 2007.

Lowenstein, Tom. *The Vision of the Buddha: Buddhism—the Path to Spiritual Enlightenment*. London: Duncan Baird, 2000.

Northeastern Illinois University, Center for Southeast Asian Studies. "Resources for Lao Studies," www.seasite.niu.edu.

Swearer, Donald. *The Buddhist World of Southeast Asia*. Albany: State University of New York Press, 1995.

Visiting Arts Cultural Profiles Project. "Laos Cultural Profile," www.culturalprofiles.org.uk/laos.

LITERATURE

Bounyavong, Outhine. *Mother's Beloved: Stories from Laos*, ed. Bounheng Inversin and Daniel Duffy. Seattle: University of Washington Press, 1997.

Dingwall, Alistair. *Traveller's Literary Companion to Southeast Asia*. Brighton, UK: Print Publishing, 1994.

Geok-lin Lim, Shirley, and Cheng Lok Chua, eds. *Tilting the Continent: Southeast Asian American Writing*. Minneapolis: New Rivers Press, 2000.

Herbert, Patricia, and Anthony Milner, eds. *Southeast Asian Languages and Literatures: A Select Guide*. Honolulu: University of Hawaii Press, 1989.

Livo, Norma J. *Folk Stories of the Hmong: Peoples of Laos, Thailand, and Vietnam*. Englewood, CO: Libraries Unlimited, 1991.

Mai Neng Moua, ed. *Bamboo among the Oaks: Contemporary Writing by Hmong Americans*. St. Paul: Minnesota Historical Society, 2002.

Northeastern Illinois University, Center for Southeast Asian Studies. "Resources for Lao Studies," www.seasite.niu.edu.

Sachai Sachchidanand. *The Rama Jataka in Laos: A Study in the Phra Lak Phra Lam*. New Delhi: B. R. Corporation, 1996.

Thao Worra, Bryan. *Touching Detonations: An E-Chapbook*. Sphinx House Press, 2004, available at members.aol.com/thaoworra/poetry.htm.

Visiting Arts Cultural Profiles Project. "Laos Cultural Profile," www.culturalprofils. org.uk/laos.

Xay Kaignavongsa and Hugh Fincher. *Legends of the Lao: A Compilation of Legends and Other Folklore of the Lao People*. Bangkok: Geodata System, 1993.

ART

Cheesman, Patricia. *Lao Textiles: Ancient Symbols—Living Art*. Bangkok: White Lotus Press, 1988.

Fisher, Robert E. *Buddhist Art and Architecture*. London: Thames and Hudson, 1993.

Ginsburg, Henry. *Thai Art and Culture*. London: British Library, 2000.

Giteau, Madelaine. *Art et archéologie du Laos*. Paris: Picard, 2001.

Howard, Michael C., Wattana Wattanapun, and Alec Gordon, eds. *Traditional Tai Arts in Contemporary Perspective*. Bangkok: White Lotus Press, 1998.

Rawson, Philip. *The Art of Southeast Asia*. London: Thames and Hudson, 1967.

Visiting Arts Cultural Profiles Project. "Laos Cultural Profile," www.culturalprofiles. org.uk/laos.

ARCHITECTURE AND DESIGN

Chihara, Daigero. *Hindu-Buddhist Architecture in Southeast Asia*. Amsterdam: E. J. Brill, 1996.

Clément-Charpentier, Sophie, and Pierre Clément. *L'habitation Lao: Dans les regions de Vientiane et de Louang Prabang*. Paris: Peeters Diffusion and J. Vrin, 1990.

Fisher, Robert E. *Buddhist Art and Architecture*. London: Thames and Hudson, 1993.

Waterson, Roxana, ed. *The Architecture of Southeast Asia Through Travellers' Eyes*. Kuala Lumpur: Oxford University Press, 1998.

Visiting Arts Cultural Profiles Project. "Laos Cultural Profile," www.culturalprofiles. org.uk/laos.

THEATER, DANCE, MUSIC, AND FILM

Lao Voices, laovoices.com.

Lockard, Craig A. *Dance of Life: Popular Music and Politics in Southeast Asia*. Honolulu: University of Hawaii Press, 1998.

Mattana Rutnin. *Dance, Drama, and Theatre in Thailand: The Process of Development and Modernization*. Chiang Mai, Thailand: Silkworm Books, 1996.

Miller, Terry E. *Traditional Music of the Lao: Kaen Playing and Mawlum Singing in Northeast Thailand*. Westport, CT: Greenwood Press, 1985.

Northeastern Illinois University, Center for Southeast Asian Studies. "Resources for Lao Studies," www.seasite.niu.edu.

Visiting Arts Cultural Profiles Project. "Laos Cultural Profile," www.culturalprofiles.
    org.uk/laos.

CUISINE AND TRADITIONAL DRESS

Alford, Jeffrey, and Naomi Duguid. *Hot, Sour, Salty, Sweet: A Culinary Journey through
    Southeast Asia*. New York: Artisan, 2000.
Bunce, Frederick W. *Buddhist Textiles of Laos, Lanna, and the Isan: The Iconography of
    Design Elements*. New Delhi: D. K. Printworld, 2004.
Chaleunsilp Phia Sing. *Traditional Recipes of Laos*. London: Prospect Books, 1995.
Daovone Xayavong. *Taste of Laos*. Hong Kong: SLG Books, 2003.
Virtual Hilltribe Museum, www.hilltribe.org.

GENDER, COURTSHIP, MARRIAGE, AND FAMILY

Cooper, Robert. *The Hmong: A Guide to Traditional Lifestyles*. New York: Times Edi-
    tions, 1998.
Hmong Studies Internet Resource Center, www.hmongstudies.org.
Ireson-Doolittle, Carol. *The Lao: Gender, Power, and Livelihood*. Boulder, CO: West-
    view Press, 2004.
Mayoury Ngaosyvathn. *Lao Women Yesterday and Today*. Vientiane: Mayoury
    Ngaosyvathn, 1995.

FESTIVALS AND FUN

Australian National University, "New Mandala: New Perspectives on Mainland
    Southeast Asia," rspas.anu.edu.au/rmap/newmandala.
Cranmer, Jeff, and Steve Martin. *Rough Guide to Laos*. London: Rough Guides, 2002.
Cummings, Joe, and Andrew Burke. *Laos*. Footscray, Australia: Lonely Planet Publi-
    cations, 2005.
Gerson, Ruth. *Traditional Festivals in Thailand*. Kuala Lumpur: Oxford University
    Press, 1996.
Griffiths, Clare, ed. *Insight Guides: Laos and Cambodia*. London: Apa Publications,
    2005.
Lao Voices, laovoices.com.
Mansfield, Stephen. *Culture Shock! A Guide to Customs and Etiquette, Laos*. Singapore:
    Times Editions, 1997.

SOCIAL CUSTOMS

Cranmer, Jeff, and Steve Martin. *Rough Guide to Laos*. London: Rough Guides, 2002.
Cummings, Joe, and Andrew Burke. *Laos*. Footscray, Australia: Lonely Planet Publi-
    cations, 2005.

Griffiths, Clare, ed. *Insight Guides: Laos and Cambodia.* London: Apa Publications, 2005.

Lao Voices, laovoices.com.

Mansfield, Stephen. *Culture Shock! A Guide to Customs and Etiquette, Laos.* Singapore: Times Editions, 1997.

Bibliography

Alford, Jeffrey, and Naomi Duguid. *Hot, Sour, Salty, Sweet: A Culinary Journey through Southeast Asia*. New York: Artisan, 2000.

Berg, Manfred, and Andreas Etges, eds. *John F. Kennedy and the Thousand Days: New Perspectives on the Foreign and Domestic Policies of the Kennedy Administration*. Heidelberg, Germany: Universitätsverlag Winter Heidelberg, 2007.

Bounheng Inversin and Daniel Duffy, eds. *Mother's Beloved: Stories from Laos*. Seattle: University of Washington Press, 1997.

Brown, Mervin. *War in Shangri-La: A Memoir of Civil War in Laos*. London: Radcliffe Press, 2001.

Brown, Robert L. *The Dvaravati Wheels of Law and the Indianization of Southeast Asia*. Leiden, the Netherlands: E. J. Brill, 1996.

Bunce, Frederick W. *Buddhist Textiles of Laos, Lanna, and the Isan: The Iconography of Design Elements*. New Delhi: D. K. Printworld, 2004.

Burton, John I. S. *Lao Close Encounters*. Bangkok: Orchid Press, 2005.

Cadet, J. M. *The Ramakien: The Thai Epic*. Tokyo: Kodansha International, 1970.

Castle, Timothy N. *At War in the Shadow of Vietnam: U.S. Military Aid to the Royal Lao Government, 1955–73*. New York: Columbia University Press, 1993.

———. *One Day Too Long: Top Secret Site 85 and the Bombing of North Vietnam*. New York: Columbia University Press, 1999.

Chaleunsilp Phia Sing. *Traditional Recipes of Laos*. London: Prospect Books, 1995.

Chazeé, Laurant. *The Peoples of Laos: Rural and Ethnic Diversities*. Bangkok: White Lotus Press, 1999.

Cheesman, Patricia. *Lao Textiles: Ancient Symbols—Living Art*. Bangkok: White Lotus Press, 1988.

Chihara, Daigero. *Hindu-Buddhist Architecture in Southeast Asia.* Amsterdam: E. J. Brill, 1996.

Clément-Charpentier, Sophie, and Pierre Clément. *L'habitation Lao: Dans les regions de Vientiane et de Louang Prabang.* Paris: Peeters Diffusion, J. Vrin, 1990.

Cooper, Robert. *The Hmong: A Guide to Traditional Lifestyles.* New York: Times Editions, 1998.

Cranmer, Jeff, and Steve Martin. *Rough Guide to Laos.* London: Rough Guides, 2002.

Cummings, Joe. *Lao Phrasebook.* Footscray, Australia: Lonely Planet Publications, 2002.

Cummings, Joe, and Andrew Burke. *Laos.* Footscray, Australia: Lonely Planet Publications, 2005.

Dakin, Brett. *Another Quiet American: Stories of Life in Laos.* Bangkok: Asia Books, 2003.

Daovone Xayavong. *Taste of Laos.* Hong Kong: SLG Books, 2003.

Daum, Andreas, Wilfried Mausbach, and Lloyd C. Gardner, eds. *America, the Vietnam War, and the World: Comparative and International Perspectives.* New York: Cambridge University Press, 2003.

Derris, Karen, and Natalie Gummer, eds. *Defining Buddhism(s): A Reader.* Oakville, ON: Equinox Publications, 2007.

Dingwall, Alistair. *Traveller's Literary Companion to Southeast Asia.* Brighton, UK: Print Publishing, 1994.

Enfield, N. J. *Linguistic Epidemiology: Semantics and Grammar of Language Contact in Mainland Southeast Asia.* London: RoutledgeCurzon, 2003.

Epstein, Steven. *Lao Folktales.* Chiang Mai, Thailand: Silkworm Press, 1995.

Evans, Grant, ed. *Laos: Culture and Society.* Chiang Mai, Thailand: Silkworm Books, 1999.

———. *The Politics of Ritual and Remembrance: Laos since 1975.* Honolulu: University of Hawaii Press, 1998.

———. *A Short History of Laos: The Land in Between.* Crows Nest, Australia: Allen and Unwin, 2002.

Fineman, Daniel. *A Special Relationship: The United States and Military Government in Thailand, 1947–1958.* Honolulu: University of Hawaii Press, 1997.

Fisher, Robert E. *Buddhist Art and Architecture.* London: Thames and Hudson, 1993.

Geok-lin Lim, Shirley, and Cheng Lok Chua, eds. *Tilting the Continent: Southeast Asian American Writing.* Minneapolis: New Rivers Press, 2000.

Gerson, Ruth. *Traditional Festivals in Thailand.* Kuala Lumpur: Oxford University Press, 1996.

Ghosh, Chitra. *The World of Thai Women.* Calcutta: Best Books, 1990.

Ginsburg, Henry. *Thai Art and Culture.* London: British Library, 2000.

Giteau, Madelaine. *Art et archéologie du Laos.* Paris: Picard, 2001.

Gombrich, Richard F. *Theravada Buddhism: A Social History from Ancient Benares to Modern Colombo.* London: Routledge, 2006.

Goscha, Christopher E., and Soren Ivarsson, eds. *Contesting Visions of the Lao Past: Lao Historiography at the Crossroads.* Copenhagen: Nordic Institute of Asian Studies, 2003.

Grant Evans, *A Short History of Laos: The Land in Between* (Crows Nest, Australia: Allen and Unwin, 2002), chap. 1.

Griffiths, Clare, ed. *Insight Guides: Laos and Cambodia.* London: Apa Publications, 2005.

Gunn, Geoffrey C. *Political Struggles in Laos, 1930–54.* Bangkok: Editions Duang Kamol, 1988.

Hamilton-Merritt, Jane. *Tragic Mountains: The Hmong, the Americans, and the Secret Wars for Laos, 1942–1992.* Indianapolis: Indiana University Press, 1993.

Hannah, Norman B. *The Key to Failure: Laos and the Vietnam War.* Lanham, MD: Madison Books, 1987.

Harris, Ian Charles, ed. *Buddhism, Power, and Political Order.* London: Routledge, 2007.

Hayashi, Yukio. *Practical Buddhism among the Tai-Lao: Religion in the Making of a Region.* Kyoto: Kyoto University Press, 2003.

Herbert, Patricia, and Anthony Milner, eds. *Southeast Asian Languages and Literatures: A Select Guide.* Honolulu: University of Hawaii Press, 1989.

Hopkins, Allen W., and John Hoskin. *Laos: The Land of a Million Elephants.* Bangkok: Post Books, 1996.

Howard, Michael C., Wattana Wattanapun, and Alec Gordon, eds. *Traditional Tai Arts in Contemporary Perspective.* Bangkok: White Lotus Press, 1998.

Ireson-Doolittle, Carol. *The Lao: Gender, Power, and Livelihood.* Boulder, CO: Westview Press, 2004.

Ivarsson, Soren, and Christopher E. Goscha. "Prince Phetsarath (1890–1959): Nationalism and Royalty in the Making of Modern Laos," *Journal of Southeast Asian Studies* 38, no. 1 (February 2007): 55–81.

Jones, John Garrett. *Tales and Teachings of the Buddha: The Jataka Stories in Relation to the Pali Canon.* Boston: Allen and Unwin, 1979.

Karber, Phil. *The Indochina Chronicles: Travels in Laos, Cambodia, and Vietnam.* Singapore: Marshall Cavendish, 2005.

Kartomi, Margaret J. "'Traditional Music Weeps' and Other Themes in the Discourse of Music, Dance and Theatre of Indonesia, Malaysia, and Thailand," *Journal of Southeast Asian Studies* 26 (September 1995): 366–400.

Keyes, Charles F. *The Golden Peninsula: Culture and Adaptation in Mainland Southeast Asia.* Honolulu: University of Hawaii Press, 1995.

Kislenko, Arne. "A Not So Silent Partner: Thailand's Role in Covert Operations, Counter-Insurgency, and the Wars in Indochina," *Journal of Conflict Studies* 25, no. 1 (Summer 2004): 65–96.

———. *Culture and Customs of Thailand.* Westport, CT: Greenwood Publishing, 2004.

Kochavi, Noam. "Limited Accommodation, Perpetuated Conflict: Kennedy, China, and the Laos Crisis, 1961–1963." *Diplomatic History* 26, no. 1 (Winter 2002): 95–135.

Kremmer, Christopher. *Bamboo Palace: Discovering the Lost Dynasty of Laos.* Sydney: Harper Collins Australia, 2003.

Livo, Norma J. *Folk Stories of the Hmong: Peoples of Laos, Thailand, and Vietnam.* Englewood, CO: Libraries Unlimited, 1991.

Lockard, Craig A. *Dance of Life: Popular Music and Politics in Southeast Asia.* Honolulu: University of Hawaii Press, 1998.

Lowenstein, Tom. *The Vision of the Buddha: Buddhism—the Path to Spiritual Enlightenment.* London: Duncan Baird, 2000.

Maha Sila Viravong. *History of Laos.* New York: Paragon Book Reprint, 1964.

Mai Neng Moua, ed. *Bamboo among the Oaks: Contemporary Writing by Hmong Americans.* St. Paul: Minnesota Historical Society, 2002.

Mallari-Hall, Luisa, and Lily Rose R. Tope, eds. *Texts and Contexts: Interaction between Literature and Culture in Southeast Asia.* Quezon City: University of Philippines Press, 1999.

Manas Chitakasem, ed. *Thai Literary Traditions.* Bangkok: Chulalongkorn University Press, 1995.

Mansfield, Stephen. *Culture Shock! A Guide to Customs and Etiquette, Laos.* Singapore: Times Editions, 1997.

———. *Lao Hill Tribes: Traditions and Patterns of Existence.* Oxford: Oxford University Press, 2000.

Martin, Rafe. *The Hungry Tigress: Buddhist Legends and Jataka Tales.* Berkeley, CA: Paralax Press, 1990.

Mattana Rutnin. *Dance, Drama, and Theatre in Thailand: The Process of Development and Modernization.* Chiang Mai, Thailand: Silkworm Books, 1996.

Mayoury Ngaosyvathn. *Lao Women Yesterday and Today.* Vientiane: Mayoury Ngaosyvathn, 1995.

———. *On the Edge of the Pagoda.* Paper No. 5, York University Working Series, Thai Studies Project, Women in Development Consortium in Thailand, 1990.

———. *Paths to Conflagration: Fifty Years of Diplomacy and Warfare in Laos, Thailand, and Vietnam, 1778–1828.* Ithaca, NY: Southeast Asian Program Publications, Cornell University Press, 1998.

Mayoury Ngaosyvathn and Kennon Breazeale, eds. *Breaking New Ground in Lao History: Essays on the Seventh to Twentieth Centuries.* Chiang Mai, Thailand: Silkworm Books, 2002.

Miller, Terry E. *Traditional Music of the Lao: Kaen Playing and Mawlum Singing in Northeast Thailand.* Westport, CT: Greenwood Press, 1985.

M. L. Jumsai Manich. *History of Thai Literature,* 3rd ed. Bangkok: Chalermnit Press, 2000.

Murphy, Dervla. *One Foot in Laos.* London: John Murray, 1999.

Nakhonkham Bouphanouvong. *Sixteen Years in the Land of Death: Revolution and Reeducation in Laos.* Bangkok: White Lotus Press, 2003.

Nguyen Thi Dieu. *The Mekong River and the Struggle for Indochina: Water, War, and Peace.* Westport, CT: Praeger, 1999.

Northeastern Illinois University, Center for Southeast Asian Studies, "Chronology of Lan Xang Dynasty," www.seasite.niu.edu/lao.

Quincy, Keith. *Harvesting Pa Chay's Wheat: The Hmong and America's Secret War in Laos*. Spokane: Eastern Washington University, 2000.

———. *Hmong: History of a People*, 2nd ed. Spokane: Eastern Washington University, 1995.

Rawson, Philip. *The Art of Southeast Asia*. London: Thames and Hudson, 1967.

Rehbein, Boike. *Globalization, Culture, and Society in Laos*. London: Routledge, 2007.

Reynolds, Craig J. *Seditious Histories: Contesting Thai and Southeast Asian Pasts*. Seattle: University of Washington Press, 2006.

Reynolds, E. Bruce. *Thailand and Japan's Southern Advance, 1940–1945*. New York: St. Martin's Press, 1994.

Robbins, Christopher. *The Ravens: The Men Who Flew in America's Secret War in Laos*. New York: Crown Publishers, 1987.

Rong Syamananda. *A History of Thailand*, 5th ed. Bangkok: Thai Watana Panich, 1986.

Sachai Sachchidanand. *The Rama Jataka in Laos: A Study in the Phra Lak Phra Lam*. New Delhi: B. R. Corporation, 1996.

Schenk-Sandbergen, Loes. "Lao Women: Gender Consequences of Economic Transformation," *International Institute for Asian Studies (IIAS) Newsletter* 9 (Summer 1996), http://www.iias.nl/iiasn/iiasn9/iiasn9.html.

Schliesinger, Joachim. *Ethnic Groups of Laos*, 4 vols. Bangkok: White Lotus, 2003.

Shigeharu Tanabe and Charles F. Keyes, eds. *Cultural Crisis and Social Memory: Modernity and Identity in Thailand and Laos*. London: Routledge Curzon, 2002.

Simms, Peter, and Sanda Simms. *The Kingdoms of Laos: Six Hundred Years of History*. Richmond, UK: Curzon Press, 1999.

Smyth, David. *The Canon in Southeast Asian Literatures: Literatures of Burma, Cambodia, Indonesia, Laos, Malaysia, the Philippines, Thailand, and Vietnam*. London: Curzon Press, 2000.

St. John, Ronald Bruce. *Revolution, Reform and Regionalism in Southeast Asia: Cambodia, Laos, and Vietnam*. New York: Routledge, 2005.

Stevenson, Charles A. *The End of Nowhere: American Policy Towards Laos since 1954*. Boston: Beacon Press, 1972.

Stieglitz, Perry. *In a Little Kingdom*. Armonk, NY: M. E. Sharpe, 1990.

Stuart-Fox, Martin. *A History of Laos*. Cambridge: Cambridge University Press, 1997.

———. *Buddhist Kingdom, Marxist State: The Making of Modern Laos*. Bangkok: White Lotus Press, 1996.

———. *The Lao Kingdom of Lan Xang: Rise and Decline*. Bangkok: White Lotus, 1998.

Sugita, Yone, Jon Davidann, and Richard Jensen, eds. *Trans-Pacific Relations: America, Europe, and Asia in the Twentieth Century*. Westport, CT: Praeger Publishers, 2003.

Swearer, Donald. *The Buddhist World of Southeast Asia*. Albany: State University of New York Press, 1995.

Tannenbaum, Nicola, and Cornelia Ann Kammerer, eds. *Founders' Cults in Southeast Asia: Ancestors, Polity, and Identity*. New Haven, CT: Yale University Press, 2003.

Tarling, Nicholas. *Nations and States in Southeast Asia*. Cambridge: Cambridge University Press, 1994.

Thao Worra, Bryan. *Touching Detonations: An E-Chapbook*. Published online by Sphinx House Press, 2004, http://members.aol.com/thaoworra/poetry.htm.

Thomson, Sheila, and Sally Baden. "Women and Development in Laos," Report No. 9, Women, Health and Population Division, Australian International Development Assistance Bureau, February 1993, Institute of Development Studies, University of Sussex, http://www.bridge.ids.ac.uk/reports/re9c.pdf.

Tongchai Winichakul. *Siam Mapped: A History of the Geo-Body of a Nation*. Honolulu: University of Hawaii Press, 1994.

U.N. Common Country Assessment (CCA). "Lao PDR (June 2006)." http://www.undplao.org/.

U.N. Conference on Trade Development. "Statistical Profiles of Least Developed Countries: Laos," http://www.unctad.org.

U.N. Development Programme, "Working with Your Lao Partner," 2003 report, http://www.seasite.niu.edu/lao/undp/wwyLp.htm.

U.N. Special Report. "Blue Book on Laos," for the Japanese Bank for International Cooperation, http://www.un.org/special-rep/ohrlls/lde/ldc-rep/LaoDemRep.htm.

U.S. Department of State, *International Religious Freedom Report 2007: Laos*, September 14, 2007, http://www.state.gov/g/drl/rls/irf/2007/90142.htm.

Van Beek, Steve. *The Arts of Thailand*. London: Thames and Hudson, 1991.

Van Esterik, Penny. "Fabricating National Identity: Textiles in Lao PDR," *Museum Anthropology* 23, no. 11 (Spring 1999): 47–55.

———. *Materializing Thailand*. Oxford, UK: Berg, 2000.

Vatthana Polsena. "Ethnic Classification and Mapping Nationhood in Contemporary Laos." *Asian Ethnicity* 3, no. 2 (September 2002): 175–197.

———. *Post-War Laos: The Politics of Culture, History, and Identity*. Ithaca, NY: Cornell University Press, 2006.

Vatthana Polsena and Ruth Banomyong. *Laos: From Buffer State to Crossroads?* Chiang Mai, Thailand: Mekong Press, 2004.

Wajuppa Tossa, trans. and ed. *Phadaeng Nang Ai: A Translation of a Thai-Isan Folk Epic in Verse*. Lewisburg, PA: Bucknell University, 1990.

———. *Phya Khankhaak, the Toad King: A Translation of an Isan Fertility Myth in Verse*. Lewisburg, PA: Bucknell University, 1996.

Warner, Roger. *Backfire: The CIA's Secret War in Laos and Its Links to the War in Vietnam*. New York: Simon and Schuster, 1995.

Waterson, Roxana, ed. *The Architecture of Southeast Asia through Travellers' Eyes*. Kuala Lumpur: Oxford University Press, 1998.

———. *The Living House: An Anthropology of Architecture in Southeast Asia*. New York: Whitney Library of Design, 1998.

Wyatt, David K. *Studies in Thai History*. Chiang Mai, Thailand: Silkworm Books, 1994.

———. *Thailand: A Short History*. New Haven, CT: Yale University Press, 1982.

Xay Kaignavongsa and Hugh Fincher. *Legends of the Lao: A Compilation of Legends and Other Folklore of the Lao People.* Bangkok: Geodata System, 1993.

WEB SOURCES

Buddhist Studies Dharma Education Association at http://www.buddhanet.net/e-learning/basic-guide.htm.

Hmong Studies Internet Resource Center, www.hmongstudies.org.

Lao Voices, http://laovoices.com.

Laos WWW Virtual Library (Coombes Australian National University Asian Studies), http://home.vicnet.net.au/~lao/mainvl.htm.

New Mandala: New Perspectives on Mainland Southeast Asia website, Australian National University, http://rspas.anu.edu.au/rmap/newmandala.

Northeastern Illinois University, Center for Southeast Asian Studies. "Resources for Lao Studies." www.seasite.niu.edu.

United Nations Educational, Scientific, and Cultural Organization (UNESCO) website at www.unescobkk.org.

Virtual Hilltribe Museum at www.hilltribe.org.

Visiting Arts Cultural Profiles Project. "Laos Cultural Profile," www.culturalprofiles.org.uk/laos.

Index

About the Author

ARNE KISLENKO is Associate Professor of History at Ryerson University and an Adjunct Professor in the International Relations Programme at the Munk Centre for International Studies, University of Toronto. His other publications include *Culture and Customs of Thailand* (Greenwood, 2004), *The Uneasy Century: International Relations 1900–1990* (with Margaret MacMillan), and numerous book chapters and articles on modern Southeast Asia and other topics in international relations history.